LIMITED EDITION

154/1,000

PERIPLUS LINE LLC

About the AUTHOR

Dr. A.V. (Sheenu) Srinivasan has resided in the United States since 1961. In addition to a long career in engineering research and education, he has developed and taught courses on the ancient Indian epics, the Ramayana and the Mahabharata, at the University of Connecticut and Wesleyan University. He is the primary founder of the Connecticut Valley Hindu Temple Society and the driving force in the establishment of the Satyanarayana Temple in Middletown, Connecticut.

Aside from books and articles in professional engineering journals, he has also published a number of articles on Hinduism and related topics in Indian American newspapers and journals. His publications include *A Hindu Primer: Yaksha Prashna,* 1984, released by Bharatiya Vidya Bhavan in 2002, and a series of booklets on Hindu religious ceremonies.

Selected publications:

How to Conduct Puja (A series of eight booklets) Periplus Line LLC, 1999-2000 :

(1) Soorya the Sun God (2) Shiva (3) SriRamachandra
(4) SriKrishna (5) MahaGanapati (6) MahaLakshmi
(7) Durgadevi (8) Saraswati

A Hindu Primer: Yaksha Prashna, 2nd Edition. Parijata Publication, 2002

Padayatra, Prayer Walk at the Satyanarayana Temple, Periplus Line LLC, 2005

Selected Journal and Newspaper articles:

Principles of Hinduism

A Thread Through the Eighteen Gems: The Srīmadbhagavadgīta

A Great Question and a Greater Answer in the Gīta

Makara Sankrānti: A Personal View

Dharmōrakṣati Rakṣita:

Hindu Philosophy of Marriage

Note: Some of these papers are available on line at www.avsrinivasan.com

THE VEDIC WEDDING
Origins, Tradition and Practice

Dedication

• To my parents
who never fully saw the fruits of their toil

• To my wife Kamla

• To my daughters Asha and Sandhya

• To the couples named below
whose weddings were performed by the author

Nina & Kevin
Jennifer & Hemamshu
Neeleshwarl & Parashar
Shilpa & Daniel
Asha & Stephen
Daya & George
Bhavini & Samir
Mary & Ravi
Anjuli & Fred
Seju & John
Sonja & Sujit
Veena & Ryan
Janine & Sunjay
Avani & Ujas
Cheryl & Sharad

Zeyneb & Sanjay
Sapna & Sean
Vandana & Arun
Ashley & Satish
Pooja & Rudresh
Anjali & Peter
Radhika & Praveen
Rachel & Sandeep
Madhuri & Magnus
Aditi & Sheel
Rebecca & Satwik
Colleen & Vishal
Joanna & Salim
Kavita & Rahul
Asha & Kumar

and

• To the second generation of Hindus in the West

THE VEDIC WEDDING
Origins, Tradition and Practice

Including a step-by-step Wedding Ceremony in Sanskrit with English transliteration and translation

by A.V. Srinivasan

भार्या दैवकृतः सखा

"A wife is a God-given friend"

The Mahabharata

PERIPLUS LINE LLC

ISBN-13: 978-0-9785443-0-0
ISBN-10: 0-9785443-0-7
Hardcover, First Edition

Inquiries should be addressed to the Publisher:
SAN: 850-8577
Periplus Line LLC
Attention: Permissions Department
P.O. Box 56, East Glastonbury, CT 06025-0056
U.S.A.

Publisher's Cataloging-In-Publication Data
(Prepared by The Donohue Group, Inc.)

Srinivasan, A. V.
The Vedic wedding : origins, tradition and practice : including a step-by-step wedding ceremony in Sanskrit with English transliteration and translation / by A.V. Srinivasan ; illustrations by Bapu.

p. : ill., facsims. ; cm.

In English and Sanskrit.
Includes bibliographical references and glossary.
ISBN: 0-9785443-0-7

1. Marriage service (Hinduism) 2. Marriage customs and rites, Hindu--History. I. Bapu, 1933- II. Title.

BL1226.82.M3 S65 2006
294.5/385

LIMITED EDITION (1,000 copies), numbered.
Illustrations by Bapu

Manufactured in India at THE BANGALORE PRESS

Hasta Milap

Kanyadanam

Mangalyadharanam

Agni Pratishtapana

Homas: Pradhana Homa; Laaja Homa

Saptapadi

Closing ceremonies: Arati; Ashirvadam; Recessional

Appendix I: Forms and Format

Appendix II: Planning and Coordination

Rehearsal/Preparatory Steps

Appendix III: Vedic Calendar

Appendix IV: Additional Ceremonies and Customs

FOREWORD

The ancient Indian marriage ritual of circumambulating the sacred fire binds two young persons together for life. It is undertaken before God Agni and the assembled relatives and friends. This ancient tradition has been kept alive in India for several thousands of years, ever since early Vedic times. The rituals as carried out today indeed go back all the way to the most ancient Vedic texts, those of the Rgvedic hymn of the marriage of the daughter of the Sun, Suryaa.

To sustain this venerable tradition in America, Dr. Srinivasan has undertaken to prepare this book, incorporating rich commentary and lavish illustrations. It clearly delineates the history and intent of the Vedic marriage rituals. The book also offers a clear layout and explanation of the many rites that constitute a Vedic marriage.

Most importantly, the book includes all the texts used, that is the mantras to be recited, both in Devanagari script as well as in Latin script, assuring correct pronunciation. The book also provides an English translation that reveals the meaning of the individual texts and makes the major constituent parts and the many individual sub-rites of the long rituals understandable. This allows all participants to follow the ceremony and the complicated rituals step by step.

As a result, the Sanskrit mantras no longer remain obscure but regain their ancient deep meaning. Only in this way, the many-sided details of the long-drawn out ceremony become clear and the ancient symbolism going back several thousand years is made understandable for the modern participants.

Dr. Srinivasan also includes some of the local variations that inevitably must occur in a huge country like India. Actually, this difference again goes back to Vedic times. For example, there is a Vedic wedding song, of quite explicit nature, that is only once fleetingly mentioned in a Sutra text, precariously preserved in Kerala, but whose actual words have been found only in a few manuscripts in Kashmir. This song was to be sung by participants in the ritual, just as today the ceremony is accompanied by music and songs.

I congratulate Dr. Srinivasan for his sustained efforts aimed at keeping the ancient Vedic traditions alive in a new setting in America, and at localizing it by including, for example, some of the American rivers in the mantras. In this way, the ancient ritual becomes alive and more meaningful for the young people of today, for whom this book is meant.

May it be a guide for many young couples in taking their first steps together.

Michael Witzel
Wales Professor of Sanskrit
Department of Sanskrit and Indian Studies
Harvard University
Cambridge, Massachusetts

AUTHOR'S NOTE

The inspiration for this book came from the young Indians in the United States who have approached me in the past three decades to seek my advice and to have me officiate at their weddings. Upon the advent of the internet these young people have sought me not only through word of mouth but also, after researching the relevant material available in cyberspace, through my website (www.avsrinivasan.com).

Most of the procedures and the corresponding mantras are, of course, in the Sanskrit language, which Hindus consider to be 'deva bhasha,' meaning the language of the gods. What is disturbing to the lover of this ancient tongue is that this most sophisticated and truly beautiful language is hardly in use nowadays except by priests who chant the mantras and by scholars.

The usual difficulties of translation have been encountered here. The subtle interweaving of sound and meaning, common to all classical languages, is such that translations can lose their spirit and intent if they do not preserve the original sense. On the other hand a vague and imprecise rendering will make the result obscure and dull. Thus it is necessary to preserve both the intent and the content intact as we transport ritualistic ideas from one culture to another.

Add to this difficulty the fact that all mantras are poetic in the original rendition and this adds another burden in that it demands preservation of some feature of sound and cadence. Thus the translator walks a fine line in taking the ancient wisdoms in these mantras and retaining their beauty in English. These are the hurdles faced in developing a treatise such as this for use by English-speaking readers.

That is not all. The authority for most of the steps followed in a Vedic wedding ceremony obviously issues out of the Vedas. And the latter are admittedly complex. Even the Pandava prince Yudhishtira admitted this when he declared: श्रुतयो विभिन्ना : (*srutayo vibhinna:)* i.e. the Vedas are abstruse *(MBh*). Fortunately we are not dealing with deep philosophies here but only the Vedic mantras that cover the events in a wedding, beginning with reception of the groom and concluding with sending the bride off to the couple's new home. Thus the context is somewhat simpler, and this is a help.

Many of the terms used in the text are transcribed from languages with differing alphabets. Over the years the best known among them have been spelled (or misspelled) in varying ways. For the sake of accuracy diacritical marks have been used in the ritual Sanskrit sequences and the Glossary. However, for the general reader's comfort, the application of diacritical marks has been minimized in the main text in favor of familiar usage. The general attempt has been to balance accuracy with ease of use, even where there may be some loss in consistency.

Apart from about a dozen or so references drawn from a variety of sources in Sanskrit, Kannada, Hindi and English that throw some light on possible interpretations of the mantras, the author has relied on the celebrated dictionary of Sir Monier Monier-Williams. No claim is made that all the translations are perfect and flawless. This text, consisting as it does, of Sanskrit shlokas, English text, English transliteration and translation, with very many complex words and phrases, is bound to contain errors. And of course the purist will no doubt pick up some violations of sandhi rules. The author would very much appreciate receiving comments pertaining to these and thanks in advance those who do take the time to review and offer suggestions for possible use when we consider a future edition.

A. V. Srinivasan,
Glastonbury, Connecticut
April, 2006

Amruthur SriChennakeshavaswami

Chapter I

INTRODUCTION : Wedding and Marriage

सुखदुःखे समेकृत्वा लाभालाभौ जयाजयौ ...

sukhaduhkhē samēkṛtvā lābhālābhau jayājayau

"through times of travail and happiness, gains and losses,
success or failure ..." *(Bhagavad Gita, II.38)*

The statement above is so reminiscent of the vow taken by Western couples married in a church or civil ceremony that one might think of it as the Sanskrit equivalent. It is, however, the wisdom imparted by Lord Krishna on the battlefield of Kurukshetra to urge the warrior Arjuna to do his duty and engage in battle in order to restore dharma. Thus although it is similar to the wedding vow, the context seems different. Or is it? After all the Kurukshetra battle may be compared to the travails a couple encounters as they embark on the journey of life together. Thus to support each other and maintain a balanced mind in times of happiness or trouble, in sickness or health, ... is the mandate which both sign onto during the wedding ceremony.

We shall start with a basic assumption that marriage is defined as the journey, through life together, of a loving, committed couple. Marriage is largely a social arrangement between two adults but is governed by laws of the land that offer protection to the essential individualities of the two persons so that the union may continue to be secure and peaceful. Through a solemn ceremony, this social arrangement also procures a religious sanction which serves as an umbrella under which the commitments made can be preserved as long as the couple shall live. In this treatise, for the sake of convenience as well as respect for many thousands of years of tradition, the marital unit is considered to be a man and a woman.

A wedding, on the other hand, is an event and a ritual. It is the formalization and acknowledgment of the basic human need for companionship and is brought about by the desire to share with family and friends the great news: the magical attraction between two individuals through an appreciation of physical features and/or an emotional bonding through shared values between the two persons. It is the process that launches a couple into the institution known as marriage, or in religious terms, holy matrimony, and this process is therefore a social-cum-religious set of procedures defined by the cultural, religious and social heritages of the partners. The process of wedding can be so vastly different from culture to culture and even within the same culture that a first view appears to rule out any commonality. Nevertheless, a careful review of approaches within and among cultures reveals an amazing degree of resemblance that only serves to confirm the essentially common hopes and aspirations of all our ancestors. In spite of some similarities and many differences, what is of special importance is the beauty and significance of the traditions of the families involved and how they are integrated into the steps taken by the couple during the wedding ritual.

I have been assisting Hindu families in the United States for nearly three decades with the wedding plans and ceremonies of their sons and daughters. Sometimes these ceremonies have involved a Hindu bride and a non-Hindu groom, or vice versa. The families have been immigrants from different parts of India including Punjab, Bengal, Uttar Pradesh, Gujarat, Andhra Pradesh, Kerala and Karnataka. The non-Hindus have included several denominations of Christianity, Jewish and Shaman faiths.

Over these years I have been impressed by the genuine interest on the part of the younger generation in understanding Vedic wedding practices and the philosophy behind them. At the same time it has become clear to me that many parents may lack basic knowledge of these practices as much as they relish the fact that their son or daughter wishes to respect their heritage. There is a very simple explanation to this dilemma. Parents who married in India four or five decades ago went through the steps in front of their own parents and supporting relatives. They were generally not expected to know the meaning of all the Sanskrit chants and rituals. No one, least of all the officiating priests, insisted that they understand the background and meaning of the several steps before they made the most personal commitment of their lives. In modern mid-twentieth century India it was even considered fashionable to look down on the rituals and consider the event as simply a social experience!

When young people approach me now asking me to perform their wedding, I am touched by their desire to understand each of the several steps they will be taking during the ceremony, and I am happy to oblige. I first make sure that they want a traditional wedding and are not doing it to please someone else. Most are concerned about the time it takes to complete the ceremony. I try to impress upon them the need to retain certain essential steps and that the time involved will depend upon how well they remember and perform what they have learned during the meetings with me and during the rehearsal prior to the wedding.

We emphasize the need for a good rehearsal to work out the logistics as well as the ceremonial steps with all the principals attending. We have tried to help families by developing a concise ceremony based on the scriptures, with necessary variations to suit individual family traditions. Through this effort I have been able to convey to the families that the solemn procedures prescribed by our ancestors are full of meaning and beauty as they charge the couple with responsibilities they inherit by virtue of the union.

The Hindu wedding ceremony is based on Vedic traditions and rituals originating in the Rig Veda, the earliest of the four ancient Sanskrit books of knowledge which form the basis of Hinduism. Variations of procedures are to be found in the Yajur, Sama and Atharva Vedas and elaborated in the Grihya Sutras. Conjugal union has always been considered an important Hindu religious and social celebration, defining the beginning of the second stage of earthly existence, the first, beyond childhood, being that of the student. These rituals, which date back at least 5,000 years, form a dramatic sequence. By involving the principals as well as the audience during the ceremonies, we have been able to maintain a sense of discipline, solemnity and joy throughout.

The format we have developed works well with modern needs and can be tailored to suit individual family traditions. In fact it is so successful that in two interfaith weddings between Hindu and Jewish principals, the entire ceremony consisting of both traditions was blended and performed as a seamless wedding to the utter delight of both families. This was possible because during initial meetings we discovered certain essentially similar steps in both traditions. It takes some effort, some research and some practice, but it can be an enjoyable cultural, social and spiritual experience that the young people and their guests will never forget. It reinforces the Hindu belief and vision as stated eloquently in the Rig Veda: ऐकं सत् विप्रा: बहुधा वदंति *(ēkam sat viprā: bahudhā vadanti)*. Truth is one, the wise utter it in different ways (*Rig Veda, Book 1, Hymn CLXIV. 46*).

May those who unite under the banner of a great tradition benefit from the beauty, pageantry and depth of human understanding that seek to bring together two families for all time.

Chapter II

HINDU PHILOSOPHY OF MARRIAGE

Friendship, Dharmapatni, Vivāha Samskāra

किंस्विन् मित्रं गृहेसतः?

kimsvin mitram gṛhēsata:?

Who is the friend of the householder?

भार्या मित्रं गृहेसतः

bhāryā mitram gṛhēsata:

One's wife

Friendship

The above question was posed to the hero Yudhishtira by a yaksha (forest spirit) as quoted in the Aranya Parva of the second great epic of India, the Mahabharata. This story from the Mahabharata has also been retold in the author's earlier publication, *A Hindu Primer:Yaksha Prashna*. The answer by the hero crystallizes the Hindu belief that friendship between a couple is the true basis for the marital union.

Centuries ago, civilized societies recognized and acknowledged the most basic instinct of all, i.e. the need for companionship, and founded the honorable institution known as marriage. Experience has shown that life is full of conflicts, questions, concerns, temptations, joys, sorrows, ups and downs, and Hindus believe that this institution of marriage can help navigate the complex ocean of life. Ancient sages, who were great thinkers, developed some guidelines to make sure that this institution was a permanent one capable of not only bringing happiness to two young people but also providing for the fullness of life within the framework they called dharma, the Hindu code of right conduct.

The July 1989 issue of Readers Digest carried an article entitled *"Surprising Key to the Happiest Couples"* written by two psychologists who conclude that "Romance 'talks' about love but it is friendship that puts love to the ultimate test." They continue: "If there is one prevailing wish that husbands and wives have for their marriage, it is to be close companions for life. While many men and women know that love is essential for such a lifelong bond, they often don't realize that love without close friendship is only a hormonal illusion. One cannot desire another person over the long haul without really being best friends with that person."

This may be a newly discovered concept for modern psychologists but the Pandava prince Yudhishtira already revealed this "secret" about four thousand years ago! According to Hindus, therefore, the basis for marriage is friendship. This friendship is the understanding, the promise and the commitment that unites a man and a woman. There is absolutely no question about the role of a woman, her importance, her position in this equation that binds them together.

Let me explain. In most Hindu wedding ceremonies, the climax is reached when a particular event takes place. That peak in the ceremony known as

Mangalyadharanam confirms for ever and seals the bond between the couple through the tying of a golden necklace or pendant around the bride's neck by the groom. Traditionally, that is the sacred moment in the wedding when they become husband and wife. But what happens later in a concluding ceremony is truly the most significant and meaningful for the rest of their marriage. Because, after the Mangalyadharanam, the bride and the groom hold hands and take seven steps together as husband and wife as they walk around Agni, the god of fire, (the kindled fire symbolic of their new hearth) and pledge to each other their eternal friendship. What they say after they have taken those seven steps is unquestionably the foundation for a successful marriage. Together they chant:

सखा सप्तपदी भव सख्यं ते गमेयं
सख्यं ते मायोशः सख्यं ते मायोष्टः

sakhā saptapadī bhava sakhyam tē gamēyam
sakhyam tē māyōśa: sakhyam tē māyōṣṭa:

"With these seven steps you have become my friend.
May I deserve your friendship.
May my friendship make me one with you.
May your friendship make you one with me." *(after Lal, P., 1996)*

Anyone who has any question about the role of a woman in a Hindu marriage should pay special attention to the charge and blessing by the presiding priest at the end of the Saptapadi. He recites:

साम्राज्ञी श्वशुरेभव
साम्राज्ञी श्वश्रुवांभव
ननान्दरि साम्राज्ञीभव
साम्राज्ञी अधिदेवृषु

sāmrājnī śvaśurēbhava
sāmrājnī śvaśruvāmbhava
nanandāri sāmrājnībhava
sāmrājnī adhidēvṛṣu

"Be queenly with your father-in-law
Be queenly with your mother-in-law
Be queenly with your husband's sisters
Be queenly with your husband's brothers"

(*after A.C. Bose, 1970*)

Nothing short of the status of a queen is what the scriptures prescribe. Hindu ancestors went even further; they blessed the bride by saying:

मूर्धानं पत्युरारोह

mūrdhānam patyurārōha

"May your husband keep you on his head"

meaning "Let him respect you."

There is another question in the Yaksha Prashna episode where this subject matter comes up:

किंस्विद् दैवकृतः सखा

kimsvid daivakṛta: sakhā

Who is a man's God-given friend?

Yudhishtira's answer was:

भार्या दैवकृतः सखा

bhāryā daivakṛta: sakhā

A man's God-given friend is his wife.

Again the basis of friendship in marriage is emphasized.

The concept of the dharmapatni

Hindu religion and culture are rooted in the Vedas, whose final composition is attributed to around 1500 B.C. or earlier. The Vedic ideal of marriage, according to Abhinash Chandra Bose (*The Call of the Vedas*, page 259, Bharatiya Vidya Bhavan, 1970) "is that of perfect monogamy, the life-long companionship of two people. This practice must have been well established, as is evident from the fact that the Vedic rishi, seeking comparisons for the perfect duality of the twin deities, the Ashvins, gives along with examples of two eyes, two lips, etc., that of a married couple."

Popular misconceptions notwithstanding, a serious study of the Vedas reveals how practical the findings of the ancient sages can be. "Vedic sages are positive in their acceptance of life and death and life's struggles and limitations, positive too in their acceptance of the ultimate values of truth, goodness and beauty... Vedic sages loved life as well as God, every wish of theirs for the good things of the earth took the form of an ardent prayer." (Bose, *ibid, 2*). Such prayers are blended into the Vedic wedding ceremony.

Certain Vedic prayers are directed towards acquiring intellectual power, wisdom, efficiency, spiritual vigor, higher skills, leading to the acquisition of what is known as brahmateja, the radiance of intellect. Certain other prayers are for strength, valor, spiritual power, victory, fearlessness and other qualities of heroism known as kshatravirya, physical prowess. The Vedas proclaim that the true goal of life is freedom and that this freedom from attachment, freedom from our lower selves, brings such joy that it is simply incomparable to the usual kinds of joy most recognize. Therefore, Hindus considered that fulfillment comes when one accomplishes four aspects of life known as dharma, artha and kama leading to complete release from bondage, that total freedom known as moksha. We have defined dharma as the moral law governing right conduct and it truly forms the very core of Hindu philosophy. The inclusion of artha (material values) and kama (sensibilities) in this series emphasizes their vital role in the life of a householder and confirms the practicality of Vedic thought. Vedic prayer included the societal and familial need for progeny as well as the individual's need for self-knowledge and redemption.

"Dharma, artha and kama conflict with each other. How can these contraries be reconciled?" This in fact was the third question on the subject asked of Yudhishtira by the yaksha:

धर्मश्चार्थश्च कामश्च परस्पर विरोधिनः
ऐषां नित्य विरुद्धानाम् कथमेकत्र संगमः

dharmaścārthaśca kāmaśca paraspara virōdhina:
ēṣām nitya viruddhānām kathamēkatra sangama:

How can a householder necessarily involved in the pursuit of the good life seeking artha and kama in raising a family and serving a community not find himself in conflict with dharma and how can he strive for moksha? Notice that artha and kama are safely sandwiched between dharma and moksha. If salvation is to be the goal, the ancient Hindus said, then by all means participate fully in the affairs of society, raise a family, enjoy the good life, serve the community–all within the framework of dharma.

How does a grihastha (a householder) reconcile these contrary requirements? According to Yudhishtira, there is only one way and that is:

यदा धर्मश्च भार्याच परस्पर वशानुगौ
तदा धर्मार्थकामानाम् त्रयाणामपि संगमः

yadā dharmaśca bhāryāca paraspara vaśānugau
tadā dharmārthakāmānām trayāṇāmapi sangama:

"When dharma and one's wife are in harmony,
then dharma, artha and kama are reconciled."

In other words, a man, in order to keep that delicate balance among the attributes of artha and kama, has to have a wife who is dharmic. It is that protection coming from such a spouse, that torchlight, that spirit of friendship and cooperation and sacrifice, that gives a reasonable chance for a couple to succeed in meeting this challenge of conflicting attributes.

The basic purpose of a Vedic wedding ceremony is to help unite a couple in the Vedic tradition. Understanding each step and the various vows is essential irrespective of the ability to repeat the mantras. Each step in the ceremony conveys implicitly or explicitly an understanding between the two. The principals inherit the burden of providing the umbrella of dharma so that the family they are about to raise, their own family, will be a dharmic one. A Hindu wife plays a major role in this, a burden that some may consider unfair. But that is the tradition and expectation. That is why a Hindu wife is not simply referred to as patni (wife) but she is a dharmapatni, a wife-in-dharma. This then is the reason for that very special, very unique, very necessary role a wife was called upon to play in the Hindu household.

Vivaha Samskara

H.T. Colebrooke, presenting a paper, *"On the Religious Ceremonies of the Hindus,"* in 1801, notes a contemporary point of deterioration in Indian society: "Among Hindus, a girl is married before the age of puberty. The law even censures the delay of her marriage beyond the tenth year." He goes on to explain this in terms of the father's obligation:

> "...it may be remarked, that it arises from a laudable motive; from a sense of duty incumbent on a father, who considers as a debt the obligation of providing a suitable match for his daughter. This notion, which is strongly inculcated by Hindu legislators, is forcibly impressed on the minds of parents."

Vivaha is easily recognized by Hindus as one of the samskaras or obligatory rites that cover a Hindu's life from conception to the funeral ceremony. The father's address to the prospective bridegroom at the time of Kanyadanam, "I offer to you, my daughter, foremost among young women, here by my side, covered with golden ornaments, so that I may obtain salvation in Brahmaloka" is also a declaration to the assembled that this sacred obligation is now being fulfilled.

Contemporary brides, unlike those in post-Vedic and post-epic times, are not children to be hastily secured in another family by parents with uncertain, usually short, life spans or bound by outworn social norms. They are usually capable of making their own choices of a mate, especially outside India where they have equal say in wedding arrangements.

Love is … an endless mystery, for it has nothing else to explain it.

Rabindranath Tagore

Bapu

Chapter III

THE ORIGINS

चतुर्णां आश्रमाणां हि गार्हस्थ्यं श्रेष्ठमाश्रमं

caturṇām āśramāṇām hi gārhasthyam śrēṣṭamāśramam

"Among the four stages of life, that of the householder is the best"

So said prince Bharata, in the Ramayana, in order to persuade his elder brother Rama to abandon his exile in the forest, as more appropriate to a later age and stage, and to return to Ayodhya to rule the kingdom and resume a normal life. Hindus divide the span of life into four parts that begin with education (student) and graduate to the status of householder. Retirement and total renunciation (sanyasin) complete the later stages. Each stage is appropriate to the age of the individual and all are considered equally important towards salvation (moksha or final release from rebirth). Barring extraordinary reasons one is urged not to abandon the responsibilities due at each stage. The householder stage is when the individual is fully equipped physically and mentally to perform his duties to himself, to his family, his community, to the country and the world and therefore this stage is considered the most important. Bharata's argument was that, as a young man and the eldest brother, Rama had a duty, appropriate to his age and station, to become king.

The charge to set up a household has its roots in the Vedas. In the following we trace the origins of this institution. An understanding of the origins and history of the Vedic wedding ceremony helps to explain not only the spirit behind the ancient words and gestures but also the reason for their continuing strong hold on young and old. Their validity over several centuries confers on these prescribed rites-of-passage (samskaras) the timeless quality of Vedic practice.

The Vedas

Veda, from the root "vid," means knowledge. The Vedas are four sacred books of knowledge, titled Rig (or Rg) Veda, Yajur Veda, Sama Veda and

Atharva Veda. The Rig Veda, consisting of 10 mandalas (books) containing 1,028 hymns (10,552 verses), is perhaps the oldest known poem of its kind, dated c. 1500 B.C. at the latest in its final form. The main theme is one of praise for Vedic gods such as Agni, Indra, Soma and Rudra. The Yajur Veda is a book of 1,975 mantras defining sacrifices used in the performance of ceremonies. The Sama Veda is a hymnal of 1,875 mantras. The Atharva Veda of 5,987 mantras describes spells and cures. The Vedas are written in early Sanskrit, a language which is the ancestor of most modern languages of India.

I. Rig Veda

The earliest Vedic reference to a wedding is found in the Rig Veda. That ceremony, which is described in some detail below, was fairly simple compared to Hindu wedding ceremonies of today. And yet the basic structure today is, as will be seen, still patterned after the wedding of Suryā (daughter of Surya, the sun god) to Soma, god of the moon. Today's bride at a wedding ceremony is symbolically Suryā herself who, in her earlier lives, as a member of a divine family, was married to Soma, later to a Gandharva and then to Agni. But in her present incarnation as a human, she is now ready to be married to another human.

सोमः प्रथमो विविदे गन्धर्वो विविद उत्तरः
तृतीयोग्निष्टे पतिस्तुरो यस्ते मनुष्यजाः

sōma: prathamō vividē gandharvō vivida uttara:
tṛtīyōgniṣṭē patisturō yastē manuśyajā:

"Soma obtained her first of all; next the Gandharva was her lord.
Agni was thy third husband; now one born of woman is thy fourth."

(*Griffith, RV 10. LXXXV. 40*)

This is the primary reason behind a practice in which the couple offer their first oblations to these former husbands in order during the fire ritual. It is important to note how the shloka refers to Suryā in the third person first and then shifts to a generic bride addressed in the second person.

An account of Suryā's wedding ceremony is found in Mandala 10, hymn 85 in the Rig Veda. The translation by Ralph T.H. Griffith *(Hymns of the Rig Veda,* 1889) is used here. The numbering corresponds to that in the Griffith reference. Each section below includes a descriptive title and commentary added here for the convenience of the reader. Both are shown in italics to distinguish the actual Vedic text from the interpretations.

Rig Veda - HYMN LXXXV. Suryā's Bridal.

Invocation/ Pravara

1 TRUTH is the base that bears the earth; by Surya are the heavens sustained. By Law the Adityas stand secure, and Soma holds his place in heaven.

2 By Soma are the Adityas strong, by Soma mighty is the earth. Thus Soma in the midst of all these constellations hath his place … The Moon is that which shapes the years.

These lines serve as either an invocation before the ceremony begins or as a statement defining place and time of the event. They also indicate the status of the giver of the bride, her father Surya, and the power and importance of the prospective bridegroom, Soma.

The bridal party

6 Raibhi was her dear bridal friend, and Narasamsi led her home. Lovely was Suryā's robe: she came to that which Gatha had adorned.

7 Thought was the pillow of her couch, sight was the unguent for her eyes: Her treasury was earth and heaven when Suryā went unto her Lord.

8 Hymns were the cross-bars of the pole, Kurira-metre decked the car: The bridesmen were the Asvin Pair Agni was leader of the train.

9 Soma was he who wooed the maid: the groomsmen were both Asvins, when The Sun-God Savitar bestowed his willing Suryā on her Lord.

17 To Surya and the Deities, to Mitra and to Varuna. Who know aright the thing that is, this adoration have I paid.

These stanzas may be interpreted as an introduction to or description of the bridal party and invocation of Vedic deities as witnesses and protectors of the new household.

Fire ceremony

18 By their own power these Twain in close succession move; They go as playing children round the sacrifice. One, of the Pair beholdeth all existing things; the other ordereth seasons and is born again.

Refers to the supposed spatial relationship between the Sun and the Moon and possibly also to circumambulation around the fire.

A blessing

19 He, born afresh, is new and new for ever: ensign of days he goes before the Mornings. Coming, he orders for the Gods their portion. The Moon prolongs the days of our existence.

This shloka is a very commonly used blessing by priests on almost every occasion including weddings.

Invocation and farewell to the Gandharva *(second husband of Suryā,* guardian of the current bride as lord of the dwelling place of her ancestors)

21 Rise up from hence: this maiden hath a husband. I laud Visvāvasu with hymns and homage. Seek in her father's home another fair one, and find the portion from of old assigned thee.

22 Rise up from hence, Visvāvasu: with reverence we worship thee. Seek thou another willing maid, and with her husband leave the bride.

"With reverence" the former suitor/guardian is asked to look for another bride or ward just before the ceremony starts.

Blessings for the witnesses and the ceremony

23 Straight in direction be the paths, and thornless, whereon our fellows travel to the wooing. Let Aryaman and Bhaga lead us: perfect, O Gods, the union of the wife and husband.

Prayer for the paths to the wedding to be unobstructed and to Aryaman and Bhaga, personifications of family honor and ancestral share.

Blessing of the bride released from her former to her new home

24 Now from the noose of Varuna I free thee, wherewith Most Blessed Savitar hath bound thee. In Law's seat, to the world of virtuous action, I give thee up uninjured with thy consort.

25 Hence, and not thence, I send these free. I make thee softly fettered there. That, Bounteous Indra, she may live blest in her fortune and her sons.

Parents' blessing and ceremony of release from her first home and obligations.

Brother of the bride as escort.

26 Let Pūsan take thy hand and hence conduct thee; may the two Asvins on their car transport thee. Go to the house to be the household's mistress and speak as lady to thy gathered people.

27 Happy be thou and prosper with thy children here: be vigilant to rule thy household in this home. Closely unite thy body with this man, thy lord. So shall ye, full of years, address your company.

Guidance from the brother of Suryā (Pusan, the guardian of roads, nourisher) and an assurance of her role as a ruler in "thy household."

Protection from possible ills carried from the previous home

31 Consumptions, from her people, which follow the bride's resplendent train These let the Holy Gods again bear to the place from which they came.

Purification ritual to counter any ill that may travel unseen from the former household to the new.

Protection during the journey

32 Let not the highway thieves who lie in ambush find the wedded pair. By pleasant ways let them escape the danger, and let foes depart.

More prayer for a trouble-free passage to her new household.

Bride is presented to the assembled

33 Signs of good fortune mark the bride: come all of you and look at her. Wish her prosperity …

This is now commonly used as the bride approaches the wedding mantap or as a signal to remove the antarpat which shields the bride from the groom.

Groom's vow

36 I take thy hand in mine for happy fortune that thou mayst reach old age with me thy husband. Gods, Aryaman, Bhaga, Savitar, Purandhi, have given thee to be my household's mistress.

The groom addresses the bride. Savitar is the Sun and Purandhi is abundance. This verse is still used as a vow.

The groom addresses the deities by whose grace he received the bride

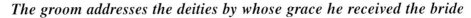

37 O Pūsan, send her on as most auspicious, her who shall be the sharer of my pleasures; Her who shall twine her loving arms about me, and welcome all my love and mine embraces.

38 For thee, with bridal train, they, first, escorted Suryā to her home. Give to the husband in return, Agni, the wife with progeny

39 Agni hath given the bride again with splendour and with ample life. Long lived be he who is her lord; a hundred autumns let him live.

40 Sōma obtained her first of all; next the Gandharva was her lord. Agni was thy third husband: now one born of woman is thy fourth.

41 Sōma to the Gandharva, and to Agni the Gandharva gave: And Agni hath bestowed on me riches and sons and this my spouse.

The groom addresses the bride

42 Be ye not parted; dwell ye here; reach the full time of human life. With sons and grandsons sport and play, rejoicing in your own abode.

43 So may Prajāpati bring children forth to us; may Aryaman adorn us till old age come nigh. Not inauspicious enter thou thy husband's house: bring blessing to our bipeds and our quadrupeds.

44 Not evil-eyed, no slayer of thy husband, bring weal to cattle, radiant, gentle-hearted; Loving the Gods, delightful, bearing heroes, bring blessing to our quadrupeds and bipeds.

Note especially the interest in the welfare of "bipeds and quadrupeds," which was usually the concern of the Ashwins, the heavenly Twins, Suryā's escort.

The groom asks for blessings for the bride

45 O Bounteous Indra, make this bride blest in her sons and fortunate. Vouchsafe to her ten sons, and make her husband the eleventh man.

Prayer for progeny, and mother-like care for the husband.

Groom to bride, conferring her domestic status, with more blessings

46 Over thy husband's father and thy husband's mother bear full sway. Over the sister of thy lord, over his brothers rule supreme.

47 So may the Universal Gods, so may the Waters join our hearts. May Matarisvan, Dhatar, and Destri together bind us close.

Verse #46 is a blessing used by priests after Saptapadi. Note that Aryaman represents the rules of society, code of honor, in this case the marriage contract. Bhaga represents the inherited share of tribal property, Savitar the sun; Pusan represents guidance and protection and Purandhi, abundance. Matarisvan is Agni as the spark of conception, Dhatar is order or sustainer, Destri, Instructress, is usually understood to be Saraswati, according to Griffith.

The above Rigvedic account confirms the ancients' emphasis on the practical aspects of the event. In addition to statement of location, the backgrounds of the couple, prayers for the success of the marriage, there are specific appeasements to former suitors of the bride, urging them to recognize the reality of the situation and seek other women to wed; and prayers for a safe travel to the bridegroom's house unencumbered by robbers and highwaymen.

II. Other Vedic Sources

A more complete description of Vedic practices in weddings is available in an excellent nineteenth century account, written by Henry Thomas Colebrooke (*Miscellaneous Essays*, Second Edition, Madras; Higginbothams and Co., 1872), which contains a detailed description of wedding ceremonies drawn from followers of the Yajur, Sama and Atharva Vedas. Selections from his essay are reproduced below. Colebrooke's 1801 account, collected from two unnamed sources, shows that the wedding process had evolved into clear and specific steps. At the outset we note that certain basic practices and steps as described below have remained intact and are important features still practiced in today's ceremonies. These include the ritual use of water and fire, chanting of the Gayatri mantra, blessings, and the charge to the groom and the bride.

As before, each selection includes a descriptive title and commentary for the convenience of the reader. Both are shown in italics to distinguish the cited actual text from the interpretations.

The arrival

> Having previously performed the obsequies of ancestors, as is usual upon any accession of good fortune, the father of the bride sits down to await the bridegroom's arrival, in the apartment prepared for the purpose; and at the time chosen for it, according to the rules of astrology. The jewels and other presents intended for him are placed there; a cow is tied on the northern side of the apartment; and a stool or cushion, and other furniture for the reception of the guest, are arranged in order.

The bride's father prepares for the arrival of the groom in procession. Not unlike the Swagatam step in today's context.

Welcome and cow worship

> On his approach, the bride's father rises to welcome him, and recites the following prayer, while the bridegroom stands before him: "May she [who supplies oblations for] religious worship, who constantly follows

her calf, and who was the milch cow when YAMA was [the votary], abound with milk, and fulfill our wishes, year after year." This prayer is seemingly intended for the consecration of the cow, which is let loose in a subsequent stage of the ceremony, instead of slaying her, as appears to have been anciently the custom.

The ceremony begins with worship of a cow. This step appears to be absent from today's wedding ceremonies, although it occurs in one form or another in housewarming ceremonies.

A dialogue between the bride's father and the groom; offer of a seat and footstool

After the prayer above-mentioned has been meditated the bridegroom sits down on a stool or cushion, which is presented to him. He first recites a text of the *Yajurveda:* "I step on this for the sake of food and other benefits, on this variously splendid footstool." The bride's father presents to him a cushion made of twenty leaves of *cusa* grass, holding it up with both hands, and exclaiming, "The cushion! the cushion! the cushion!" The bridegroom replies, "I accept the cushion," and, taking it, places it on the ground under his feet, while he recites the following prayer: "May those plants over which SOMA presides, and which are variously dispersed on the earth incessantly grant me happiness while this cushion is placed under my feet." Another is presented to him, which he accepts in the same manner, saying, "May those numerous plants over which SOMA presides, and which are salutary a hundred different ways, incessantly grant me happiness while I sit on this cushion." Instead of these prayers, which are peculiar to the *Brahmanas* that use the *Samaveda,* the following text is commonly recited: "I obscure my rivals, as the sun does other luminaries; I tread on this, as the type of him who injures me."

The details shown above and below are somewhat akin to the Vara Puja of modern times. A seat is offered. Note how the approach varies from Yajur Veda to Sama Veda.

Ablutions; offer of water to wash hands and feet

The bride's father next offers a vessel of water, thrice exclaiming, "Water for ablutions!" The bridegroom declares his acceptance of it, and looks into the vessel, saying, "Generous water! I view thee; return in the form of fertilizing rain from him, from whom thou dost proceed:" that is, from the sun; for it is acknowledged, says the commentator, that rain proceeds from vapors raised by the heat of the sun. The bridegroom takes up water in the palms of both hands joined together, and throws it on his left foot, saying, "I wash my left foot, and fix prosperity in this realm:" he also throws water on his other foot, saying, "I wash my right foot, and introduce prosperity into this realm:" and he then throws water on both feet, saying, "I wash first one and then the other, and lastly both feet, that the realm may thrive and intrepidity be gained." The following is the text of the *Yajush,* which is generally used instead of the preceding prayers: "Thou dost afford various elegance; I accept thee, who dost so: afford it for the ablution of my feet."

An *arghya* (that is, water, rice, and *dūrva* grass, in a conch, or in a vessel shaped like one, or rather like a boat) is next presented to the bridegroom in a similar manner, and accepted by him with equal formality. He pours the water on his own head, saying, "Thou art the splendor of food; through thee may I become glorious." This prayer is taken from the *Yajush;* but the followers of that *Veda* use different texts, accepting the *arghya* with this prayer, "Ye are waters *(ap);* through you may I obtain *(ap)* all my wishes:" and pouring out the water with this

text, "I dismiss you to the ocean; return to your source, harmless unto me, most excellent waters! but my beverage is not poured forth."

Offer of and use of water as a part of the ceremony is in use today. Both arghya (washing hands) and padya (washing feet) are included. The use of a conch, although not common in practice today, is interesting, because it is one of the first items worshipped after worshipping earth (Bhoomimāta, Mother Earth) in the performance of Satyanārayana Puja.

Offer of achamana (water to drink)

A vessel of water is then offered by the bride's father, who thrice exclaims, "Take water to be sipped:" the bridegroom accepts it, saying, "Thou art glorious, grant me glory;" or else, "Conduct me to glory, endue me with splendor, render me dear to all people, make me owner of cattle, and preserve me unhurt in all my limbs."

Madhuparka (sweetened food or drink)

The bride's father fills a vessel with honey, curds, and clarified butter; he covers it with another vessel, and presents it to the bridegroom, exclaiming three times, "Take the *mad'huparca."* The bridegroom accepts it, places it on the ground, and looks into it, saying, "Thou art glorious; may I become so." He tastes the food three times, saying, "Thou art the sustenance of the glorious; thou art the nourishment of the splendid: thou art the food of the fortunate; grant me prosperity." He then silently eats until he be satisfied.

Although these texts be taken from the *Yajush,* yet other prayers from the same *Veda* are used by the sects which follow it. While looking into the vessel, the bridegroom says, "I view thee with the eye of the sun [who draws unto himself what he contemplates]." On accepting the *mad'huparca* the bridegroom says, "I take thee with the assent of the generous sun; with the arms of both sons of *Aswini;* with the hands of the cherishing luminary." He mixes it, saying, "May I mix thee, O venerable present! and remove whatever might be hurtful in the eating of thee." He tastes it three times, saying, "May I eat that sweet, best, and nourishing form of honey; which is the sweet, best, and nourishing form of honey; and may I thus become excellent, sweet-tempered, and well nourished by food." After eating until he be satisfied, and after sipping water, he touches his mouth and other parts of his body with his hand, saying, "May there be speech in my mouth, breath in my nostrils, sight in my eye-balls, hearing in my ears, strength in my arms, firmness in my thighs; may my limbs and members remain unhurt together with my soul."

The offering of madhuparka is still in practice in many families.

Offer of gifts

Presents suitable to the rank of the parties are then presented to the guest. At the marriage ceremony, too, the bride is formally given by her father to the bridegroom, in this stage of the solemnity according to some rituals, but later according to others.

The cow is released

The hospitable rites are then concluded by letting loose the cow at the intercession of the guest. A barber who attends for that purpose exclaims, "The cow! the cow!" Upon which the guest pronounces this text: "Release the cow from the fetters of VARUNA. May she subdue my foe: may she destroy the enemies of both him (the host) [and me]. Dismiss the cow, that she may eat grass and drink water."

Hasta milap

After the bridegroom has tasted the *Mad'huparca* presented to him, as above mentioned, the bride's right hand is placed on his, both having been previously rubbed with turmeric or some other auspicious drug. A matron must bind both hands with *cuśa* grass amidst the sound of cheerful music.

Both hasta milap and "cheerful music" are part of the modern ceremony.

Kanyadanam

The bride's father, bidding the attendant priests begin their acclamations, such as "happy day! auspicious be it! prosperity attend! blessings!" &c., takes a vessel of water containing *tila (Sesamum Indicum)* and *Cusa (Poa cynosuroides*) grass, and pours it on the hands of the bride and bridegroom, after uttering the words, *"O'm tat sat!"* "God the existent!"

The description comes close to the current practice of Kanyadanam; the *notable difference is that in the above description the bride's mother does not play a role in pouring water. The use of tila is interesting as it is always used in offering sacrifices such as during Tarpan (sacrifices during ceremonies honoring ancestors.)*

Pravara Recital

... and after repeating at full length the names and designations of the bridegroom, of the bride, and of himself; and then solemnly declaring, "I give unto thee this damsel adorned with jewels and protected by the lord of creatures." The bridegroom replies, "Well be it!" The bride's father afterwards gives him a piece of gold, saying, "I this day give thee this gold, as a fee for the purpose of completing the solemn donation made by me." The bridegroom again says, "Well be it!" and then recites the text below:

This is similar to current practice although specific mention is not made here of reciting three lineages, three times, for each side as in use today. The part of the mantra "this damsel adorned with jewels..." is familiar.

Vows

"Who gave *her?* to whom did he give *her?* Love (or free consent) gave *her.* To love he gave *her.* Love was the giver. Love was the taker. Love! may this be thine! With love may I enjoy *her!*" The close of the text is thus varied in the *Sāmaveda:* "Love has pervaded the ocean. With love I accept *her.* Love! may this be thine." In the common rituals another prayer is directed to be likewise recited immediately after thus formally accepting the bride: "May the ethereal element give thee. May earth accept thee."

The above shlokas are sometimes used now as part of the vows.

Promise and appeal

Being thus affianced, the bride and bridegroom then walk forth, while he thus addresses her: "May the regents of space, may air, the sun, and fire, dispel that anxiety which thou feelest in thy mind, and turn thy heart to me." He proceeds thus, while they look at each other: "Be gentle in thy aspect and loyal to thy husband; be fortunate in cattle, amiable in thy mind, and beautiful in thy person; be mother of valiant sons; be fond of delights; be cheerful, and bring prosperity to our bipeds and quadrupeds. First [in a former birth] SOMA received thee; the sun next obtained thee; [in successive transmigrations] the regent of fire was thy third husband: thy fourth is a human being. SOMA gave her to the sun; the sun gave her to the regent of fire; fire gave her to me; with her he has given me wealth and male offspring. May she, a most auspicious cause of prosperity, never desert me," &c.

Bridegroom's promise and special appeal to the bride. These shlokas are used in today's ceremony also.

The knot; gift of apparel

It should seem that, according to these rituals, the bridegroom gives a waistcloth and mantle to the bride before he is affianced to her; and the ceremony of tying the skirts of their mantles precedes that of her father's solemnly bestowing her on the bridegroom. But the ritual of the *Samavedi* priests makes the gift of the damsel precede the tying of the knot; and, inconsistently enough, directs the mantles to be tied before the bridegroom has clothed the bride. After the donation has been accepted as above mentioned, the bride's father should tie a knot in the bridegroom's mantle over the presents given with the bride, while the affianced pair are looking at each other. The cow is then released in the manner before described; a libation of water is made; and the bride's father meditates the *Gayatri,* and ties a knot with the skirts of the bride's and bridegroom's mantles, after saying, "Ye must be inseparably united in matters of duty, wealth, and love."

Tying the bride and groom together through a knot in their upper garments is still practiced in many weddings. Note especially the charge to the bridegroom from the bride's father: "Ye must be inseparably united in matters of duty, wealth, and love." This is the reference to the chaturvidha phala purushartha *and a promise extracted from the bridegroom that he shall not cross the boundaries implied in dharma, artha and kama.*

The fire ritual

He goes to the principal apartment of the house, prepares a sacrificial fire in the usual mode, and hallows the implements of sacrifice. A friend of the bridegroom walks round the fire, bearing a jar of water, and stops on the south side of it: another does the same, and places himself on the right hand of the first. The bridegroom then casts four double handfuls of rice, mixed with leaves of *sami,* into a flat basket: near it he places a stone and mullar, after formally touching them, and then entering the house, he causes the bride to be clothed with a new waistcloth and scarf, while he recites the subjoined prayers: "May those generous women who spun and wound the thread, and who wove the warp and weft of this cloth, generously clothe thee to old age: long-lived woman! put on this raiment." "Clothe her: invest her with apparel: prolong her life to great age. Mayest thou live a hundred years. As long as thou livest, amiable woman! revere [that is, carefully preserve] beauty and wealth." The first of these prayers is nearly the same with that which is used by the followers of the *Yajush,* when the scarf is put on the bride's shoulder. It is preceded by a different one, which is recited while the waistcloth is wrapped round her: "Mayest thou reach old age. Put on this raiment. Be lovely: be chaste. Live a hundred years. Invite [that "is, preserve and obtain] beauty, wealth, and male offspring. Damsel! put on this apparel." Afterwards the following prayer is recited: "May the assembled gods unite our hearts. May the waters unite them. May air unite us. May the creator unite us. May the god of love unite us."

The bridegroom conducts a homa or fire ritual. Upon entering the main room of the bride's parent's house he presents gifts of clothing to the bride and prays for her prosperity and longevity as is done today. In families that perform elaborate ceremonies over a period of two to three days, this is still practiced in the form of Gṛhapravesham. The bride may also take leave for a while during the ceremony to change into the gifted garment and return. A stone slab is still used in the ceremony known as Ashmarohana. Prayers offered at the end of this ceremony are still in use.

The homas

But, according to the followers of the *Samaveda,* the bridegroom, immediately after the scarf has been placed on the bride's shoulder, conducts her towards the sacrificial fire, saying, "SOMA [the regent of the moon] gave her to the sun: the sun gave her to the regent of fire: fire has given her to me, and with her, wealth and male offspring." The bride then goes to the western side of the fire and recites the following prayer, while she steps on a mat made of *Virana* grass* and covered with silk: "May our lord assign me the path by which I may reach the abode of my lord." She sits down on the edge of the mat; and the bridegroom offers six oblations of clarified butter, reciting the following prayers, while the bride touches his shoulder with her right hand. 1. "May fire come, first among the gods; may it rescue her offspring from the fetters of death; may VARUNA, king [of waters], grant that this woman should never bemoan a calamity befalling her children." 2. "May the domestic perpetual fire guard her; may it render her progeny long-lived: may she never be widowed: may she be mother of surviving children; may she experience the joy of having male offspring." 3. "May heaven protect thy back; may air, and the two sons of ASWINI, protect thy thighs; may the sun protect thy children while sucking thy breast; and VRIHASPATI protect them until they wear clothes; and afterwards may the assembled gods protect them." 4. "May no lamentation arise at night in thy abode; may crying women enter other houses than thine; mayest thou never admit sorrow to thy breast; mayest thou prosper in thy husband's house, blest with his survival, and viewing cheerful children." 5. "I lift barrenness, the death of children, sin, and every other evil, as I would lift a chaplet off thy head; and I consign the fetters [of premature death] to thy foes." 6. "May death depart from me, and immortality come; may [YAMA] the child of the sun, render me fearless. Death! follow a different path from that by which we proceed, and from that which the gods travel. To thee who seest and who hearest, I call, saying, hurt not our offspring, nor our progenitors. And may this oblation be efficacious."

The homas described above and the mantras are very similar to those in use today.

Changing sides

The bridegroom then presents oblations, naming the three worlds, separately and conjointly, and offers either four or five oblations to fire and to the moon. The bride and bridegroom then rise up, and he passes from her left side to her right, and makes her join her hands in a hollow form.

Note the familiar practice of changing sides in which the bride now is on the groom's left. Some traditions interpret this as her being closer to his heart!

Ashmarohana

The rice, which had been put into a basket, is then taken up, and the stone is placed before the bride, who treads upon it with the point of her right foot, while the bridegroom recites this prayer: "Ascend this stone; be firm like this stone; distress my foe, and be not subservient to my enemies."

The bride is asked to step on a stone, a symbolic assurance of stability of the alliance.

Bride's oblations

The bridegroom then pours a ladleful of clarified butter on her hands; another person gives her the rice, and two other ladlefuls of butter are poured over it. She then separates her hands, and lets fall the rice on the fire, while the following text is recited: "This woman, casting the rice into the fire, says, May my lord be long lived, may we live a hundred years, and may all my kinsmen prosper: be this oblation efficacious."

The bride's prayer for her husband's longevity, "May my lord be long lived, may we live a hundred years..." is identical. In practice today, it is common to have her brother or cousin be "another person" (mentioned below) who gives her the rice for offering to Agni.

Circumambulation

Afterwards the bridegroom walks round the fire, preceded by the bride, and reciting this text: "The girl goes from her parents to her husband's abode, having strictly observed abstinence [for three days from factitious salt, &c,] "Damsel! by means of thee we repress foes, like a stream of water." The bride again treads on the stone and makes another oblation of rice, while the subjoined prayer is recited: "The damsel has worshiped the generous sun and the regent of fire; may he and the generous sun liberate her and me from this [family]; be this oblation efficacious." They afterwards walk round the fire as before. Four or five other oblations are made with the same ceremonies and prayers, varying only the title of the sun, who is here called *Pushan,* but was entitled *Aryaman* in the preceding prayer. The bridegroom then pours rice out of the basket into the fire, after pouring one or two ladlefuls of butter on the edge of the basket; with this offering he simply says, "May this oblation to fire be efficacious."

The couple walk around the fire, a signal ceremony in most weddings. Factitious, a word more common in 1801 English, means manufactured (possibly refined from sea water) rather than rock salt.

Approaches to Pradhana Homa

The oblations and prayers directed by the *Yajurveda,* previous to this period of the solemnity, are very different from those which have been here inserted from the *Samaveda;* and some of the ceremonies, which will be subsequently noticed, are anticipated by the priests, who follow the *Yajush.*

Twelve oblations are made with as many prayers. 1. "May this oblation be efficacious, and happily conveyed to that being who is fire in the form of a celestial quirister, who is accompanied by truth, and whose abode is truth; may he cherish our holy knowledge and our valour." 2. "Efficacious be this oblation to those delightful plants, which are the nymphs of that being who is fire in the form of a celestial quirister, who is accompanied by truth, and whose abode is truth." 3. and 4. The foregoing prayers are thus varied: "To that being who is the sun, in the form of a celestial quirister, and who consists wholly of the *Samaveda."* "Those enlivening rays, which are the nymphs of that sun." 5. and 6. "That being who is the moon in the form of a celestial quirister, and who is a ray of the sun, and named *Sushmana."* "Those asterisms which are the nymphs of the moon, and are called *"Bhecuri."** 7. and 8. "That being who is air, constantly moving and traveling every where." "Those waters which are the nymphs of air, and are termed invigorating." 9. and 10. "That being who is the solemn sacrifice in the form of a celestial quirister; who cherishes all beings, and whose pace is elegant." "Those sacrificial fees, which are the nymphs of the solemn sacrifice, and are named thanksgivings." 11. and 12. "That being who is mind in the form of a celestial quirister, who is the supreme ruler of creatures, and who is the fabricator of the universe." "Those holy strains *(Rich* and *Saman)* who are the nymphs of mind, and are named the means of attaining wishes." Thirteen oblations are next presented, during the recital of as many portions of a single text. "May the supreme ruler of creatures, who is glorious in his victories over [hostile] armies, grant victory to INDRA, the regent of rain. All creatures humbly bow to him; for he is terrible:

to him are oblations due. May he grant me victory, knowledge, reflection, regard, self-rule, skill, understanding, power, [returns of] the conjunction and opposition of the sun and moon, and holy texts *(Vrihat* and *Rat'hantara.)"*

Eighteen oblations are then offered, while as many texts are meditated; they differ only in the name of the deity that is invoked. 1. "May fire, lord of [living] beings, protect me in respect of holiness, valour, and prayer, and in regard to ancient privileges, to this solemn rite, and to this invocation of deities." 2. "May INDRA, lord or regent of the eldest (that is, of the best of beings) protect me," &c. 3. "YAMA, lord of the earth." 4. "Air, lord of the sky." 5. "The sun, lord of heaven." 6. "The moon, lord of stars." 7. "VRIHASPATI, lord [that is, preceptor] of BRAHMA [and other deities]." 8."MITRA (the sun), lord of true beings." 9. "VARUNA, lord of waters." 10. "The ocean, lord of rivers." 11. "Food, lord of tributary powers." 12. "SOMA (the moon), lord of plants." 13. "SAVITRI (the generative sun), lord of pregnant females." 14. "RUDRA (SIVA), lord of [deities, that bear the shape of] cattle." 15. "The fabricator of the universe, lord of forms." 16. "VISHNU, lord of mountains." 17. "Winds *(Maruts)*, lords of *(ganas)* sets of divinities." 18. "Fathers, grandfathers, remoter ancestors, more distant progenitors, their parents, and grandsires."

Oblations are afterwards made, with prayers corresponding to those which have been already cited from the Samaveda. 1. "May fire come, first among the gods," &c. 2: "May the domestic perpetual fire guard her," &c. 3. "Fire, who dost protect such as perform sacrifices! Grant us all blessings in heaven and on earth: grant unto us that various and excellent wealth, which is produced on this earth and in heaven." 4. "O best of luminaries! Come, show us an easy path, that our lives may be uninjured. May death depart from me, and immortality come. May the child of the sun render me fearless." 5. "Death! Follow a different path," &c. The bride offers the oblations of rice mixed with leaves of sami, letting fall the offerings on the fire in the manner before mentioned, and with the same prayers, but recited in a reversed order and a little varied. 1."The damsel has worshipped the generous sun in the form of fire; may that generous sun never separate her from this husband. 2. "This woman, casting the rice into the fire, says, May my lord be long-lived; may my kinsmen reach old age." 3. "I cast this rice into the fire, that it may become a cause of thy prosperity: may fire assent to my union with thee."

According to the followers of the Yajurveda, the bridegroom now takes the bride's right hand, reciting a text which will be subsequently quoted. The bride then steps on a stone while this text is recited: "Ascend this stone: be firm like this stone. Subdue such as entertain hostile designs against me, and repel them." The following hymn is then chanted. "Charming SARASWATI, swift as a mare! whom I celebrate in face of this universe; protect this [solemn rite]. O thou! in whom the elements were produced, in whom this universe was framed, I now will sing that hymn [the nuptial text] which constitutes the highest glory of women." The bride and bridegroom afterwards walk round the fire, while the following text is recited: "Fire! thou didst first espouse this female sun (this woman, beautiful like the sun); now let a human being again espouse her by thy means. Give her, O fire! with offspring, to a [human] husband." The remainder of the rice is then dropped into the fire as an oblation to the god of love.

Differences between Yajur and Sama are expounded above. Individuals may be able to choose depending on the family tradition or a combination of the two after studying the spirit and meaning of the oblations.

Saptapadi

The next ceremony is the bride's stepping seven steps. It is the most material of all the nuptial rites; for the marriage is complete and irrevocable, so soon as she has taken the seventh step, and not sooner. She is conducted by the bridegroom, and directed by him to step successively into seven circles, while the following texts are uttered: 1. "May VISHNU cause thee to take one step for the sake of obtaining food." 2. "May VISHNU cause thee to take one step for the sake of obtaining strength." 3. "Three steps for the sake of solemn acts of religion." 4. "Four steps for the sake of obtaining happiness." 5. "Five steps for the sake of cattle." 6. "Six steps for the sake of increase of wealth." 7. "Seven steps for the sake of obtaining priests to perform sacrifices." The bridegroom then addresses the bride, "Having completed seven steps, be my companion. May I become thy associate. May none interrupt thy association with me. May such as are disposed to promote our happiness, confirm thy association with me." The bridegroom then addresses the spectators: "This woman is auspicious: approach and view her; and having conferred [by your good wishes] auspicious fortune on her, depart to your respective abodes."

The Hindu Marriage Act of 1955 passed by the Indian Parliament now mandates that a marriage is considered legal only upon completion of the seventh step in this ritual, thus drawing on and validating the Vedic sacrament.

The spirit of friendship is explicitly stated with the words translated here as "companion" and "associate." The concluding shloka addressed to the audience: "This woman is auspicious: approach and view her ...;" is used today exactly as it is here and as it was in the Vedic period.

Concluding prayers and vows

Then the bridegroom's friend, who stood near the fire bearing a jar of water, advances to the spot where the seventh step was completed, and pours water on the bridegroom's head, and afterwards on the bride's, while a prayer abovementioned is recited: "May waters and all the Gods cleanse our hearts; may air do so; may the creator do so; may the divine instructress unite our hearts."

Panigrahana (Holding Hands)

The bridegroom then puts his left hand under the bride's hands, which are joined together in a hollow form, and taking her right hand in his, recites the six following texts: 1. "I take thy hand for the sake of good fortune, that thou mayest become old with me, thy husband: may the generous, mighty, and prolific sun render thee a matron; that I may be a householder." 2. "Be gentle in thy aspect and loyal to thy husband; be fortunate in cattle, amiable in thy mind, and beautiful in thy person; be mother of surviving sons; be assiduous at the [five] sacraments; be cheerful; and bring prosperity to our bipeds and quadrupeds," 3. "May the lord of creatures grant us progeny, even unto, old age; may the sun render that progeny conspicuous. Auspicious deities have given thee to me; enter thy husband's abode, and bring health to our bipeds and quadrupeds." 4. O INDRA, who pourest forth rain! render this woman fortunate and the mother of children: grant her ten sons; give her eleven protectors." 5. "Be submissive to thy husband's father, to his mother, to his sister, and to his brothers." 6. "Give thy heart to my religious duties: may thy mind follow mine; be thou consentient to my speech. May "VRIHASPATI unite thee unto me."

Yajurvedic version of Panigrahana

The followers of the *Yajurveda* enlarge the first prayer and omit the rest, some of which, however, they employ at other periods of the solemnity. "I take thy hand for the sake of good fortune, that thou mayest become old with me, thy husband; may the deities, namely, the divine sun *(Aryaman),* and the prolific being *(Savitri),* and the god of love, give thee as a matron unto me, that I may be a householder. I need the goddess of prosperity. Thou art she. Thou art the goddess of prosperity. I need her. I am the *Saman [veda]:* thou art the *Rich [veda].* I am the sky: thou art the earth. Come; let us marry: let us hold conjugal intercourse: let us procreate offspring: let us obtain sons. May they reach old age. May we, being affectionate, glorious, and well disposed, see during a hundred years, live a hundred years, and hear a hundred years." The taking of the bride's hand in marriage is thus completed.

Most of the above vows are still in use.

The Pole Star

The bride and bridegroom rise up; and he shews her the polar star, reciting the following text: "Heaven is stable; the earth is stable; this universe is stable; these mountains are stable; may this woman be stable in her husband's family." The bride salutes the bridegroom, naming herself and family, and adding a respectful interjection. The bridegroom replies, "Be long-lived and happy." Matrons then pour water, mixed with leaves, upon the bride and bridegroom, out of jars which had been previously placed on an altar prepared for the purpose; and the bridegroom again makes oblations with the names of the worlds, by way of closing this part the ritual, which conforms to the *Samaveda,* the bridegroom sits down near the fire with the bride, and finishes this part of the ceremony by making oblations while he names the three worlds severally and of the ceremony.

The sighting of Dhruva, the pole star, by the bride signifies stability and steadiness. This is still in practice performed symbolically if the timing of the wedding ceremony is not right for the actual viewing. This is also the occasion to view the Arundhati star as Arundhati, wife of sage Vasishta, considered to be of spotless character, is a Hindu ideal for the newlywed. See the "Charge to the bride" in a later chapter.

Wedding meals

The bridegroom afterwards eats food prepared without factitious salt. During this meal he recites the following prayers: 1. "I bind with the fetters of food thy heart and mind to the gem [of my soul]; I bind them with nourishment, which is the thread of life; I bind them with the knot of truth." 2. "May that heart, which is yours, become my heart; and this heart, which is mine, become thy heart." 3. "Since food is the bond of life, I bind thee therewith." The remainder of the food must be then given to the bride.

Arrival at the new home

Alighting from the carriage, the bridegroom leads the bride into the house, chanting the hymn called *Vamadevya.* Matrons welcome the bride, and make her sit down on a bull's hide of the same [red] color, and placed in the same manner as before. The bridegroom then recites the following prayer: "May kine here produce numerous young; may horses and human beings do so; and may the deity sit here, by whose favour sacrifices are accomplished with gifts a thousand fold."

The women then place a young child in the bride's lap; they put roots of lotus, or else fruit of different kinds, in his hand. The bridegroom takes up the child, and then prepares a sacrificial fire in the usual manner, and makes eight oblations with the following prayers, preceded and followed by the usual oblations to the three worlds. 1."May there be cheerfulness here." 2. "May thine own [kindred] be kind here." 3. "May there be pleasure here." 4. "Sport thou here." 5. "May there be kindness here with me." 6. "May thine own [kindred] be here, benevolent towards me." 7. "May there be here delight towards me." 8. "Be thou here joyous towards me." The bride then salutes, her father-in-law and the other relatives of her husband.

Reception: The bride leaves for her new home on the fourth day. She is received with appropriate ceremony. This resembles the Grihapravesham of modern day practice. Blessings in the new home are conferred on the bride.

More fire rituals and purification ceremonies in the new home

Afterwards the bridegroom prepares another sacrificial fire, and sits down with the bride on his right hand. He makes twenty oblations with the following prayers, preceded and followed as usual by oblations to the three worlds: The remainder of each ladleful is thrown into a jar of water, which is afterwards poured on the bride's head. 1. " Fire, expiator of evil! thou dost atone evils for the gods themselves. I, a priest, approach thee, desirous of soliciting thee to remove any sinful taint in the beauty of this woman." 2. "Air, expiator of evil!" &c. 3. "Moon, expiator of evil!" &c. 4. "Sun, expiator of evil!" &c. 5. "Fire, air, moon, and sun, expiators of evil! ye do atone evils for the gods. I, a priest, approach thee, desirous of soliciting thee to remove any sinful taint in the beauty of this woman." 6, 7, 8, 9, 10. "soliciting thee to remove any thing in her person which might destroy her husband." 11, 12, 13, 14, 15, "any thing in her person which might make her negligent of cattle."

The priests who use the *Yajurveda,* make only five oblations with as many prayers addressed to fire, air, the sun, the moon, and the *Gandharba* or celestial quirister; praying them to remove any thing in the person of the bride which might be injurious to her husband, to her offspring, to cattle, to the household, and to honour and glory. The following text is recited while the water is poured on the bride's head: "That blameable portion of thy person which would have been injurious to thy husband, thy offspring, thy cattle, thy household, and thy honour, I render destructive of paramours: may thy body [thus cleared from evil] reach old age with me." The bride is then fed with food prepared in a caldron, and the following text is recited; "I unite thy breath with my breath; thy bones with my bones; thy flesh with my flesh; and thy skin with my skin."

The bride is ritually assimilated into her new home.

Colebrooke's summary

The ceremonies of which the nuptial solemnity consists may be here recapitulated. The bridegroom goes in procession to the house where the bride's father resides, and is there welcomed as a guest. The bride is given to him by her father in the form usual at every solemn donation, and their hands are bound together with grass. He clothes the bride with an upper and lower garment, and the skirts of her mantle and his are tied together. The bridegroom makes oblations to fire, and the bride drops rice on it as an oblation. The bridegroom solemnly takes her hand in marriage. She treads on a stone and mullar [*upper, handheld grindstone]*. They walk round the fire. The bride steps seven times, conducted by the bridegroom, and he then dismisses the spectators, the marriage being now complete and irrevocable. In the evening of the same day the bride sits down on a bull's hide, and the bridegroom points out to her the polar star as an emblem of stability. They then partake of a meal. The bridegroom remains three days at the house of the bride's father; on the fourth day he conducts her to his own house in solemn procession. She is there welcomed by his kindred; and the solemnity ends with oblations to fire. [*The Colebrooke passages end here.*]

Based on the study so far, we may state that, as will be evident throughout this book, the ceremonies of long ago have served as a firm basis for today's practices, the very many variations notwithstanding. Also it will be noted that the rituals do not all take place at one time. The ceremony appears to have been spread over several days. Building a fire and offerings to Agni and other gods, chanting of the Gayatri, prayers for longevity, health and wealth have remained essentially intact. Stepping "on a stone or mullar" is still practiced by some traditions as Ashmarohana. Saptapadi appears to have been the concluding event upon which the bridegroom "dismisses the spectators." There appears to have been a preoccupation with keeping "rivals" and "enemies" at bay with the bridegroom reciting a verse at almost the very beginning of the ceremony when the bride's father presents a cushion of grass: "I obscure my rivals, as the sun does other luminaries; I tread on this, as the type of him who injures me" (Colebrooke, *ibid*). Charges to the bride concerning her responsibility, her position in the new family and prayers for progeny to be sons are included. We may attribute the worries concerning "rivals" and "enemies" and highway robbers to "kāladharma," the temporal dharma of the nineteenth century and earlier when personal security varied widely from region to region. The concerns today are different and our prayers, although drawn from the same scriptures, are directed elsewhere.

On the whole one gets the impression from Suryā's wedding described in the Rig Veda and Colebrooke's essay that prescriptions for the wedding day during the Vedic period were specific, covering a wide range from ritual baths and purifications, clothing, invocations, vows and fire ceremonies, blessings, to sending off the bride. The tying of the mangalasutra which plays a significant part in traditional South Indian weddings is not to be found in these accounts. Perhaps this ritual has its origins in the swayamvara weddings (discussed in the next section of the book), practiced by kshatriyas, especially royalty, in which the bride garlands either her choice of a bridegroom from a group of suitors or the winner of a physical contest. Garlanding is now the most common early step. The tying of the golden necklace may have been a further development signifying prosperity, or even a custom borrowed from a non-Vedic Indian cultural source.

The initial welcoming ceremony as described by Colebrooke emulates many acts of hospitality offered to a guest. The use of water is also preserved although the practice of washing the feet with the offered water (pādya) has yielded to simple achamanam (ceremonial sipping of the sanctified water offered by the bride's father three times, each sipping preceded by a prayer to Achyuta, Ananta and Govinda respectively) although in some families the bride's father or mother do indeed wash the feet of the bridegroom.

The Dharmashastras:

Another important source in the quest for the origins of the concept and rituals of the Hindu wedding is the Manusmrti or Manava Dharma Shastra. The date of original composition is unknown but some scholars place the final version between 200 B.C. and 100 A.D.

Manu specifies eight forms of weddings and arranges them hierarchically as follows:

ब्रह्मो-दैवस्तथैवर्षः प्रजापत्य-स्तथासुरः
गंधर्वो राक्षसश्चैव पैशवस्तमः स्मृतः

brahmō-daivastathaivarṣa: prajāpatya-stathāsura:
gandharvō rākśasaścaiva paiśavastama: smṛta:
(MDS, 3. 21)

They are the rite of Brahman (Brahma), that of the Gods (Daiva), that of the Rishis (Arsha), that of the Lord of Progeny (Prajapatya), that of the Titans (Asura), that of the Guardians (Gandharva), that of the Demons (Rakshasa), and that of the Fiends (Paisacha).

The highest form is defined as the Brahma type in which the governing principle is advancement of dharma through a requisite samskara, that is, a marriage that unites two families. The bride is given away as a Kanyadana (gift of a bride) with absolutely no exchange of worldly goods. The union is considered sacred and fulfilling in itself and nothing else matters. The bride is sought by the groom's family which arranges the wedding.

In the second category known as Daiva, the bride's family goes in search of a groom and offers her to a priest engaged in a yagna. This type is inferior to the Brahma type only because the initiating family is the bride's side. Again there is no exchange of worldly goods.

In the third kind known as Arsha, a bride is given in marriage in exchange for a couple of cows from the groom.

Prajapatya was driven by social pressure to arrange an early marriage and the desire for progeny in the short term. The initiators are from the bride's side.

In the Asura type of marriage the initiator is the groom who may force a claim on a bride by offering tempting sums of money and other goods to the bride's family. It is in essence an open business transaction and thus its inferiority. The dowry system that still plagues Hindu society, in which a bride's family is forced to fulfill demands from the groom's family, can be considered an Asura type of marriage.

Gandharva marriage is love marriage, pure and simple, and the respective families may not be involved in the initial stages.

The so-called Rakshasa type appears to be a misnomer because no less an authority than the royal patriarch Bhishma "rather startlingly proclaims it as the best type of marriage for warriors (See Stephanie W. Jamison, "Draupadi on the Walls of Troy: Iliad 3 from an Indic Perspective" *Classical Antiquity,* Volume 13. No. 1. August 1994). It is therefore a form prescribed for kshatriyas. In this type of marriage the groom claims the bride and fights for her literally. In fact it is a requirement of the kshatra dharma. More about this later.

The Paishacha is the lowest form and is downright brutal and ugly. The bride is simply snatched and taken away against her will after physical harm is inflicted on her family. This so called union can hardly be graced with the term marriage as it represents rape, bondage or kidnaping. Except for the sake of completeness in this discussion of the category of sexual unions, this type of "marriage" deserves no space anywhere.

If we were to examine the above classification and omit the Paishacha from further discussion in the context of 21st century definitions of marriage, it is possible to view the practices of today, especially in North America, as a composite of the remaining seven categories in general. The Gandharva approach is predominant in the initial stages where two young people court each other and fall in love. Except in cases of elopement, the later stage, when the families get into the equation and the ceremony is planned, evolves into a combination of Brahma and Rakshasa, minus any violence and acts of valor. As stated earlier, the term Rakshasa seems rather harsh especially when, for example, it was the mode used by (1) Bhishma when he secured Amba, Ambika and Ambalika, not for himself but for his brother Vichitravirya, (2) Arjuna when he carried off Subhadra and (3) again when he won Draupadi. In these cases, undoubtedly there were acts of valor and violence but the ensuing wedding ceremonies, especially in Draupadi's case, were elaborate and glamorous with Vedic rituals discussed below.

Remnants of the "Rakshasa" type remain in today's weddings, especially in North Indian families. The arrival to "snatch" the bride is implied dramatically with the groom riding a horse (sometimes with his brother behind) and processing towards the wedding hall with considerable fanfare accentuated by loud music and joyous dance by the accompanying relatives and friends. This is an entirely welcome replacement of the "valor" and "violence" implicit in the "Rakshasa" mode. More about this type of marriage may be found in the following section. An excellent and concise summary of the types is found in the Grihya Sutras and is reproduced in the section below for the sake of completeness.

The Grihya Sutras

The Grihya Sutras are rules of domestic ceremonies and serve as manuals with more specific instructions although the basic mantras pertaining to Vedic weddings are still largely drawn from the Vedas, especially from the Rig Veda (X. Hymn 85, Suryā's Bridal). Some vows ("I seize thy hand ...") and blessings ("Be queenly to your father-in-law ...") from the Hymn above are reproduced, as is a verse from the Atharva Veda ("I am He, you are She..."). Types of marriages (see below) are also stated much as found in the Manu Smrti *(MDS)*. Ashmarohana is described here as well as Saptapadi. The distribution of fried grain by the bride's brother during the Laja Homa fire ritual is also noted. It is specifically stated that the fire used during the wedding rites is kept as a sacred domestic fire by the couple subsequent to the ceremony. More details may be found in Kandika 6 of Adhyaya 1 of the Asvalayana-Grihya Sutra:

1. (The father) may give away the girl, having decked her with ornaments, pouring out a libation of water: this is the wedding (called) Brahma. A son born by her (after a wedding of this kind) brings purification to twelve descendants and to twelve ancestors on both (the husband's and the wife's) sides.

2. He may give her, having decked her with ornaments, to an officiating priest, whilst a sacrifice with the three (Srauta) fires is going on: this (is the wedding called) Daiva. (A son) brings purification to ten descendants and to ten ancestors on both sides.

3. They fulfill the law together: this (is the wedding called) Prajapatya. (A son) brings purification to eight descendants and to eight ancestors on both sides.

4. He may marry her after having given a bull and a cow (to the girl's father): this (is the wedding called) Arsha. (A son) brings purification to seven descendants and to seven ancestors on both sides.

5. He may marry her, after a mutual agreement has been made (between the lover and the damsel): this (is the wedding called) Gandharva.

6. He may marry her after gladdening (her father) by money: this is (the wedding called) Asura.

7. He may carry her off while (her relatives) sleep or pay no attention: this (is the wedding called) Paishacha.

8. He may carry her off, killing (her relatives) and cleaving (their) heads, while she weeps and they weep: this (is the wedding called) Rakshasa.

The Epics

The two great epics of India, the Ramayana and the Mahabharata, still exercise such a firm grip on the minds of Hindus that nearly every aspect of life is influenced or illuminated by the thousands of events illustrated in the stories. This includes weddings, principally the kshatriya type, as the heroes in both the epics were princes whose weddings were governed by the principles of swayamvara and kshātravirya. Thus it is instructive for us to note the practices that prevailed then and observe how they have been absorbed into our current rites.

The Ramayana

In this, the earlier epic, when princes Rama and Lakshmana are "borrowed" by sage Vishvamitra to obtain protection from asuras who were interrupting his penance, they happen to visit Mithila, the kingdom of King Janaka. This is where they learn about the "divine bow." They are told of the enormous strength required to string the bow and the failures of many princes who have made the attempt. The reason why so many have vied for this feat becomes obvious to them when Janaka declares that his daughter Sita is the virya shulka (price of bravery). Vishvamitra urges Rama to try it and lo and behold the bow is strung! Upon which Janaka declares (translation based on the online Valmiki Ramayana by Desiraju Hanumantha Rao and K.M.K. Murthy, 1998-2003):

अस्मै देया मया सीता वीर्य शुल्का महात्मने

प्रतिज्ञां तर्तुं इच्छामि तत् अनुज्ञातुं अर्हसि

asmai dēyā mayā sītā vīrya śulkā mahātmanē

pratigñām tartum icchāmi tat anugñātum arhasi 1-68-10

"I shall offer Sita to the noble-souled Rama as the reward for bravery and I beg you to give your consent as I intend to keep my solemn promise."

That said, the wedding plans are under way. King Dasharatha, the father of the groom, and his entourage arrive from Ayodhya and the date is set as follows:

माघा हि अद्य महाबाहो त्रितीये दिवसे प्रभो फल्घुण्यां उत्तरे

māghā hi adya mahābāhō tṛtīyē divasē prabhō phalghuṇyām uttarē

(I.71.24)

"This month is Magha but the day after tomorrow is Phalguni ..." the implication being that Phalguni is an auspicious month and therefore that date is preferred. Similarly, the auspicious moment, the muhurta, is also set when Rama arrives at the "*yukte muhuurte vijaye* i.e. a muhurta known as Vijaya is chosen for the wedding. *(I.73.9)*

A very detailed account of the lineages of both families is recited and is concluded by

नाभागस्य भभूव अज अजात् दशरथो अभवत्
अस्मात् दशरथात् जातौ भ्रातरौ रामलक्ष्मणौ

nābhāgasya bhabhūva aja ajāt daśarathō abhavat
asmāt daśarathāt jātau bhrātarau rāmalakshmaṇau

"Dasharatha's father was Aja and Aja's father was Nābhāga and Rama and Lakshmana are Dasharatha's children." *(1.70.43)*

The presiding sage Vasishta sets up the fire altar at the center of the sacred space as stated by प्रपा मध्ये तु विधिवत् वेदीं कृत्वा *(prapā madhyē tu vidhivat vēdīm kṛtvā)* upon which he proceeds to sanctify a variety of vessels and spoons for use during the ceremony. This step is not unlike what is practiced today.

Then the bride is conducted towards the fire altar:

ततः सीतां समानीय सर्वाभरणभूषितां ।
समक्षं अग्नेः संस्थाप्य राघवा अभिमुखे तदा ॥

tata: sītām samānīya sarvābharaṇabhūṣitām
samaksham agnē: samsthāpya rāghavā abhimukhē tadā

"The father of the bride brings forth the beautifully adorned Sita and positions her in front of the bridegroom Rama." *(1.73.25)*

The ceremony begins thus with the bride's father declaring:

इयं सीता मम सुता सहधर्मचरी तव
प्रतीच्छ च ऐनां भद्रं ते पाणिं गृह्णीश्व पाणिना

iyam sītā mama sutā sahadharmacarī tava
pratīccha ca ēnām bhadram tē pāṇim gṛhṇīśva pāṇinā (1.73.26)

"This my daughter Sita will be your partner in the practice of dharma and therefore accept her willingly and take her hand in yours." This is clearly the Hasta Milap ceremony of today.

Then the bride is given away.

पतिव्रता महभागा छाय इव अनुगता सदा
इति उक्त्वा प्रक्षिपत् राजा मंत्रपूतं जलं तदा

pativratā mahabhāgā chāya iva anugatā sadā
iti uktvā prakṣipat rājā mantrapūtam jalam tadā (1.73.27)

"This prosperous and devoted wife will follow you like a shadow. So saying, the king poured the sanctified water."

The current version of this step is the kanyadanam, the equivalent of giving the bride away.

The episode concludes with अग्निम् प्रदक्षिणं कृत्वा वेदिम् (*agnim pradakśiṅam kṛtvā vēdim*) that is, with circumambulations around the fire.

The Mahabharata

Reference to a wedding ceremony in the Mahabharata can be found in the Vaivahika section of the Adi Parva covering the swayamvara of Draupadi who chose Arjuna as her husband. Swayamvara appears to be a form of marriage or marriage-related custom in its own right and is worthy of further discussion. It seems to precede a rather diluted form of Manu's Rakshasa mode because it involves choice, and violence is not a requirement. The primary feature of the Rakshasa type of marriage is established, according to Jamison (*ibid*) in the Manava Dharma Shastra, as follows:

हत्वा छित्वा च भिथ्वा च क्रोषंतिं रुदतिं गृहात्
प्रसह्य कन्याहरणं राक्षसो विधिरुच्यते

hatvā chitvā ca bhithvā ca krōśantim rudatim gṛhāt
prasahya kanyāharaṇam rākshasō vidhirucyate (MDS III.33)

"The abduction by force of a maiden, weeping and wailing, from her house, after smashing and cleaving and breaking [her relatives and household], this is called the Rakshasa rite."

Jamison cleverly argues that even though the above requirements spell mayhem and chaos, they do follow certain rules. One of the rules is an interesting component of kshatra dharma which prohibits accepting gifts and is therefore the presumed reason for "taking the girl by force, not accepting her." There are other rules including performing an act of valor "that serves as bride price *(virya shulka)* in a Rakshasa marriage." *Virya shulka* is indeed evident in Sita's swayamvara in the Ramayana where Rama is chosen upon successfully performing an impossible feat. In the example of Draupadi referred to above, an "act of valor" was a requirement. Also the violence component, built into Rakshasa bridals, may arise in a swayamvara but only if things turn ugly and the losers decide to attack the winner, as happened to Arjuna.

The Pandavas had assembled at this event disguised as Brahmins as they had just escaped their cousin Duryodhana's attempt on their lives through the burning of the "wax" palace while they were asleep. They were now traveling incognito in order to leave the impression that they had actually been burned alive. The Pandavas were drawn into the required contest only when none of the assembled princes succeeded in striking with "these decorated arrows" a contraption "suspended high up" at whose center was the target visible through a hole (P. Lal, 1970.) The feat required piercing the eye of an artificial fish in a rotating device, just by seeing its reflection in a pool of water below. Not only did Arjuna succeed but both he and Bhima fought off the annoyed crowd of princes who could not bear humiliation at the hands of a mere Brahmin. Thus violence became necessary on that occasion.

The wedding ceremony was then performed by the officiating priest, sage Dhaumya, who "lit the sacred fire, poured the libations to the chanting of mantras, called the eldest of the Pandavas, Yudhishṭira, to the fire, and united him to lovely Krishnā" (Draupadi). There is further reference to how they circled the fire holding each other's hands, "and were married" (Lal, *ibid*; section 200, 11, 12). Another important aspect from the Mahabharata account that has remained essentially intact in today's wedding is the series of affectionate blessings by Kunti when "beautiful Draupadi, graced with all the auspicious marks" stands before her mother-in-law "reverently and silently" (Lal, *ibid*, section 201, 3-7).

Kunti's blessings as a "charge to the bride" (Lal, *ibid,* 201, 5-6) are still used today immediately following a climactic event such as the tying of the mangalasutra:

यथेंद्राणि महेंद्रस्य	*yathendrāṇi mahēndrasya*	As Shachi to Indra,
स्वाहाचैव विभावसोः	*svāhācaiva vibhāvasō:*	as Swaha to Agni,
रोहिणीच यथा सोमे	*rōhiṇīca yathā sōmē*	as Rohini to Chandra,
दमयंती यथा नळे	*damayantī yathā naḷē*	as Damayanti to Nala,
यथा वैवस्वते भद्रा	*yathā vaivasvatē bhadrā*	as Bhadra to Vivasvat,
वसिष्ठे चापि अरुंधती	*vasiṣṭhē cāpi arundhatī*	as Arundhati to Vasishta,
यथा नारायणी लक्ष्मी	*yathā nārāyaṇī lakśmī*	as Lakshmi to Vishnu,
तथा त्वं भवभर्तारि	*tathā tvam bhavabhartāri*	may you be to your husband.

If the bride is Hindu, the priest may address the bride and say "I, in the name of your and my ancestors charge you as follows" and read the English version first and then chant the shloka that Kunti used. If the bride is not Hindu, the blessing is still relevant.

Chapter IV

TRADITIONS AND CUSTOMS

"I don't want to utter anything that I do not fully understand, appreciate and approve..." said the bride's father during initial discussions pertaining to an interfaith wedding.

I couldn't agree more. It makes sense as individuals, especially those with non-Hindu traditions, struggle to come to grips with their son's or daughter's decision to marry a Hindu.

When the spirit and content of the steps and procedures are explained, more often than not, they can be seen objectively and all is well. In fact during discussions with ministers or priests or rabbis we have found that certain steps in other traditions are so identical in spirit, intent and content that we have been able to substitute one or more steps with those of the other tradition without any loss to the continuity. Thus one could accomplish a seamless ceremony with some planning. A study of both traditions will establish the fact that ancestors around the world must have thought along the same lines to make sure the couple understood their responsibilities when they commit to each other for life. This is the interesting part of this beautiful process in which two people come together as husband and wife.

The ceremonial aspects of the Hindu wedding have evolved over centuries into a hundred or more varieties depending on regional and family traditions and beliefs. Yet there is a central thread that ties the steps together with invocation of Agni, god of fire and preserver of the domestic hearth, implicit or explicit display of respect to deities and gurus venerated by the families, respect shown to elders in the two families and the officiating priest, and above all a commitment to dharma and friendship. The evolution has little intellectual basis, the overwhelming driver being mostly those traditions that may have been in vogue at the wedding of the parents themselves. Also the changes, on the whole, are minor and the basic procedures have remained unaffected by other cultures except perhaps the modern practice of exchanging rings. Additions of a social nature include the dinner and dance following a reception and the toasting and roasting common in Hindu weddings in North America these days. Our experience has been to note the strong desire evident on the part of Hindu families to see their sons and daughters observe the familiar customs and a similar desire on the part of the young couple to understand the procedure and the rituals.

It is quite natural to love one's own customs and thus it is important to listen and try to integrate the ideas of the families as far as possible. Preserving family traditions is as old as time and is independent of cultural background. Consider the conversation between Bhishma and Shalya when the former sought, in behalf of King Pandu, the hand of the latter's sister.

पूर्वैः प्रवर्तितं किंचित्कुले अस्मिन् नृपसत्तमै
साधु वा यदि वा साधु तन्नातिक्रान्तुमुत्सहे

pūrvai: pravartitam kimcitkulē asmin nṛpasattamai
sādhu vā yadi vā sādhu tannātikrāntumutsahē

Sambhava-ādi Parva, 106-22

[Shalya:] *"We have a custom that is strictly followed.*
Call it good or bad, we happen to follow it."

Good or bad, this is our custom! That is the position of Shalya, brother of princess Madri whose hand was sought. In a subtle way the "custom" being discussed here was to give away the bride, not as a gift, but to expect something in return. Bhishma sensed this accurately when he proclaimed, "I am aware of this custom and I know that an observance honored by tradition has the approval of wise and virtuous men." That "something in return" ended up to be "vast treasures of pure gold, thousands of precious stones of all colors, elephants and horses and chariots, robes and ornaments, pearls and corals and other gems. Happy with the dowry, Shalya gave his sister to Bhishma, ..." (Lal, *ibid*, Sambhava (105-120), Adi Parva, Mahabharata)

Thus kuladharma (family tradition) may always be invoked and it is important to consider and retain as many of the family traditions/requirements as possible in planning modern weddings.

A review of publications in modern Indian languages confirms the extent of variations dictated by geography and changing times. The question then is which steps to consider when planning a particular modern Hindu wedding. Based on the Vedic sources and a desired framework of space and time, one may define the following basic steps as essential to satisfying most of the ritualistic needs of those raised in the Hindu faith. It is worth repeating that a final program may be developed around this suggested framework to suit individual family practices and desires. Again the words used below may sometimes be different to describe the same steps as will be evident later.

- Swagat or Swagatam/ Milni (The meeting/greeting of both families. Bride is not present)
- Vara Puja (Dialogue between bride's father and the groom)
- Jayamala (Exchange of garlands)
- Pravara (Announcement of lineage)
- Kanyadanam (Giving away the bride)
- Mangalyadharanam (Tying the mangalasutra)
- Agni/Homas (Fire rituals)
- Mangal Phera (Circling the fire)
- Saptapadi (Seven steps)
- Ashirvadam (Blessings)

Hindu weddings, as we have seen, are based on the Vedas. In ancient India, and to some extent in modern times, each family has had allegiance to a particular Veda. That is why one hears about Rigvedis, Yajurvedis or even Trivedis and Chaturvedis, i.e. adherents to either three or all the four Vedas. As pointed out in Colebrooke's analysis the mantras chanted during a particular step in a wedding ceremony depended on the particular Vedic tradition inherited by the family. As discussed there, the mantras used and their interpretation can be vastly different for the same step in the ceremony. As an example, recall the step in which the bridegroom was presented a cushion. The mantras uttered could either be in praise of Soma as the god of all plants including the kusha grass from which the cushion was made or could be the occasion to wish that the enemies of the groom be trampled as he steps (tramples) on the grass cushion. Clearly the intent and emphasis are quite different in different Vedas for the same ritualistic step.

Included in the basic structure listed above are sacred chants and mantras, many of which have remained unchanged from Vedic and epic times, as described in the Origins section. These prescribed procedures and instructions are then combined with regional, family and modern variations to make sure both families feel fulfilled and comfortable.

The final program developed thus will involve the use of natural elements such as water and fire along with rice, turmeric, kumkum, ghee, puffed rice, fruits, flowers and incense. The specific use of garments, threads, grasses, jewelry and powders for anointing usually play a role in the ceremonies.

The particular traditions and customs of the individual family may be woven around the basic framework listed above. First we review examples of some preliminary overtures:

- Exchange of horoscopes leading to a determination of compatibility of the couple, also to an appropriate and ideal setting of a date and range of time (muhurtam) for the predetermined climactic step which proclaims the authority and sanction for the union. Our experience is that the date and time couples choose in North America are driven by parameters other than the above and depend very much on the convenience of the principals, availability of space for the event as well as hotel rooms for guests. With some care it is possible to meet both the above requirements but it does require a knowledge base as well as early planning. See Appendix III.
- Pre-wedding celebrations on days preceding the wedding and in particular the evening before may include formal/ informal musical renditions, mehendi application to palms and feet of the bride and her female relatives and friends from both families.

- Pujas performed at the bride's and bridegroom's quarters. Typically a Gauri Puja by the bride and Ganapati Puja by the bridegroom are held separately in their own quarters. See Appendix VI.

- Clothing and jewelry for the bride vary depending upon individual tastes. Brides appear to prefer shades of red or gold with highly decorative gold/silver trims and ends with an additional equally festive shawl. Color choices may vary from pink and gold to deeper shades as well as the traditional reds or even gold bordered whites. Floral crowns are still popular, especially with South Indian brides. See Appendix V.

We now give a brief introduction to some of the rituals.

- Pravara. This step is a formal public announcement of the of the names of the bridegroom and the bride in front of the assembled. They are introduced by declaring their lineage beginning with great-grandfather and proceeding with grandfather and father from both families. This serves as an opportunity to remember the ancestors on this auspicious occasion and seek their blessing. Normally the practice is to repeat the Pravara recital three times. But it can also be done just once.

  Generally only patriarchal names are included. We have developed the practice of including the name of the bride's mother as can be seen below. On one occasion when a family (non-Hindu) requested inclusion of the names of all female members from their side, we were happy to oblige in order to respect those wishes.

  It is the general Hindu belief that each Hindu family tree can be traced back to a sage. Some families trace spiritual descent to three or five or even seven sages. Although few records go back thousands of years, elders in the family usually remember their gotra which refers to the name of a sage and this is what is used in the Pravara recital.

- Kanyadanam: This is the ceremony where the bride's parents give the bride away. Three decades ago, during a discussion before the very first wedding I performed between the daughter of good friends who were Hindus and a local young man who was Christian, the bride's mother posed the following question: "Is she a thing to be gifted away?" A great lesson in diversity of views and practices among Indians struck home at this very first attempt. It is a legitimate question pertaining to the concept of giving the bride away which in Sanskrit uses the phrase kanyaadaan, the literal meaning of which is "gift of a bride." The objection to the phrase was understandable although somewhat unexpected from Hindu parents. "Is she a thing to be gifted away?" Of course not! The problem is not in the mantras as will be clear later in the book but it is the name given to the step. We continue to use this as an essential step and define it as the ritual equivalent of leaving one's family to establish one's own home and thus begin a new life. This guard against literal interpretation of the title has helped and all appears to be well. However this is a never-ending and stimulating process of learning, adopting and adapting. And it is important always to pay attention to the views and wishes of the principals.

- Agni/Homas (Fire rituals). One of the most revered rituals that Hindus love to see practiced in important ceremonies is Homa, or Havan as it is popularly known among Hindus from North India. In every temple in the United States devotees look forward to seeing and participating in the celebration of Agni Homa for a variety of gods and goddesses. People appear to experience a great deal of satisfaction in making offerings to the fire god and enjoy viewing the pouring of oblation, including the climax where brand new colorful clothing (a saree or blouse piece), dipped in ghee is offered. The whole ceremony brings alive the concept of sacrifice and is especially meaningful in weddings as the new couple symbolically acknowledge that material possessions are of little importance to them by declaring that the offerings are not theirs at all but belong to Agni himself and therefore they simply offer the "possessions" to Agni. There is also a recognition that the flame that one builds during the sacrifice is the same as the inner flame in individuals. Thus it becomes a practice towards enhancing self awareness which is the very goal of the Vedas.

- Saptapadi. Irrespective of the region of India from which Indians have come and settled in the United States, Europe or Canada, they all recognize this ritual as the indispensable component of a Hindu wedding ceremony. While there may be discussion on the relevance of any other step, this ritual is highly revered and never questioned. As mentioned earlier, this ceremony is held by Indian civil law to be the defining step, the completion of which seals the husband-wife relationship between a couple. Each step of seven taken by the couple specifies a separate blessing, for food, strength, austerity, love, welfare of cattle, prosperity, and sacred illumination.

Within this tradition, there are different versions. One version prescribes that seven circles be drawn to the north of the agni kunda (fire vessel) and that the couple step into each circle holding hands, led by the bridegroom as the latter chants the appropriate verses. Again, the circles may be of raw rice, or, as in another version they may be large circles defined with rice or rice flour as the boundary (rangoli) so that the couple need not step onto the rice. In yet another version, as the bridegroom recites the mantras, he bends down to hold, with his right hand, the right toe of the bride to help her take each step. At each step he prays that Mahavishnu follow and bless the bride and grant the wishes stipulated in that step. And perhaps there may be other versions.

Some parents remember circling around the fire seven times. Perhaps the confusion comes from a shloka which refers to circles (mandala) which is intended to refer to the circles into which the bride and the groom step.

- Kashiyatra. The assumptions and the spirit that are built into each step should be understood before choices are made rather than simply following a "tradition." Consider for example the step defined in some Brahmin traditions as "Kashi Yatra" in which the bridegroom, attired as a mendicant (usually clad in a dhoti, uttareeyam or upper cloth worn on a bare back (both dipped in turmeric water and dried), triple-string thread signifying bachelorhood, an umbrella and a fan to protect him from the sun and heat during the long journey, a vessel for water and a pair of sandals on his feet) begins his mock journey to the holy city of Benares (Kashi) with the declared purpose of dedicating himself to a life of learning and celibacy. The assumption built into this step is that the young man is already well versed in the four Vedas and is keen on skipping the "grhasthashrama" i.e. the stage of the householder and is now proceeding to take sanyas, the last stage in the Hindu cycle of life on earth. The procession, by the way, according to South Indian practice, is led by musicians playing on pipes and drums–the same troupe that might accompany a kshatriya groom on horseback on his way to "abduct" his bride. The bride's father interrupts the

journey when an accompanying priest describes the young man as someone who has "mastered the four Vedas and is now intent on advanced studies leading to a pious life" upon which the bride's father successfully persuades the "scholar" to return to marry his daughter. It is an interesting piece of theater and in fairness is not unlike some other steps of equivalent drama in the wedding rituals. However, the basic assumption that raises the question pertaining to adopting it as an essential step is the reference to the mastery of the Vedas.

Does this mean that one should abandon this or other similar steps in the ceremonies altogether? It depends on the family and how strongly a family feels it needs to enact this drama. Also a relevant question is the extent of void felt by the families by omitting this or similar steps. A good comparison is with a step that is more familiar, i.e. the groom's arrival on horseback. Using that as a yardstick, we would conclude that the void is minimal but care must be exercised before these steps are integrated into a ceremony.

First and foremost, one needs to have a basis to work with and that basis can be the family tradition. That is always the best place to start in planning a wedding ceremony. We have found that, by prodding and probing, parents generally remember some key events that serve as a framework from which the wedding rites appropriate to that family can be developed. Furthermore, we need to appreciate that most ritual prescriptions deserve to be examined in the light of passing centuries so that we retain what is most essential and consistent with the concept of sthaladharma (i.e. consistent with the location). Young persons we have worked with appreciate this aspect.

Tradition has it that parents have an obligation to arrange for a daughter's marriage.

It has always been considered a responsibility whose fulfillment brought a sense of relief. Tensions used to be high due to fear that something might go wrong and relief was felt only upon completion of a climactic step after which there was no going back. Of course in these modern times the level of concern is the same but the sources of tension may be different.

Chapter V

The Wedding Ceremony

- Preliminaries
- Assemblies: The Bridegroom's Family, The Bride's Family
- Processionals and Milni
- An Overview
- Preparatory Chants
- Sankalpam
- Bride's Arrival, Garland Exchange
- Hasta Milap
- Kanyadanam
- Mangalyadharanam
- Agni Pratishtapana
- Homas: Pradhana Homa; Laaja Homa
- Saptapadi
- Closing ceremonies: Arati; Ashirvadam; Recessional

PRELIMINARIES

In this chapter, we begin with a discussion of the preparatory steps the families may take a day or two before in order to make sure the wedding proceeds smoothly.

Pujas

Some families desire to perform pujas to their ishtadevata (family godhead) either at home or at the location of the wedding. These are best done the day or night before. Generally pujas to Mahaganapati and Maheshwara are requested by either family and Gauri Puja by the bride's family. Again this depends upon family traditions. These pujas can be performed, under the direction of a priest, by the bride and the groom separately in their own quarters with their immediate families and friends attending.

It is quite adequate to perform these pujas by offering shodashopachaaraas (invocation, respectful greeting and prayer steps) described in the Appendix and along the lines discussed in my puja booklets (see www.avsrinivasan.com). Normally each of these pujas should take about an hour using the materials, plans and procedures recommended in Appendix VI. The chanting of the ashtothara (108 names of the deity being worshipped) and Mantrapushpa are appropriate before the concluding aarati, followed by blessings by the assembled elders. Many families have expressed their feeling that performing and participating in these worship services helped reduce stress and brought about a sense of peace. Thus some time devoted to this activity prior to the wedding may help in more sense than one.

Materials and other ritual arrangements used at the pujas may be brought to the mantap later for use during the processionals and the main ceremony. See Appendix I.

Abbreviated pujas to Mahaganapati and Gauri are included in Appendix VI.

Rehearsal

A rehearsal is unheard of in Hindu weddings. It is mandatory in Western practice. Over the years we have found that the second generation growing up in North America, having previously observed or participated in the Christian or Jewish weddings of their friends, are puzzled at what sometimes appears to be a chaotic scene at Hindu weddings. When young Indians visit India and attend weddings, they report being shocked as they observe some ritual taking place on a stage with the immediate family surrounding the scene of action and milling around the stage, fetching this and conveying that, while the audience engages in multiple conversations waiting for the thing to end. Blaring music to which no one pays attention, a fully functioning kitchen that serves food as needed, and a blatant lack of involvement are all accepted as normal and perhaps it may be. This has been the author's experience too.

But we strongly believe that the beauty and grandeur of the scriptural mandates and the ceremonies are too important to ignore on a day which is so special to the principals. Therefore we have developed a format that has established without doubt that we can integrate discipline with joy and thus the sanctity of the samskara can indeed be preserved. To that end a rehearsal is considered mandatory where a talk-through and a walk-through pertaining to the main steps may take place. Thus all those participating the following day do indeed understand the sequence of the steps and the meaning of each ritual. Obviously, actual garlanding and homas do not take place during the rehearsal. Again experience here has shown, with a well coordinated rehearsal, how enjoyable and successful the wedding can be. It has also shown how things can go wrong when the information received at the rehearsal was either not really understood or not followed or principal helpers were absent. But there is no question about the value of this strategy and therefore we highly recommend it. There has generally been complete understanding of this need on the part of the families even when both are of the Hindu faith. See Appendix II

Mantap

The arrangement of the mantap (mandapam), the sacred space, can vary from an extremely simple space defined in subtle ways to a very elaborately decorated wood or metal structure with posts, garlands and cloth or ceiling covered with Indian motifs. The choice is up to individual taste and budget. Some have used the traditional four pillars or just flower stands to define a rectangular space, some have used gazebos available on the premises and decorated them with flowers. Any of these will do as long as the space is made special and distinct. In North America some entrepreneurs have recognized a business opportunity in this and families are now aware of their service. For a fee, they are able to bring the necessary components and assemble a mantap and disassemble it after the ceremony. Many families use this service as well as a variety of catering and DJ services.

Outdoor mantaps need to be firmly anchored, especially when the ceremony is held on a beach. Plates, flowers and other materials may need to be weighted down and deepas (lamps or candles) may need glass mantles or protectors.

Organization of materials at the mantap

For greeting the bridegroom:

- Seven metallic plates containing (a) five types of fruit, (b) a ceremonial cup of water, uddharana (ceremonial spoon), akshata, (c) madhuparkam, deepa, kumkum, haldi, flower petals and akshata, (d) flowers, (e) agarbattis, perfumes, (f) the garland for the bridegroom and (g) a kalasha on a bed of raw rice, filled to about a third with water, topped with a decorated coconut on a fringe of leaves (mango or other fruit tree leaves). These should be placed at the front of the mantap in a row and ready to be picked up when the processional to receive the bridegroom starts.

For use at the mantap:

- A table on the side of the mantap towards the back is needed to place the plates described above upon return to the mantap after bringing the bridegroom in the processional. Note: Some of these plates (fruits, flowers) can be conveyed to thc bride's entourage quarters to be used in their processional and placed again on this table. The only additional plates that will accompany the bride are (a) a plate with the mangalasutra (necklace) on a silk cloth with a few petals of flowers, kumkum, haldi and a few grains of akshata and (b) a garland for the bridegroom.

- A second table on the other side of the mantap to place materials to be used in the havan: (four small cups of puffed rice, small jar of ghee with a spoon, few small sticks about 2 to 3 inches long, akshata cup); the sheet/saree to be used as antarpat, an extra bowl of akshata; an extra container with water and a basin to collect water poured down during the Kanyadanam ceremony.
- A third table (about 24 inch diameter) at the left front corner (from the vantage of the audience), with (1) a plate of flowers, (2) a plate containing small cups of kumkum, haldi and (3) a bowl of akshata, pancha patra (copper vessels used in pujas) with uddahrana (spoon), (4) a silver or copper vessel with water, for exclusive use by the officiator.
- Havan kund (fire receptacle), with a small table to hold it, havan samagree (mixture for offering), small wood sticks/twigs, cube/s of fire-starter, candle stub, matches or lighter. A fire extinguisher and a small bucket of sand in the vicinity but out of obvious sight.

The mantap should be easily accessed when the groom's party and later the bride's entourage arrive to enter the mantap. One or two firm steps may be needed if the mantap is raised above the floor level. Make sure they are firm, safe and easy to use. A chair may be needed for use by the bride and her entourage to remove shoes gracefully before they mount the mantap.

It is best to have all the plates arranged before they are brought to the site. It is important that the entire mantap along with tables as described above be in place and checked out at least thirty minutes before the ceremony begins. Also the point of Milni, that is, the location (an entrance or archway) where the bridegroom and party are met may also be decorated.

PREPARATORY CHANTS

As stated before, upon arrival at the sacred space and after a brief overview, all is set to begin. Here we propose to begin with a Vedic chant. The particular

shloka chosen is the most appropriate beginning because it combines prayer and praise for the Vedic gods but also affords an opportunity for the principals (and the audience if they can join in the chanting) to make statements of their value system ("I shall speak the truth, ...") setting a stage worthy of a grand alliance between two families. This verse induces bhakti as well as declaration and determination to subscribe to one's heritage.

Assembly of the Bride's Family/First Processional

An assembly is formed from among the bride's family (minus the bride) with the bride's parents, five ladies selected from the family and the officiating priest. Each carries a plate as described below:

Bride's father: A garland in a plate. Bride's mother: plate with a lamp (deepa), petals, madhuparkam in a small cup, kumkum and haldi in containers. Each of the other ladies carries a plate that may consist of fruits, flowers, agarbattis and perfume sprinkler, lamps and a copper or silver vessel with water and decorated coconut. The priest will carry a plate with akshata, a panchapatra (a silver or copper bowl used in rituals) with water, and uddharana (ceremonial spoon). Minor variations from the above are acceptable as long as they are decided apriori during the rehearsal.

At the moment appointed for the beginning of the ceremony, two or more rows of the processional are formed with the priest at the front row center and the bride's mother on one side and the father on the other side. The five ladies (other family members and friends may also join in) form the second and third rows. As nadaswaram, shehnai or any other form of selected music begins to play, the assembly proceeds towards the previously designated place where the bridegroom's party is met. The timings should be such that the bride's party arrives at the meeting place a couple of minutes before the groom's party reaches there.

Baraat

It is customary for the bridegroom's family to assemble outside the wedding hall before beginning the procession to be greeted later by the bride's family. Depending on the tradition, a choice is made by family and friends to have the groom ride a decorated animal (usually a horse) or in a decorated vehicle (usually a convertible) and process towards the wedding hall in order to arrive at the previously agreed point where the other family's principals and the priest wait. This procession is usually quite lively with loud music and especially folk dance, and results in an appropriately joyous and festive mood. Depending upon the families such a procession may take a few minutes to as long as half an hour or more. It is important to designate a person to keep track of the time so that the party is at the designated place at the appointed hour. Timing of the steps in the ceremony may be set back if there is delay in this clearly free-for-all event. It is therefore best for the designated person to make an announcement, ten minutes before the main ceremony begins, requesting that the guests proceed to the wedding hall and take their seats. Also it is helpful to have ushers hand out the program note and guide the guests to their seats to help keep the pace. It is best to direct the groom's party to the right side of the mantap (from the audience vantage) and the bride's party to the left side. A subtle requirement is that the bride's side arrive just a few seconds before the bridegroom's side arrives to adhere to the protocol of greeters.

As discussed earlier in the chapter on Traditions and Customs, if the families decide to have the groom proceed on a Kashiyatra, then the bride's party interrupts the "journey." In this case the priest accompanies the groom and a dialogue ensues as described earlier. The rest of the process may remain intact and the entire group (bride's and groom's parties) now proceeds towards the mantap.

Greeting of the Groom/Milni/Swagatam

Upon arrival of the groom and his family at the pre-determined meeting point (Milni), the priest blesses the groom and chants "*śuklāmbharadharam viṣnum...*" and concludes by saying: "*avighnamastu* (May there be no obstacles)." He then directs the bride's mother to apply tilak to the forehead of the groom and perform an arati using the lamp in her plate. The bride's father garlands the groom and shakes his hand. If there is a perfume sprinkler on one of the plates, it is customary to sprinkle a few drops generally in the direction of the groom and his party.

At this point some families use this Milni as the occasion to honor close relatives and garland previously selected family members from each side. Upon completion of this formality, the bride's welcoming group turns around, proceeding towards the mantap with the groom at the center now flanked by both sets of parents and the priest and followed by all the rest of the party.

Processional towards the Mantap

The processional reaches the mantap and the principals, (bridegroom and his parents, bride's parents or other elder in charge of bestowal), and any other family members previously agreed to, get up on the platform and face the

audience. It is best to have the bridegroom and his parents stand (or sit) on the left side of the priest facing the assembly and the bride's parents on the right. The latter is the side from which the bride will enter the mantap. This is important because after the Mangalyadharanam (or other defining step) the bride is asked to move to the left of the groom and stay there for the rest of the ceremony. Those who have plates in their hands may place them on the tables and take their seats nearby. Groomsmen may stay on the mantap if they wish and if there is space. Otherwise they may be seated nearby. While some may still be ushering guests at this point, they may soon be needed to help with the antarpat or fire preparation.

The number of family members who remain at the mantap is decided by the families. It can be limited to just the couple's parents but may include more from each side. Friends and family members who are designated to help at the mantap should have reserved seats in the front row or may prefer to stand at designated locations.

When everyone is settled the officiant begins to give an overview.

This should serve as the cue for the bridal party to leave their quarters and approach close enough to the entrance but not within site of the mantap, and wait for the final signal to begin their own processional.

Wedding Overview

The overview concept suggested here was developed by the author over the years and has been used in about thirty weddings. It works very well. The concept replaces the need to stop the ceremony often to "describe" each step before or after it is taken, so that the flow of the process is smooth. Generally we have found our wedding audiences to be intelligent, curious and fully capable of absorbing the spirit and meaning of the procedures as long as they are given a broad background and philosophy of the rituals. With an overview of the type shown below and a program note in hand, the assemblage can follow the dynamics of the wedding process quite well.

The following is the general overview that the author has used with minor modifications and which may be used as a basis by another officiant with his or her own embellishments.

Good afternoon! My name is Srinivasan and in behalf of the two families that are about to be united through the solemn ceremony of a wedding, it is a pleasure for me to welcome all of you to participate in the ceremonies.

For the benefit of those in the audience who may be new to our Vedic wedding rites, I would like to give a brief overview of the several steps the two young persons are about to take. The program you have received is a condensed version of the procedures and you may wish to refer to it from time to time.

The Hindu wedding ceremony is based on Vedic traditions and rituals originating in the Rig Veda, the earliest of the four ancient Sanskrit books of knowledge which form the basis of Hinduism.

Our ancestors set up guidelines to make sure that this institution known as marriage is a permanent one capable of not only bringing happiness to two young people, but also providing a delicate balance so that the new family enjoys the fullness of life within the framework of what we call dharma, the Hindu code of right conduct. Dharma is one of the four aspects of life that Hindus strive to live for. The other three are artha and kama, which underline the financial and aesthetic aspects, and the final goal is liberation or moksha. All the rituals that comprise the wedding ceremony, directly or indirectly charge the couple to strive for these four aspects, known as चतुर्विध फल पुरुषार्थ (chaturvidha phala purushartha). As you will see, we have successfully preserved the principal elements and spirit of the traditional wedding program which, in the not-too-distant past, took as many as five days. The rituals, which date back at least 5,000 years, form a significant dramatic sequence.

We begin our ceremonies with a Vedic chant of benediction. The Vedic chant ends with a prayer for peace. The traditional seven Great Rivers are then invoked, because one of the principal elements in Hindu ritual is water. The invocation is followed by a purification chant.

The groom has been received and honored by the bride's family. The sacred space, the mantap, has been prepared. We will locate this time and space and invoke the principal Hindu Gods.

In just a couple of minutes, after the formal greetings, I shall instruct the bride's father and request him to declare his intention to honor the groom and his family, and to give away the bride to the trust and care of the bridegroom's family at this moment in time and space as specified. We will then receive the bride and her entourage accompanied by some members of her immediate family.

These initial steps pave the way for a ceremony known as Kanyadanam, the ritual equivalent of leaving one family and setting the stage for the new family to establish its own home and thus begin a new life.

As with many world traditions, Hindu tradition also assumes that as an assembly of family and friends, you have acquired a special, although temporary, authority to grant permission when sought and offer blessings at appropriate intervals. Both these are granted by your free and firm declaration of a single word in Sanskrit तथास्तु (Tathaastu), meaning "It shall be so." When I seek such permission through words such as अनुगृह्णंतु (Anugrnhantu) or अधिब्रुवन्तु (Adhibruvantu), please respond by saying, तथास्तु (Tathaastu).

I shall occasionally remind you of this sacred authority and it is therefore essential that you remain alert until the ceremony is complete.

The principal seal or bond between the bridegroom and the bride is a golden necklace, the mangalasutra, which the bridegroom places around the bride's neck. This particular necklace first receives the blessings of the elders in the two families, and it is the power of that blessing that we believe will sustain this couple for all time.

The latter ceremony known as मांगल्यधारणं (Mangalyadharanam) is of deep significance. It begins with an invocation to all the Hindu Gods and Goddesses and, as I recite a chant of blessing, with an intense sound of music in the background, the bridegroom offers the necklace and puts it around the neck of the bride. This ceremony indeed is considered the climax in the series of steps.

The couple is then declared husband and wife for all time.

It is an ancient practice of Hindus to invoke Agni, Fire, and the purifier of all, to serve as witness to the wedding vows. Holding hands, and with fire as witness, the couple pledge their love to each other.

Into the fire symbolic sacrifices through offerings of grain, herbs, clarified butter, incense, sandalwood are made in a gesture of gratitude and worship to the gods and symbolizing the offer of all their worldly possessions to God's grace. Initially, the couple goes around Agni four times. The first three rounds led by the bridegroom signify the pledge to adhere to the practice of dharma, artha and kama but in the final round, the bride leads the bridegroom confirming the Hindu belief that salvation is impossible without the leadership of the lady of the house or the धर्मपत्नी (dharmapatni). Mutual wishes for prosperity, for children and for a long, happy life together follow in a series of ceremonial offerings to the fire.

This is followed by a ceremony called सप्तपदी (Saptapadi) in which the couple take seven steps together in front of Agni, and pledge to each other their eternal friendship. The friendship element is important in our weddings, and signifies the nature of the promise and the commitment that bind a couple. This seventh step is also the event which makes the marriage legal in Indian law.

We will then ask you to witness this wedding and bless the couple with long life and prosperity, and again your approval will be sought.

We are ready to begin and we urge you to relax, enjoy the ceremonies and help us through the process.

Invocation/Vēda Mantrās
Chanting led by priest

The priest begins with the invocation which forms the first verse of the first chapter of Part One of the *Taittirīya Upanishad:*

ॐ शं नो मित्रः शं वरुणः
शं नो भवत्वर्यमा
शं न इंद्रो ब्रुहस्पतिः
शं नो विष्णुरुरुक्रमः
नमो ब्रह्मणे
नमस्ते वायो
त्वमेव प्रत्यक्षं ब्रह्मासि
त्वामेव प्रत्यक्षं ब्रह्म वदिष्यामि
ऋतं वदिष्यामि
सत्यं वदिष्यामि
तन्मामवतु
तद्वक्तारमवतु
अवतु माम्
अवतु वक्तारं
ॐ शांतिः शांतिः शांतिः

Salutations to the assembly:
Chanting led by priest

ॐ नमस्सदसे नमस्सदसस्पतये
नमस्सखीणां पुरोगाणां चक्षुषे
नमोदिवे नमः पृथिव्यै
सप्रथसभांमे गोपाय
येचस्सभ्यास्सभासदः
तानिंद्रियावतः कुरु
सर्वमायुरुपासतां
सर्वेभ्यो महांतेभ्यो नमो नमः

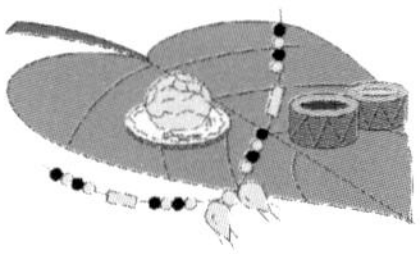

ōm śam nō mitra: śam varuṇa:
śam nō bhavatvaryamā
śam na indrō bṛhaspati:
śam nō viṣṇururukrama:
namō brahmaṇē
namastē vāyō
tvamēva pratyakṣam brahmāsi
tvāmēva pratyakṣam brahma vadishyāmi
ṛtam vadiṣyaami
satyam vadiṣyaami
tanmāvavatu
tadvaktāramavatu
avatu mām
avatu vaktāram
ōm shānti: shānti: shānti:

OM, may the sun god Mitra and other Vedic gods–Varuna, Aryama, Indra, Bṛhaspati and the all pervading MahaVishnu and all the devatas shower their blessings upon us.
Salutations to Brahma, salutations to Vayu. You are a personification of Brahma. I shall proclaim you as Brahma. I shall always abide by dharma. I shall always speak the truth.
May THAT protect us all
OM peace, peace, peace!

ōm nama:ssadasē namassadasa spatayē
nama:ssakhīnām purōgāṇām chakshuṣē
namōdivē nama: pṛthivyai
saprathasabhāmē gōpāya
yēchasabhyāssabhāsada:
tānindriyāvata: kuru
sarvamāyurupāsatām
sarvēbhyō mahāntēbhyō: namō nama:

Salutations to the assembly and its leader (presider), friends, family and other leaders present here. Salutations to heaven and earth. May all the honorable and powerful belonging to the family (present or absent) in this assembly be blessed with long life and be protected.

Prayers/Salutations

These prayers may be chanted by the priest and principals as well as Hindus in the audience familiar with these salutations.

प्रार्थना

श्रीमन्महागणाधिपतये नमः
लक्ष्मी नारायणाभ्याम् नमः
उमा महेश्वराभ्याम् नमः
श्री सत्यनारायण स्वामिने नमः
वाणी हिरण्यगर्भाभ्यां नमः
शची पुरंदराभ्यां नमः

माता पितृभ्यो नमः
इष्ट देवताभ्यो नमः
कुल देवताभ्यो नमः
ग्राम देवताभ्यो नमः
स्थान देवताभ्यो नमः
वास्तु देवताभ्यो नमः

आदित्यादि नवग्रहदेवताभ्यो नमः
सर्वेभ्यो देवेभ्यो नमः
ऐतत्कर्म प्रधान देवताभ्यो नमः

अविघ्नमस्तु

शुक्लांबरधरं विष्णुं शशिवर्णं चतुर्भुजं
प्रसन्न वदनं ध्यायेत् सर्व विघ्नोपशांतये

prārthana

Prayers

śrīmanmahāgaṇādhipatayē nama:
lakṣmī nārāyaṇābhyām nama:
umā mahēśvarābhyām nama:
śrī satyanārāyaṇa swāminē nama:
vāṇī hiraṇyagarbhābhyām nama:
śachī purandarābhyām nama:

Salutations to Mahaganapati, Lakshminarayana, Umamaheshwara, Satyanarayana, Vanihiranyagarbha, Shachipurandara.

mātā pitṛbhyō nama:
iṣta dēvatābhyō nama:
kula dēvatābhyō nama:
grāma dēvatābhyō nama:
sthāna dēvatābhyō nama:
vāstu dēvatābhyō nama:

Salutations to the mothers and fathers, my chosen godhead, family deity, deity presiding over this town, deity presiding over this place, deity presiding over this building.

ādityādi navagrahadēvatābhyō nama:
sarvēbhyō dēvēbhyō nama:
ētatkarma pradhāna dēvatābhyō nama:
avighnamastu

Salutations to the nine planets, salutations to all godheads, salutation to the godhead presiding over this ceremony.
May there be no obstacles.

śuklāmbaradharam viṣṇum
śaśivarṇam caturbhujam
prasanna vadanam dhyāyēt
sarva vighnōpa śāntayē

I meditate on Vishnu who is clothed in white, the color of the moon, four-armed and smiling, to lessen all obstacles.

Sankalpam

The father of the bride, repeating after the priest, declares his intention publicly thus:

This is a declaration of the time and place specified for the rite, here assumed to take place in North America.

संकल्पं

शुभे शोभन मुहूर्ते आद्य ब्रह्मणः द्वितीय
परार्धे श्री श्वेत वराह कल्पे वैवस्वत मन्वन्तरे
कलियुगे प्रथमे पादे क्रौन्च द्वीपे अमेरिका
वर्षे उत्तर अमेरिका खंडे व्यवहारिके
चांद्रमानेनास्य षष्टि संवत्सराणां मध्ये ---
-------संवत्सरे, -----------
- आयने, --------- ऋतौ,-----
------- मासे, ------------
पक्षे, ----------- तिथौ, -----
----- नक्षत्रे, ----------वासर
युक्तायाम्, ऐवं गुण विशेषण विशिष्ठायां
अस्याम् शुभ तिथौ, ------------
----- नामधेयः अहं मम धर्मपत्नी ---
------ देवी सहित मम पुत्री चिरन्जीवी
सौभाग्यवती------- देवी नाम्नि शुभ
विवाह महोत्सवांगाय --------
गोत्रोद्भवस्य ---------नामधेयः अस्य
वरं तथा तस्य कुटुम्बकम् कन्यादान समये
सुस्वागतं तथा वरपूजांच करिष्ये

Sankalpam

śubhē śōbhana muhūrtē, ādya brahmaṇa:, dvitīya parārdhē, śrī śvēta varāha kalpē, vaivasvata manvantarē, kaliyugē, prathama pādē, kraunca dvīpē, amerikā varṣē, uttara amerikā khanḍē, vyavahārikē, cāndramānēnasya ṣaṣṭhi samvatsarāṇām madhyē, ---------------samvatsarē, -------------------āyanē, ----------- ṛtau,------------ māsē, ------------ pakṣē, ----------- tiṭhau, -----------nakṣatrē,-----------vāsara yuktāyām, ēvam guṇa viśēṣaṇa viśiṣṭhāyām asyām śubha tiṭhau, ----------------- nāmadhēya: aham mama dharma patnī --------- dēvī sahita mama putrī ciranjīvi saubhāgyavati ---------- -------dēvī nāmni śubha vivāha mahōtsavāngāya ----------------------- gōtrōdbhavasya ---------------------------nāmadhēya: asya varasya taṭhā tasya kutumbānām kanyādāna samayē susvāgatam taṭhā vara pūjāmca kariṣyē.

Declaration of Space/Time

At this most auspicious time in the earliest part of the second half of Brahma's term of Vaivasvata in the White Boar's millennium, in the first segment of Kali Yuga, in North America, in the general region of America, in the island of Krauncha (Heron), specifying, under normal practice, among the sixty Chāndramana years beginning with Prabhava, ------------ year, ----------------solstice, ------------ season, ---------------month, -------------- position of the moon, ------------- the lunar day, ------------star, ---------------- day, on such superior time and particular day,

I -----------------along with --------------my wife-in-dharma, declare my intention to welcome this bridegroom ------------------------, born in ------------gotra, and his family, in order to offer Vara Puja in connection with the auspicious wedding of my daughter Chiranjeevi Saubhaagyavati --------------------- Devi.

Vara Puja

Short Version

This dialogue may take place at the Milni stage if an elaborate version will be used at the mantap. Otherwise this version is all that is necessary and will suffice for use at the mantap.

The dialogue begins with a greeting from the bride's father and continues as shown with a final mandate from the priest.

वर पूजा

कर्तृ : ॐ साधु भवान् आस्ताम्
वर : व्रतोस्मि – ॐ साधुं अहमासे
कर्तृ : अर्चयिष्यामो भवंतं
वर : अर्चय

पुरोहितः
गृहस्थाश्रम सिध्यर्थं चतुर्विध
फल पुरुषार्थ सिध्यर्थं
शुभ विवाह विधिं
यथा विहितं कर्म कुरु

वरः यथा ज्ञानं करवाणि

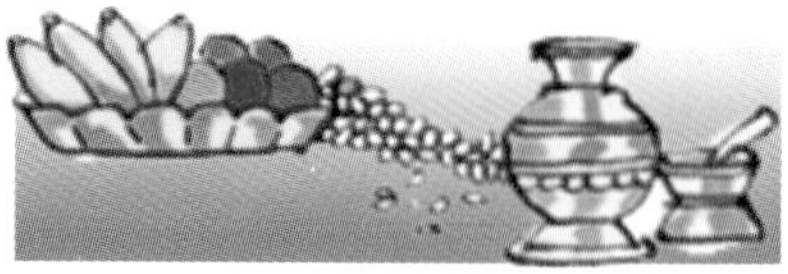

Vara Puja

kartṛ : *ōm sādhu bhavān āstām*
vara : *vṛtōsmi - ōm sādhum ahamāsē*
kartṛ : *arcayiśyāmō bhavantam*
vara : *arcaya*

purōhita:

gṛhasṭhāśrama sidhyarṭham
caturvidha phala puruṣārṭha
sidhyarṭham śubha vivāha vidhim
yaṭhā vihitam karma kuru

***vara**: yaṭhā jnānam karavāṇı*

(after Lal, P. 1996)

Vara Puja (Short Version)

The initiator : (bride's father): May you receive this honor from us.
Bridegroom : I am satisfied. I am honored.
Bride's father: We worship your virtues.
Bridegroom : I am honored.

Priest:

In order to attain the next stage of Householder and in order to attain the fruits of the four aspects of life, prepare yourself to perform the auspicious wedding rites according to prescribed shastras.

Groom: I shall do so to the best of my knowledge (ability).

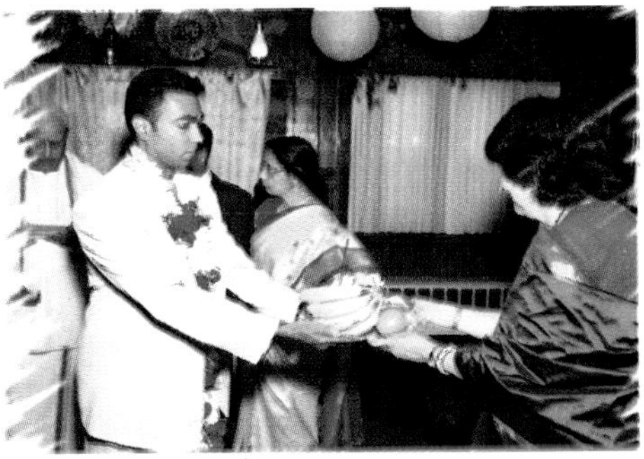

Vara Puja

(Longer Version)

In this version the dialogue is longer and covers the shodashopacharas i.e. the steps used in performing a puja to a deity except that in this case the object of the worship (the groom) responds in appreciation of the puja rendered to him.

Note that the step in which the bride's mother offers an arati may be omitted if she has already taken this step at the Milni

दाता

मम कुमार्या: उद्वाहार्थं आगतं श्री लक्ष्मीनारायण स्वरूप वरं तुभ्यं गंध पुष्प अक्षताभिः पूजयिष्ये

वरः अस्तु

दाता

श्री लक्ष्मीनारायण स्वरूपस्य इदमासनं

वरः सुखासनं

दाता

श्री लक्ष्मीनारायणं भवत्सु आवाहयिष्ये

वरः आवाहय

दाता

भागशः अमीवो गंधाः

वरः सुगंधाः

दाता

इमानिवपुष्पाणि पुष्प मालिकाम्

वरः सुपुष्पाणि

दाता

अयंवो धूपः

वरः सुधूपः

दाता

अयंवो दीपः

वरः सुदीपः

कन्या माता

श्री लक्ष्मीनारायण स्वरूप वरस्य इदं नीराजनं

वरः सुनीराजनं

dātā

mama kumāryāha udvāhārṭham
āgatam śrī lakshmīnārāyaṇa
svarūpāya varam
tubhyam gandha puṣpa akṣatābhi:
pūjayiśyē

***vara**: astu*

dātā

śrī lakshmīnārāyaṇa svarūpasya
idamāsanam

***vara**: sukhāsanam*

dātā

śrī lakshmīnārāyaṇam bhavatsu
āvāhayiṣyē

***vara**: āvāhaya*

dātā

bhāgaśa: amīvō gandhā:

***vara**: sugandhā:*

dātā

imānivapuṣpāṇi puṣpa mālikām

***vara:** supuṣpāṇi*

***dātā:** ayamvō dhūpa:*

***vara**: sudhūpa:*

***dātā**: ayamvō dīpa:*

***vara**: sudīpa:*

kanyā mātā

śrī lakshmīnārāyaṇa svarūpāya
varasya idam nīrājanam

***vara**: sunīrājanam*

Giver

I offer sandal paste, flowers, akshata in worshipping you the very embodiment of Lakshminarayana in the course of my daughter's wedding rituals.

Groom: May it be so.

Giver

This is the seat for you in the form of Lakshminarayana.

Groom: A comfortable seat.

Giver

I invoke you in the form of Lakshminarayana.

Groom: Please do.

Giver

As part (of the worship) here is sandal paste.

Groom: Good fragrance.

Giver

Here is the garland of flowers.

Groom: Good flowers.

Giver: Here is fragrance.

Groom: Good fragrance.

Giver: Here is the light.

Groom: Good light.

Bride's mother

Here is arati to the groom in the form of Lakshminarayana.

Groom: Good arati.

The Vara Puja is complete with the final offerings as shown here and the stage is now set for the arrival of the bride.

The coordinator signals the person in charge of conducting the bride to the hall, traditionally her maternal uncle, close to the moment when the bride's mother conducts the arati (in the elaborate version). As stated earlier if the brief version is chosen then the cue for the coordinator is when the brief Vara Puja dialogue begins on stage.

दाता
गंध पुष्प धूप दीप सकलाराधनैः स्वर्चितं

वर
अस्तु

dātā

gandha puṣpa dhūpa dīpa
sakalāradhanai: svarcitam

Giver

We worship you elaborately with sandal,
flowers, fragrance and lamp.

Vara

astu

Groom

May it be so.

Antarpat*

As the bridal procession approaches the mantap, the bride, escorted by her maternal uncle or other relative, is helped by her maid of honor while the other bridesmaids take previously planned positions. The bride stands in front of the cloth shield (antarpat), facing the groom.

The ceremony begins with the groom reciting the mantras shown here or repeating after the priest.

Remove the curtain at the end of this chant.

* Note: If the family practice is to omit Antarpat, then the garlanding ceremony may proceed in the way described here by omitting all actions pertaining to the curtain

अंतर्पट

आनः प्रजां जनयंतु प्रजापतिः
आजरसाय समनक्त्वर्यमा
अभ्रातृघ्नीं वरुणा
अपतिघ्नीं बृहस्पते
इन्द्रा पुत्रघ्नीं
लक्ष्म्यंतामस्यै सवितस्सुव

अघोर चक्षुर् अपतिघ्न्येधि
शिवा पतिभ्यस्सुमना स्सु वर्चाः
वीरसूर् देवकामा स्योना शंनो भव
द्विपदे शंचतुष्पदे

Antarpat

āna: prajām janayantu prajāpati:
ājarasāya samanaktvaryamā
abhrātṛghnīm varuṇā apatighnīm
bṛhaspatē indrā putraghnīm
lakṣmyamtāmasyai savitassuva

aghōra cakṣur apatighnyēdhi śivā
patibhyassumanā ssu varcā:
vīrasūr dēvakāmā syōnā śamnō
bhava dvipadē śamcatuśpadē

Antarpat Blessing

May Prajaapati bless her with children, May Aaryama bless her jewelry, May Varuna and Bṛhaspati protect her husband and his brothers, May Indra protect her children, May Savitr grant her wealth.

O Bride, may your peaceful demeanor and compassion provide peace in my family. May you bear brave children and bring happiness to both humans and animals.

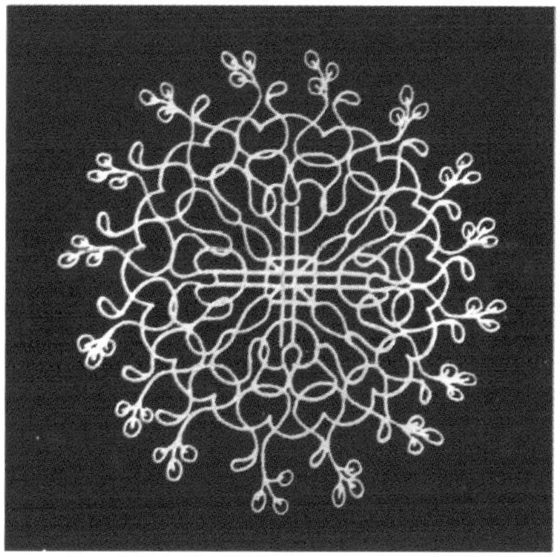

Jayamala

The couple face each other.
The maid of honor hands a garland to the bride while at the same time the best man assists the groom to take off the garland that is now on his neck.

The bride garlands the groom who in turn takes the garland from the hand of the best man and garlands the bride. With both garlanded now they face the audience with the bride standing to the right of the groom.

I have taken the liberty of using सोहम् अस्मि instead of amoahamasmi because in context सोहम् appears to be more appropriate and in tune with सा त्वं.

(Atharva Veda 14.2.71)

जयमाल

संज्ञानं विज्ञानं प्रज्ञानं जानदभि जानत्
संकल्पमानं प्रकल्पमानं उपकल्पमानं
उपक्लुप्तं क्लुप्तं
श्रेयोवसीयः आयुस्संभूतं भूतं
चित्रकेतुः प्रभानाथ्संभानां
ज्योतिष्मागस्तेजस्वानातपग्
स्तपन्नभितपन्
रोचनो रोचमानश्शोभन श्शोभमानः कल्याणः

सुमंगलीरियं वधूरिमां समेत पश्यत

सोहम् अस्मि सा त्वं सामाहमस्म्य
ऋक्त्वं द्यौरहं पृथिवी त्वं ताविह
संभवाव प्रजामा जनयावहै

samjnānam vijnānam prajnānam
jānadabhi jānat, sankalpamānam
prakalpamānam upakalpamānam
upakluptam kluptam
śrēyōvasīya āyussambhūtam
bhūtam citrakētu: prabhānāṭh
sambhānām
jyōtiṣmāgamstējasvānātapag
stapannabhitapan rōcanō
rōcamāna śśōbhana
śśōbhamāna: kalyāṇa:

sumangalīriyam vadhūrimām
samēta paśyata

sōham asmi sā tvam
sāmāhamasmya ṛktvam
dyauraham pṛthivī tvam
tāviha sambhavāva prajāmā
janayāvahē

This bride possesses superior
intelligence to bring harmony
between the families; decisive,
honorable, desirous of and ready to
make a home.
She arrives truly beautiful,
distinguished as a bright shining
light, gleaming with luster,
charming, pleasing and lovely;
Hail this bride.

Let all look at this bride who is
auspicious.

I am He, you are She
I am Song, you are Verse
I am Heaven, you are Earth.
Let us both dwell together here,
parents of future children

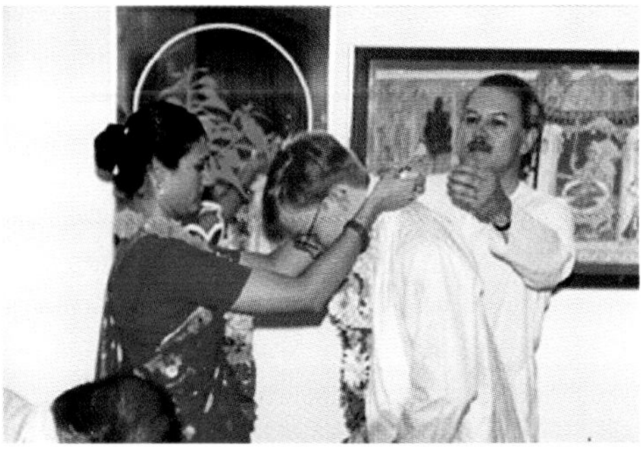

Hasta Milap

Subsequent to garlanding and as the bride and groom turn to face the audience, the bride's father steps up and places the right hand of his daughter in the right hand of the groom.

The groom is instructed to chant the mantra.

Pravara Recital

This step is a formal public announcement of the of the names of the bridegroom and the bride in front of the assembled. They are introduced formally declaring their lineage beginning with great grandfather and proceeding with grandfather and father. This serves as an opportunity to remember the ancestors in both families on this auspicious occasion. Normally the practice is to repeat the Pravara recital three times. But it may be done only once

हस्तमिलाप्

गृभ्णामि ते सुप्रजास्त्वाय हस्तंमया
पत्या जरदश्टिर्यथाअसः
भगोअर्यमा सविता
पुरंधिर्मह्यंत्वादुर्गार्हि पत्याय देवाः

प्रवर

त्रया ऋषयः (पंचार्षयः, सप्तार्षयः)
प्रवरान्विताय .... गोत्रोत्पन्नयां
.....................प्रपौत्रायां, ... पौत्रायां,
श्रीमान् .... तथा श्रीमती
सौभाग्यवती .... देवी पुत्रायां,
श्रीधर रूपिणी चिरंजीवी ....
नाम्ने वराय,
त्रया ऋषयः (पंचार्षयः) प्रवरोपेतां
......................गोत्रोत्पन्नां
.................प्रपौत्रीं, ...पौत्रीं,
श्रीमान् .... तथा श्रीमति
सौभाग्यवती .... देवी पुत्रीं,
श्री रूपिणी, चिरंजीवी सौभाग्यवती
.... नाम्नी कन्यां,
प्रजापति दैवत्यां प्रजोत्पादनार्थं तुभ्यमहं
संप्रददे नमम.

gṛbhṇāmi tē suprajāstvāya hastam
mayā patyā jaradaśṭir yaṭhāasa:
bhagōaryamā savitā
purandhirmahyamtvādurgārha
patyāya dēvā:

O bride, I shall hold your hand in order to live long with you and our progeny through the grace of Aryama, Savitr and Indra who have granted us the status of householders.

trayā ṛṣaya: (pancārṣaya: ,
saptārṣaya:) pravarānvitāya ....*
gōtrōtpannayām...........prapautrāyām,
...............pautrāyām, śrīmān ....
taṭhā śrīmati saubhāgyavati ....
dēvi putrāyām, ciranjīvi ....
nāmnē varāya,

Spiritual descendent of three sages (five or seven sages*), born in the -------------gotra, the great grandson of --------------, --------------, grandson of -----------------, son of Mr.----------------- and Mrs. Saubhagyavati ---------------------------, Chiranjivi -----------------------------------, the bridegroom

trayā ṛṣaya: pravarōpētam ....
gōtrōtpannam
...................prapautrīm, ...
........pautrīm, śrīmān .... taṭhā
śrīmati saubhāgyavatī .... dēvi
putrīm, ciranjīvi saubhāgyavatī
.... nāmnī kanyām,

Spiritual descendent of three sages (five or seven sages), born in the -------------- gotra, great granddaughter of ----------------------, granddaughter of ---------------, and daughter of Mr. ------------------ and Mrs. Saubhagyavati --------------------, Chiranjivi Saubhagyavati -----------, the bride,

prajāpati daivatyām
prajōtpādanārṭham tubhyamaham
sampradadē namama

And in order to propitiate Brahma, the lord of progeny, and in order to continue my lineage, I bestow this young woman on you without any reservation. Please accept her. She is all yours.

* Some gotras refer to 5 or 7 sages.

Kanyaadaanam

This important ritual begins with a call to the audience to bless this moment to be auspicious. This and similar requests throughout the ceremony not only engage the audience but serve notice that the assembled are witness to an important commitment being made at the mantap. Everyone present is requested to respond with "tathaastu" at the end of each phrase.

With this set of permissions granted the Kanyadanam ceremony may now begin.

कन्यादानं

अनुज्ञ

अयं मुहूर्तस्सुमुहूर्तोस्त्विति
भवन्तो महांतो अनुगृह्णंतु

कर्तव्ये अस्मिन् शुभविवाह कर्मणि
भवन्तो महांतो अधिब्रुवंतु

ॐ पुण्याहं भवंतो अधिब्रुवंतु
ॐ ऋध्धिं भवंतो अधिब्रुवंतु
ॐ स्वस्ति भवंतो अधिब्रुवंतु

कन्यां कनकसंपन्नां कनकाभरणैर्युतां
दास्यामि विष्णवे तुभ्यं ब्रह्मलोक जिगीषया
कन्ये ममाग्रतो भूयात् कन्येमे देविपार्श्वयोः
कन्येमे सर्वतो भूयात् त्वद्दानान्मोक्षमाप्नुयां

विश्वंभराः सर्वभूतः साक्षिण्यः सर्वदेवताः
इमां कन्य्यां प्रदास्यामि पितृणां तारणायच
कन्यां सालंकृत्वा साध्वीं सुशीलाय सुधीमते
प्रयतोहं प्रदास्यामि धर्म काम्यार्थ सिद्धये

anujne

ayam muhūrtassumuhūrtōstviti
bhavantō mahāntō anugṛṇhantu

kartavyē asmin śubha vivāha karmaṇi
bhavantō mahāntō adhibruvantu

om puṇyāham bhavantō
adhibruvantu
om ṛdhdhim bhavantō adhibruvantu
om svasti bhavantō adhibruvantu

kanyādānam

kanyām kanakasampannām
kanakābharaṇairyutām
dāsyāmi viṣṇuvē tubhyam brahma
lōka jigīśayā kanyē mamāgratō
bhūyāt kanyēmē dēvipārśvayō:
kanyēmē sarvatō bhūyāt tvaddānān
mōkṣamāpnuyām

viśvambharā: sarvabhūta: sākṣiṇya:
sarvadēvatā: imām kanyām
pradāsyāmi pitṛṇām tāraṇāyaca
kanyām sālamkṛtvā sādhvṝm suśīlāya
sudhīmatē prayatōham pradāsyāmi
dharma kāmyārṭha siddhayē

Permission

May you, the great assembled, grant this present time to be auspicious.

May you, the great assembled, express that this wedding task be auspicious.

May you cxprcss this day to be auspicious.
May you express this to be successful.
May you express your blessings.

Gift of the bride

May I offer to you, the embodiment of Vishnu, this, my daughter, foremost among all young women, by my side, covered with golden ornaments, so that I may obtain salvation in Brahmaloka.

With all gods and other beings as witness, in order to liberate my ancestors and to accomplish dharma, artha and kama, I give away this gift, my daughter who is virtuous, intelligent and beautifully adorned.

Upon these statements of purpose the priest arranges the hands of the principals as follows:

On the outstretched palms of the bride, place the outstretched palms of the groom and on the palms of the groom, place those of the bride's father. On the the topmost palms (bride's father's) place a coconut smeared with kumkum and haldi.

The three stand such that the assembly gets a clear view.
The bride's mother is now positioned behind the three and is facing the audience squarely.

As the priest (or the bride's father) chants the following mantras the bride's mother pours water over the coconut in a thin stream and the audience is requested once again to say "tathastu" (it shall be so) at the end of each phrase.

A child needs to be positioned to hold a bowl below to collect the water. The water should continue to be poured in a thin stream until all the phrases are chanted.

During this sequence the mangalasutra is taken around to be blessed by the elders present.

श्रीरूपिणीं इमां कन्यां श्रीधर रूपिणे
तुभ्यं इत्युक्त्व उदक पूर्वांतां
कायेनवाचामनसा ददाम्यस्मै

कन्या तारयतु
पुण्यं वर्धतां
सौमनस्यमस्तु
अक्षतं चरिष्टं चास्तु
दीर्घमायुः श्रेयः शान्तिः पुष्टिः तुष्टिः चास्तु
यच्छ्रेयस्तदस्तु
यत् पापं तत्प्रतिहतस्तु
पुण्याहं भवंतो ब्रुवन्तु
स्वस्ति भवंतो ब्रुवंतु
ऋध्धिं भवंतो ब्रुवंतु
श्रीरस्त्विति भवंतो ब्रुवंतु

śrīrūpiṇīm imām kanyām śrīdhara
rūpiṇē tubhyam ityuktva udaka
pūrvāntām kāyēnavācā manasā
dadāmyasmai

kanyā tārayatu
puṇyam vardhatām
saumanasyamastu
akśatam cāriśṭam cāstu
dīrghamāyu: śrēya:
śānti: puṣṭi: tuṣṭi:cāstu
yacchrēyastadastu
yat pāpam tatpratihatastu
puṇyāham bhavantō bruvantu
svasti bhavantō bruvantu
ṛdhdhim bhavantō bruvantu
śrīrastviti bhavantō bruvantu

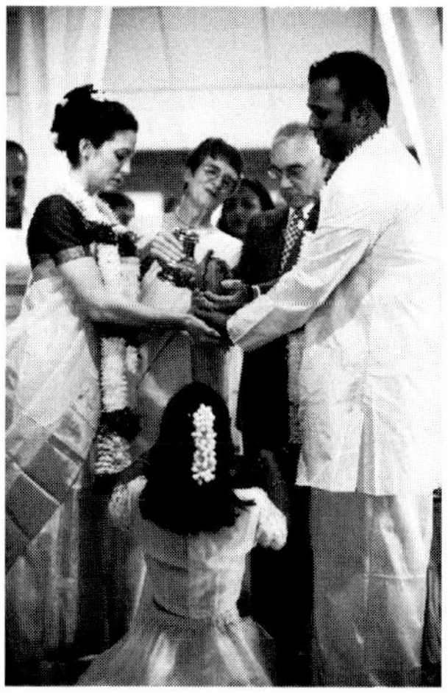

With this in my mind, with these words and with this act before the ceremonial water is poured, May I offer you, who are in the form of Vishnu, this my daughter in the form of Lakshmi.

May my daughter gain protection
May holiness prosper
May there be joy
May she be whole
May she live long, flourish, be at peace, well nourished and content
May prosperity prevail
May any ills be struck down
May you grant this day to be a happy one
May you bless her wellbeing
May you grant her abundance
May you grant her respect and status

मांगल्य धारणं/Māngalyadhāraṇam

Among the various traditions practiced in wedding ceremonies, the South Indian tradition considers the tying of the mangalasutra necklace by the groom around the bride's neck as the point at which the couple is declared married. In the old days, in India, unuttered sighs of relief could be seen on the faces of the bride's family upon completion of this step because the "responsibility" to care for the young woman was now officially transferred from the parents of the bride to the young man.

Ritualistic requirements in this ceremony include the following:

1. The māngalyam is taken around, prior to the ceremony, to be blessed by the elders in both families. The designated person upon cue (as Kanyādānam water is being poured) from the coordinator takes the plate on which the necklace rests on a colorful silk cloth and shows it to the elder as if it is being offered to the person. The elder then simply places both of his/her hands, palms down, on the plate as if to cover it. That gesture is blessing and is considered imperative.
2. The groom worships the māngalya godhead because the belief is that a goddess protects it.
3. Approval of the assembled is sought.
4. The bride is blessed by the priest.
5. The groom ties the necklace, as he prays for his longevity, assisted by his sister who positions herself behind the bride to make sure the knot (or the clasp) is tied securely. Some traditions require her to tie a second and third knot.

Generally the practice has been to increase the volume of music (a particularly loud drum roll in South Indian tradition) to mark the climactic moment. Upon completion of the tying, the bride's father once again confirms the offer of the bride and stipulates and extracts a promise that the groom lead a virtuous life and not transgress the boundaries of dharma, artha and kama. The groom gives his word and thus he is now a husband and she is his wife.

Māngalyadhāraṇam

The groom first does achamanam that is, he sips water three times after praying to Acyuta, Ananta and Govinda respectively.

The mangalya, blessed by elders, is brought to the priest.

The groom offers worship to the mangalya:

The priest seeks permission of the assembly to grant the moment to be auspicious.

The priest puts akshata on the bride's head as he blesses her just prior to the tying of the mangalasutra.

मांगल्य धारणं

वरः आचमनं

मांगल्य देवताभ्यो नमः; ध्यायामि,
आवाहयामि ; आसनं समर्पयामि
नानाविध परिमळ पत्र पुष्प फलानि
समर्पयामि

अनया पूजया भगवती श्री मांगल्य
महालक्ष्मी देवी सुप्रीता सुप्रसन्ना वरदा
भवतु

ध्रुवंते राजा वरुणो ध्रुवं देवो बृहस्पतिः
ध्रुवंत इंद्रश्चाग्निश्च राष्ट्रं धारयतां ध्रुवं ध्रुवं

अनुज्ञा

मांगल्य धारण मुहूर्तस्सुमुहूर्तोस्त्विति
भवन्तो महांतो अनुगृह्णंतु
सुमुहूर्तोस्तु

अक्षत/वधु

दीर्घ सुमंगली भव आयुरारोग्य ऐश्वर्य
संपत् समृद्धा भव गृहस्थाश्रमे शुभनि
वर्धतां

Māngalyadhāraṇam

Tying the Maangalya

māngalya dēvatābhyō nama:
dhyāyāmi, āvāhayāmi
āsanam samarpayāmi
nānāvidha parimaḷa patra puṣpa
phalāni samarpayāmi

Salutations to the goddess of this maangalya. I meditate upon her, invoke her, offer her a seat and a variety of perfumes, leaves, flowers and fruits.

anayā pūjayā bhagavatī śrī
māngalya mahālakṣmī dēvī suprītā
suprasannā varadā bhavatu

May you goddess Mahalakshmi of this maangalya be pleased with this puja.

dhruvantē rājā varuṇō dhruvam dēvō
bṛhaspati: dhruvanta indraścāgniśca
rāṣtram dhārayatām dhruvam
dhruvam

May your realm be as firm as that of King Varuna, gods Brhaspati, Indra and Agni.

Anujna

Permission

māngalya dhāraṇa
muhūrtassumuhōrtōstviti
bhavāntō mahāntō anugṛṇhantu
sumuhūrtōstu

May all the great assembled grant this moment of tying the maangalya to be especially auspicious.
May this be a specially auspicious moment.

dırgha sumangalī bhava
āyurārōgya aiśvarya
sampat samṛddhā bhava
gṛhasṭhāśramē śubhāni vardhatām

May your husband live long. May you both live long and may your life be filled with health, wealth and be plentiful. May your life as a householder prosper well.

The Tying of the Māngalya

The groom picks up the necklace and chants.

The groom ties the sutra around the bride's neck with two knots. Some traditions require a third knot tied by the sister of the groom.

Priest sprinkles flowers on the bride.

Bride's father puts flower petals on her head and chants.

Bride's father charges the groom asking him not to transgress the boundaries of dharma, artha and kama.

The groom responds affirmatively.

Then the bride is instructed to move to his left.

धारणं

मांगल्यं तंतुनानेन मम जीवन हेतुना
कण्ठे बध्नामि सुभगे त्वं जीव शरदश्शतं
मंगळं भगवान् विष्णुः मंगळं मधुसूदनः
मंगळं पुंडरीकाक्षो मंगळं गरुडध्वजः

वधु/पुष्पं दाताः

गौरीं कन्यां इमां विप्र यथा शक्ति
विभूषितां ...... गोत्रोद्भवस्य ......

तुभ्यं दत्तां विप्र समाश्रय कन्ये ममाग्रतो
भूयाः कन्येमे देवि पार्श्वयोः

कन्येमे षष्ठतो भूयाः त्वद्दानान् मोक्षमाप्नुयां
मम वंश कुले जाता पालिका

वत्स रा कं तुभ्यं विप्र मया दत्त पुत्र पौत्र
प्रवर्धिनीं धर्मेंचार्थेच कामेच नाति चरितव्या
त्वमेयं

वरः नाति चरामि

Dhāraṇam

The Tying of the Maangalya

māngalyam tantunānēna mama
jīvana hētunā kanṭē badhnāmi
subhagē tvam jīva śaradaśśatam

The yellow thread here (mangalasutra) will enhance my longevity. I tie it on your neck as I pray that you live happily for a hundred years.

mangaḷam bhagavān viṣṇu:
mangaḷam madhusūdana:
mangaḷam pundarīkākṣō
mangaḷam garudadhvaja:

May it please the gods, the various avatars of Vishnu; Madhusudana, Pundareekaakshа and Krishna.

vadhu/puṣpam/dātā

dātā

Giver (of the bride):

gaurīm kanyām imām vipra yaṭhā
śakti vibhūṣitām ....
gōtrōdbhavasya ...... tubhyam
dattām vipra samāśraya kanyē
mamāgratō bhūyā: kanyēmē dēvi
pārśvayō: kanyēmē ṣaṣṭhatō bhūyā:
tvaddānān mōkṣamāpnuyām
mama vamsha kulē jātā pālikā vatsa
rāṣtakam tubhyam vipra mayā datta
putra pautra pravardhinīm
dharmēcārṭhēca kāmēca
nāti caritavyā tvamēyam

So that I may get liberation and so that you may have children and grandchildren, I offer you, the gentleman born in ....gotra, this foremost among young women, my daughter, born and brought up in my family, standing near me here prominently, adorned to the best of our ability. Provide support and comfort to her and never transgress the boundaries of dharma, artha and kaama.

vara: nāti carāmi

Bridegroom: I shall not transgress

Blessing the Bride

The priest chants a charge to the bride and blesses her, reciting the same blessing used by Queen Kunti. (See the Origins chapter):

फुरोहित

यथेंद्राणि महेंद्रस्य
स्वाहाचैव विभावसोः
रोहिणीच यथा सोमे
दमयंती यथा नळे
यथा वैवस्वते भद्रा
वसिष्ठे चापि अरुंधती
यथा नारायणी लक्ष्मी
तथा त्वं भवभर्तारि

दीर्घ सुमंगली भव

Purōhita	**Priest's blessing**
yathēndrāṇi mahēndrasya	As Shachi to Indra,
svāhāchaiva vibhāvasō:	as Swaha to Agni,
rōhiṇīca yathā sōmē	as Rohini to Chandra,
damayantī yathā naḷē	as Damayanti to Nala,
yathā vaivasvatē bhadrā	as Bhadra to Vivasvat,
vasiṣṭhe cāpi arundhatī	as Arundhati to Vasishta,
yathā nārāyanī lakṣmī	as Lakshmi to Vishnu,
tathā tvam bhavabhartāri	may you be to your husband.

Pradhāna Homa

Primary Fire Ritual

The priest begins this ceremony with a prayer to Agni by touching the front of the kunda with both palms and bringing the palms to the eyes to show reverence to the fire god. The most appropriate shloka chosen for this beginning prayer is the very first shloka in the very first hymn in the very first book of the Rig Veda. The beauty and relevance of this stanza is that it hails Agni and acknowledges him as the priest.

Next using the ceremonial spoon (uddharana) the priest sprinkles water as the following four appeals are made by reciting each phrase successively along with the sprinkling as described below:

First sprinkle on the right side of the agnikunda going from lower side to the upper side, then on the lower side going from right to left and the third from lower side to upper side on the left of the agnikunda. The final sprinkling is clockwise all around.

प्रधान होमः

ॐ अग्निमीळे पुरोहितं
यज्ञस्य देवमृत्विजं
होतारं रत्न धातमं

परिषेचनम्

ॐ अदितेनुमन्यस्व
ॐ अनुमतेनुमन्यस्व
ॐ सरस्वतेनुमन्यस्व
ॐ देव सवितः प्रसुव

Pradhānahoma :

ōm agnimīḷē purōhitam
yajnasya dēvamṛtvijam
hōtāram ratna dhātamam

pariṣēcanam

ōm aditēnumanyasva
ōm anumatēnumanyasva
ōm saraswatēnumanyasva
ōm dēva savita: prasuva

Primary Fire Ritual

Om Praise be to Agni, the domestic priest, God, minister of ritual, the invoker and lavisher of wealth upon his devotees

Rig Veda (1.1.1)

Ceremonial sprinkling

OM, O Aditi, appear on this side here
OM, O Anumati, appear on this side here
OM, O Saraswati, appear on this side here
OM, O Sun God, appear completely here

The Homas

An assistant must now be ready with the samagris (offerings of ghee, rice, incense) for use by the couple. First the priest instructs the groom to declare his intention to perform the homas.

The particular aspect of Agni invoked is Yojaka who, in this context, means Preparer, i.e. Agni whose grace is sought to prepare for the new status and for a secure union.

The groom chants all mantras or repeats after the priest. He offers oblations with the samagris handed over to him by the assistant.

Note : These first offerings are to the former husbands (guardians Soma, Gandharva and Agni) of the bride and thus acknowledges them at the very beginning of this yajna (sacrifice).

प्रतिगृहीतायां अस्यां वध्वां
भार्यात्व सिध्धये गृह्यात्व सिध्धयेच
विवाह होमं करिष्ये
तदंग योजक नामाग्नि प्रतिष्ठापने विनियोगः

ॐ अग्नये स्वाहा– अग्नय इदं नमम
ॐ सोमाय स्वाहा – सोमाय इदं नमम
ॐ बूर्भुव स्वाहा – प्रजापतय इदं नमम

ॐ सोमाय स्वाहा – सोमाय इदं नमम
ॐ अग्नये स्वाहा– अग्नय इदं नमम
ॐ बूर्भुव स्वाहा – प्रजापतय इदं नमम

सोमाय जनिविदे स्वाहा
सोमाय जनिविद इदं नमम
गंधर्वाय जनिविदे स्वाहा
गंधर्वाय जनिविद इदं नमम
अग्नये जनिविदे स्वाहा
अग्नये जनिविद इदं नमम

pratigṛhītāyām asyām vadhvām
bhāryātva siddhdhayē gṛhyātva
siddhayēca
vivāha hōmam kariṣyē
tadanga yōjaka nāmāgni
pratiṣṭhāpanē viniyōga:

So that I may receive this bride, to gain her as a wife and to gain the status of a householder, I shall perform the wedding sacrificial rites. And as a part of the ceremony, I shall take the task of establishing Agni of the name Yojaka.

Towards the north of the Agnikunda:

ōm agnayē svāhā- agnaya idam namama
ōm sōmāya svāhā - somayē idam namama
ōm būrbhuva svāhā - prajāpataya idam namama

Hail to Agni: this is yours, not mine
Hail to Soma: this is yours, not mine
Hail to the three worlds: this is that of the divinity of procreation, not mine.

Towards the south of the Agnikunda:

ōm sōmāya svāhā - sōmayē idam namama
ōm agnayē svāhā- agnaya idam namama
ōm būrbhuva svāhā - prajāpataya idam namama

Hail to Soma: this is yours, not mine
Hail to Agni: this is yours, not mine
Hail to the three worlds: this is that of the divinity of procreation, not mine.

sōmāya janividē svāhā sōmāya
janivida idam namama
gandharvāya janividē svāhā
gandharvāya janivida idam namama
agnayē janividē svāhā agnayē
janivida idam namama

This oblation is to Soma who knew this bride as a wife. This belongs to that knowledge, not mine.

This oblation is to the Gandharva who knew this bride as a wife. This belongs to that knowledge, not mine.

This oblation is to Agni who knew this bride as a wife. This belongs to that knowledge, not mine.

कन्यला पितृभ्यो यती पतिलोकमव
दीक्षामदास्थ स्वाहा
वध्वै सूर्याय इदं नमम

प्रेतोमुंचाति नामुतस्सुबध्धाममुतस्करत्
यथेयमिन्द्र मीढ्व स्सुपुत्रा सुभगासति
स्वाहा
इंद्राय मीढुष इदं नमम

इमांत्वं इन्द्रमीड्व स्सुपुत्रागं् सुभगां कृणु
दशास्यां पुत्रानाधेहि पतिमेकादशं
कृधिस्वाहा
इंद्राय मीढुष इदं नमम

अग्निरैतु प्रथमो देवतानागं् सोस्यै प्रजां
मुंचतु मृत्युपाशात्
तदयगं् राजा वरुणोनुमन्यतां
यथेयग्गं् स्त्री पौत्रमघं नरोदात्स्वाहा
अग्नी वरुणाभ्यामिदं नमम

इमामग्नि स्त्रायतां गार्हपत्यः प्रजामस्यै
नयतु दीर्घमायुः अशून्योपस्था जीवतामस्तु
माता पौत्रमानंदमभि प्रभुध्यतामियं स्वाहा
अग्नये गार्हपत्यायेदं नमम

kanyalā pitṛbhyō yatī patilōkamava
dīkṣāmadāstha svāhā
vadhvai sūryāya idam namama

This young woman is on her way to her husband's family leaving behind her own. Thus this oblation belongs to Sooryaa in the form of this bride, not to me.

prētōmuncāti
nāmutassubaddhāmamutaskarat
yathēyamindra mīḍhva ssuputrā
subhagāsati svāhā
indrāya mīḍhuṣa idam namama

May Indra who blesses the earth with rain grant her a stable and prosperous life with children and prosperity. This therefore is Indra's oblation, not mine.

imāmtvam indramīḍva ssuputrāgm
subhagām kṛṇu
daśāsyām putrānādhēhi
patimēkādaśam kṛdhisvāhā
indrāya mīḍhuṣa idam namama

O Indra, bestow on this bride virtuous sons and prosperity. Grant her ten sons and let her husband be the eleventh. This oblation is therefore Indra's, not mine.

agniraitu prathamō dēvatānāgm
sōsyai prajām muncatu mṛtyupāśāt
tadayagm rājā varuṇōnumanyatām
yathēyaggm strī pautramagham
narōdātsvāhā agnī
varuṇābhyāmidam namama

Let Agni, the first among devatas, be present to protect her children from the noose of death. Let Varuna follow suit. Thus protected, let the bride never weep for her progeny. This therefore is Agni's and Varuna's oblation, not mine.

imāmagni strāyatām gārhapatya:
prajāmasyai
nayatu dīrghamāyu: aśūnyōpasthā
jīvatāmastu
mātā pautramānandamabhi
prabhudhyatāmiyam svāhā
agnayē gārhapatyāyēdam namama

Let the sacrificial fire Gaarhapatya (householder's fire) protect this bride and her children for a long time. Let her live as a mother and awaken to the bliss of progeny. This therefore is Gaarhapatya's oblation, not mine.

मा तेगृहे निशिघोष उत्थादन्यत्र त्वद्रुदत्य
स्संविशंतु मात्वं विकेष्युर आवधिष्ठा जीवपत्नी
पतिलोके विराज पश्यन्ती प्रजागं्
सुमन्स्यमानां स्वाहा
वध्वै सूर्यायेदं नमम

द्यौस्ते पृष्ठगं् रक्षतु वायुरूरू
अश्विनौच स्तनं धयन्तगं सविताभिरक्षतु
आवाससः परिधानात् बृहस्पतिर् विश्वे देवा
अभि रक्षंतु पश्चात् स्वाहा
द्यौर्वायुरश्च सवितृ बृहस्पतिर्विश्वेभ्यो
देवेभ्य इदं

अप्रजस्तां पौत्रमृत्युं पाप्मानमुतवाघं
शीर्ष्णस्स्रजमिवोन्मुच्य द्विषद्भ्यः प्रति मुंचामि
पाशं स्वाहा वध्वै सूर्यायेदं

mā tēgṛhē niśighōṣa utthādanyatra
tvadrudatya ssamviśantu mātvam
vikēṣyura āvadhiṣṭhā jīvapatnī
patilōkē virāja paśyantī prajāgm
sumansyamānām svāhā
vadhvai sūryāyēdam namama

Let there be no sharp cries of distress in your home. May you not weep with disheveled hair and beating on your chest. May you be illustrious in your own home with your husband. May there be no reason not to enjoy seeing your virtuous children. This then is Suryaa's oblation, in the form of this bride, not mine.

dyaustē pṛṣṭhagm rakṣatu vāyurūrō
aśvinauca stanam dhayantagam
savitābhirakṣatu
āvāsasa: paridhānāt bṛhaspatir viśvē
dēvā abhi rakṣantu paścāt svāhā
dyaurvāyuraśva savitṛ
bṛhaspatirviśvēbhyō
dēvēbhya idam

May Heaven protect your back, Vayu your thighs, Ashvins your breasts, the Sun your children, Brhaspati when you are fully dressed in your abode, and Visvedeva hereafter.

aprajastām pautramṛtyum
pāpmānamutavāgham
śīrṣṇassrajamivōnmucya
dviṣadbhya: prati muncami
pāśam svāhā
vadhvai sūryāyēdam

May you have progeny who live long and suffer no calamity. I shall prevent any attempt by enemies to harm you with a noose by removing it as easily as the garland around your neck. This therefore is the oblation to Suryaa in the form of the bride

इमं मे वरुणश्रुधीहव मद्याचमृडय
त्वामवस्यु राचके स्वाहा वरुणायेदं नमम

तत्वायामि ब्रह्मणा वंदमानस्तदाशास्ते
यजमानो हविर्भिः अहेडमानो
वरुणेहबोध्युरुशगंसमान आयुः प्रमोषी स्वाहा
वरुणायेदं नमम

त्वंनो अग्ने वरुणस्य विद्वान् देवस्य हेडो
अवयासिसीष्ठाः
यजिष्ठोवह्नितमश्योशुचानो विश्वाद्वेषागं्सि
प्रमुमुग्ध्यमत् स्वाहा
अग्नीवरुणाभ्यामिदं नमम

सत्वन्नो अग्ने अवमो भवोती नेदिष्ठो
अस्या उषसोव्युौ अवयक्ष्वनो वरुणगं्
रराणो वीहि मृडीकगं् सुहवोन ऐधि
स्स्वाहा अग्नीवरुणाभ्यांमिदं नमम
त्वमग्ने अयास्ययासन् मनसाहितः
अयासन् हव्यमूहिषे अयानोधेहि भेषजं स्वाहा
अग्नये अयस इदं नमम

imam mē varuṇaśrudhīhava
madhyācamṛḍaya
tvāmavasyu rācakē svāhā
varuṇāyēdam namama

O Varuna, listen to this invocation. Bring happiness to us now. I pray to you and seek your protection. This oblation therefore is Varuna's and not mine.

tatvāyāmi brahmaṇā
vandamānastadāśāstē
yajamānō havirbhi: ahēḍamānō
varuṇēhabōdhyuruśagamsa
māna āyu: pramōṣī svāhā
varuṇāyēdam namama

Adored by many with Vedic mantras and homa samagrees, O Varuna, increase our longevity. This oblation therefore is Varuna's and not mine.

tvamnō agnē varuṇasya vidvān
dēvasya hēḍō avayāsisīśṭhā:
yajiśṭhōvahnitamaśyōśucānō
viśvādvēṣāgmsi
pramumugdhyamat svāhā
agnīvaruṇābhyāmidam namama

O Agni! You are the wisest and most splendid of all the gods to whom sacrificial offerings are made through you. Let Varuna be appeased and let all enmities cease. This oblation is Agni's and Varuna's, not mine.

satvannō agnē avamō bhavōtī nēdiṣṭhō
asyā uṣasō vyuṣṭhau avayakṣvanō
varuṇagm rarāṇō vīhi mṛḍīkagm
suhavōna ēdhi ssvāhā
agnīvaruṇābhyāmidam namama

O Agni you are the first among gods as described above. Be with us in the dawn and remain close to protect us from Varuna's ire. Help us obtain sacrificial foods to offer gods. This oblation is Varuna's and Agni's, not mine.

tvamagnē ayāsyayāsan manasāhita:
ayāsan havyamūhiṣē ayānōdhēhi
bhēṣajam svāhā agnayē ayasa idam
namama

O Agni, please come close to your devotees and convey our oblations and bring us remedies. Thus this oblation is Agni's and not mine.

Mangal Phera/Laaja Homa

This ritual following the primary homas has the bridegroom hold the right hand of the bride while together they walk around the agnikunda with garments knotted. We have interpreted the four rounds or circumambulations as dedication to the chaturvidha phala purushaartha, i.e. dharma, artha, kama and moksha. As stated in the overview the first three rounds are dedicated to the first three aspects and the final round to moksha. The groom leads the bride and chants the mantras as the couple circumambulate the fire. When they return to the starting point they offer laaja (puffed rice) to Agni.The fourth round, however, praying for moksha, is led by the bride.

While a variety of havan samagris (materials for yajna) are offered in the primary fire ritual, during laaja homa only parched/puffed rice (laaja) is offered. The bride's brother (or a friend) positions himself to one side at the head of the kunda with a bowl of parched/puffed rice and fills the open palms of the bride with it at the end of each round. The groom adds a spoon of ghee to the handful of parched rice in the bride's palms. As the mantras are chanted by the groom or the priest on his behalf, the bride offers the contents to the fire while the groom offers a spoon of ghee.

The mantra indicated by * is repeated before beginning each round.

मंगळ फेरा/ लाजा होमः

तुभ्यमग्ने पर्यहवन् थ्सूर्यां वहतु नासः
पुनः पतिभ्यो जायादा अग्ने प्रजया सहः
पुनः पत्नीमग्निरदा दायुषा सह वर्चसा
दीर्घायुरस्यायः पतिस्स ऐतु शरदश्शतं *

इयं नार्युपब्रूते कुल्पान्याव पंतिका
दीर्घायुरस्तु मे पतिर्जीवातु शरदश्शतं स्वाहाः
अग्नये आर्यम्ण इदं नमम
वध्वै सूर्याय नमः

Repeat *

आर्यमणं नु देवं कन्या अग्निमयक्षत
स इमां देवो अध्वरः प्रेतो मुंजातिना
मुत स्सुबध्धा मुमुतस्करथ्स्वाहाः
अग्नये आर्यम्ण इदं नमम

Repeat *

त्वमर्यमा भवसि यत्कनीनां नाम
स्वधावत् स्वर्यं भिभर्शि अंजंति वृक्शगं सुधितं
नगोभिर्यद्दंपती समनसौ कृणोषि स्वाहा
अग्नये आर्यम्ण इदं नमम

Repeat *

प्रजापतये स्वाहा
प्रजापतय इदं नमम

Lājahōma

tubhyamagnē paryahavan thsūryām
vahatu nāsa: puna: patibhyō jāyādā
agnē prajayā saha:
puna: patnīmagniradā dāyuṣā saha
varcasā dīrghāyu rasyāya: patissa
*ētu śaradaśśatam **

iyam nāryupabrūtē kulpānyāva
pantikā dīrghāyurastu mē patirjīvātu
śaradaśśatam svāhā: agnayē
āryamṇa idam namama vadhvai
sūryāya nama:

*[Repeat *]*

āryamaṇam nu dēvam kanyā
agnimayakṣata sa imām dēvō
adhvara: prētō munjātinā muta
ssubaddhā mumutaskarathsvāhā
agnayē āryamṇa idam namama

*[Repeat *]*

tvamaryamā bhavasi yatkanīnām
nāma svadhāvat svaryam bhibharśi
anjanti vṛkśagam sudhitam
nagōbhiryaddampatī samanasau
kṛṇōṣi svāhā agnayē āryamṇa idam
namama

*[Repeat *]*

prajāpatayē svahā
prajāpataya idam namama

Lāja Hōma

O Agni you received Suryaa, the goddess and authority for wedding ceremonies in the form of bridal dower wealth. Now please bestow upon us that wealth and progeny through this bride.

Agni has given this radiant husband with long life. May this bride's husband live for a hundred years. [Repeated 3 times below]

This bride, while offering this oblation, prays for a life of a hundred years for her husband. This oblation is Suryaa's in the form of this bride, not mine.

Brides worshipped Aryama in the past and obtained husbands quickly. Let Aryama now effect her release from the family of her parents and help her enter her own family in a stable manner. This oblation therefore is Aryama's, not mine.

Aryama! You are named Aryama since you have the power to unite partners in a firm bond. Bring the minds of this couple together with the strength of a well-fixed and firmly rooted tree. This oblation is for Aryama in Agni's form, not mine.

Oblations to Prajaapati.
This is Prajaapati's, not mine.

Saptapadi

Saptapadi, the ceremony of seven steps, is the essential and pivotal element in a Vedic wedding. In law as well as generally held Hindu belief, the bride and the groom attain the status of husband and wife only after the seventh step is taken. Each step taken by the couple specifies that they be blessed with food, strength, ritual knowledge, love, welfare of cattle, prosperity, and sacred illumination.

Either all the steps are taken at the northern side of the fire, sometimes by having the bride step into seven circles or mounds of rice, or the couple may complete the seven steps in a single circumambulation.

The ritual begins with the couple standing with hands joined and with the agnikunda on their right. The groom leads the bride through each step forward, reciting the chant after the priest before each step. The paces are measured such that after the seventh step the couple is back at the front of the agnikunda facing the assembly.

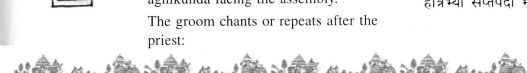

The groom chants or repeats after the priest:

सप्तपदी

सामामनुव्रता भव पुत्रान् विंदावहै
बहूस्ते संतु जरदुश्टयः [*]

ईष ऐक पदी भव –इति प्रथमं

[*]
ऊर्जे द्विपदी भव –इति द्वितीयं

[*]
व्रताय त्रिपदी भव –इति तृतीयं

[*]
मायो भवाय चतुश्पदी भव – इति चतुर्थं

[*]
पशुभ्यो पंचपदी भव – इति पंचमं

[*]
रायस्पोषाय षट्पदी भव – इति षष्ठं

[*]
होत्रेभ्यो सप्तपदी भव – इति सप्तमं

Saptapadī

sāmāmanuvratā bhava
putrān vindāvahai
bahūstē santu jaradusṭhaya: [*]

īṣa ēka padī bhava -iti prathamam

Repeat [*]
ūrjē dvipadī bhava -iti dvitīyam

Repeat [*]
vratāya tripadī bhava -iti tṛtīyam

Repeat [*]
māyō bhavāya catuśpadī bhava
iti caturtham

Repeat [*]
paśubhyō pancapadī bhava - iti
pancamam

Repeat [*]
rāyaspōṣāya ṣatpadī bhava - iti
ṣaṣṭam

Repeat [*]
hōtrēbhyō saptapadī bhava - iti
saptamam

Seven Steps

Please follow me here. May we gain many sons and grandsons. And may they reach old age (live long).

*[This verse is repeated before each step is taken.]

Take this first step for the sake of nourishment.

Take this second step for the sake of strength.

Take this third step for the sake of ritual austerities.

Take this fourth step for the sake of love.

Take this fifth step for the sake of cattle.

Take this sixth step for the sake of prosperity.

Take this seventh step to be sacredly illumined.

Both the bride and groom chant or repeat after the priest the mantra:

सखा सप्तपदी भव
सख्यंते गमेयं
सख्यंते मायोशः
सख्यां ते मायोश्टाः

After the seventh step, the couple face the audience (bride on groom's left) and the priest requests that each repeat the following mantra:

पुरोहित

Then the priest puts a few grains of akshata on the bowed head of the bride and blesses her as shown:

सम्राज्नी श्वशुरेभव
सम्राज्नी श्वश्रुवांभव
ननान्दरी सम्राज्नीभव
सम्राज्नी अधिदेवृषु

After this the agnikunda is removed.

The priest instructs the couple to be ready to receive general blessings from the entire assembly. The priest instructs the audience to respond with "tathastu" at the end of each of the seven phrases of blessing.

संप्रियौ रोचिष्णू सुमन्स्यमानौ
पश्येम शरदः शतं
जीवेम शरदः शतं
श्रुणुयाम शरदः शतं

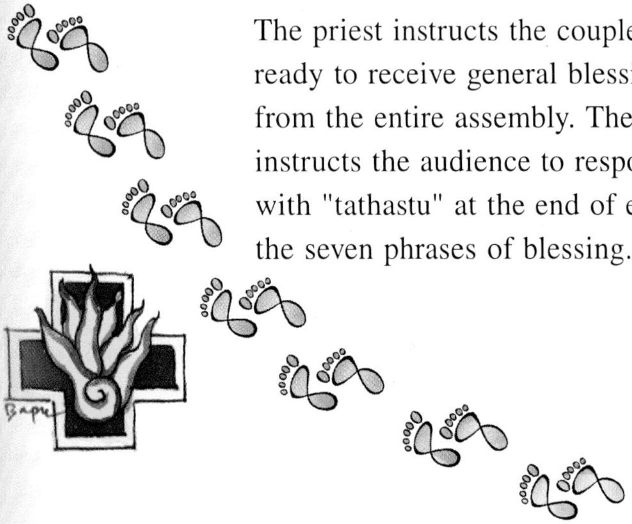

sakhā saptapadī bhava
sakhyamtē gamēyam
sakhyamtē māyōśa:
sakhyām tē māyōśtā:

purōhita

samrājnī śvaśurebhava
samrājnī śvaśruvāmbhava
nanāndari samrājnībhava
samrājnī adhidēvṛṣu

sampriyau rōciṣṇū sumansyamānau
paśyēma śarada: śatam
jīvēmā śarada: śatam
śruṇuyāma śarada: śatam
[Vājasanēya Samhita]

With these seven steps may you become my friend.
May I deserve your friendship. May my friendship make me one with you. May your friendship make you one with me.

Priest

Be queenly with your father-in-law
Be queenly with your mother-in-law
Be queenly with his sisters
Be queenly with his brothers

Let us live as a loving, vigorous, happy couple enjoying each other's company, listening to each other for a hundred years.

आशीर्वादं

Ashirvadam/Blessings

This is the very final ritual step when the audience is requested to grant their approval to the blessings chanted by the priest by responding in unison with the word "tathāstu" (it shall be so), as before, at the end of each phrase. These blessings combine melody and significance; they cover all aspects of the new life begun by the couple. The elders in both families as well as all friends assembled to witness the occasion have the opportunity to offer their final good wishes by uttering "tathāstu." It is customary for everyone to offer (throw) akshata on to the heads of the couple but logistics and size of audience may prevent this practice. In that case the immediate families may do the honors as they say "tathāstu" while the rest of the audience may simply utter the word. Another option for the audience is to bless the couple with the akshata as they walk down the aisle.

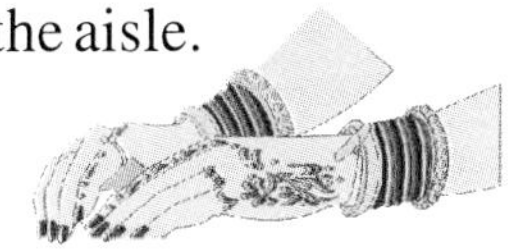

Final Blessings

The priest instructs the couple to bend their heads down to receive the akshata.

While the priest chants each phrase, the assembly responds with *"tathaastu"

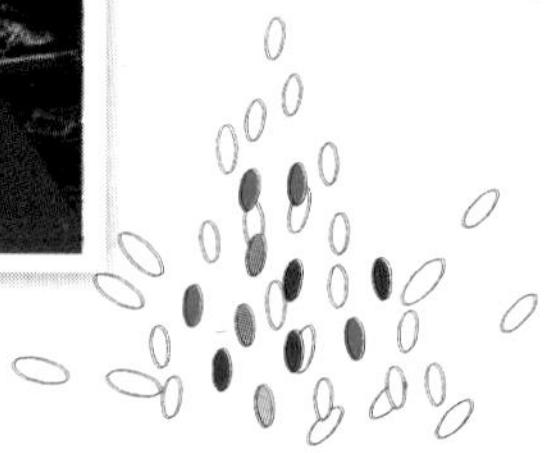

आशीर्वादं

स्वामिनः

स्वस्ति मंत्रार्थास्सत्यास्सफला स्संत्विति
भवन्तो महान्तो अनुगृह्णंतु

अनयोर्दंपत्योः वेदोक्तं दीर्घमायुष्यं भूयादिति
भवन्तो महान्तो अनुगृह्णंतु

इमौ दंपती भास्करवदारोग्यवंतौ,
मृकन्डवत् आयुश्मंतौ, कुबेर पुरंदरवदैश्वर्यवंतौ,
सौभाग्यवंतौ, काश्यप सौभरी वत्संतानवन्तौ,
भाग्याभिवृध्धि मुंतौच, भूयास्तामिति भवन्तो
महान्तो अनुगृह्णंतु

इमौ दंपती लोपामुद्रागस्त्यौ, अहल्या गौतमौ,
अरुंधती वशिष्ठौ, शांता ऋष्यशृंगौ,
अनसूयात्रिमुनिवराविव, सप्तपाकयज्ञ,
सप्तहविर्यज्ञ, शतमख वरिष्ठानुष्ठानपरौ,
चंद्रमती हरिश्चंद्रौ, दमयंती नळौ,
सौभरितद्भार्याविव, तेजस्विनौ, वर्चस्विनौ,
यशस्विनौ, भूयास्तामिति भवन्तो महान्तो
अनुगृह्णंतु

Ashirvadam

svāmina: svasti mantrārthāssatyā
ssaphalā ssantviti
*bhavantō mahāntō anugṛhṇantu **

anayōrdampatyō: vēdōktam
dīrghamāyuṣyam bhūyāditi
*bhavantō mahāntō anugṛhṇantu **

imau dampatī
bhāskaravadārōgyavantau,
mṛkandavat āyuśmantau,
kubēra purandaravadaiśvaryavantau,
saubhāgyavantau, kāśyapa
saubharī vatsantānavantau,
bhāgyābhivṛddhi muntauca,
bhūyāstāmiti bhavantō
*mahāntō anugṛhṇantu **

imau dampatī lōpāmudrāgastyau,
ahalyā gautamau, arundhatī
vaśiṣṭhau, śāntā ṛṣyaśṛngau, anasūyā
trimunivarāviva, saptapākayajna,
saptahaviryajna, shatamakha
variṣṭhānuśṭānaparau
candramatī hariścandrau,
damayantī naḷau,
saubharitadbhāryāviva,
tejasvinau, varcasvinau, yaśasvinau,
bhūyāstāmiti bhavantō mahāntō
*anugṛhṇantu **

Blessings

O great assembled:
May you grant that thc good wishcs bestowed on this couple be indeed true and effective!

May you grant that this couple have a long life as enjoined in the Vedas.

May you grant that this couple enjoy as much health as the sun, as much longevity as Mrukanda, as much wealth and happiness as Kubera and Purandara, progeny as strong as those of Kashyapa and Saubhari, and increasing prosperity.

May you grant that this couple carry out a hundred sacrifices including cooked sacrifices of seven forms with ghee as performed by the sage couples Agastya and Lopamudra, Gautama and Ahalya, Vasishta and Arundhati, Rishyashringa and Shanta, and Atri and Anasuya.
May you grant that this couple be as illumined, as vigorous and successful as the couples Harishchandra and Chandramati, Nala and Damayanti, and Saubhari and his wives

इमौ दंपती सुवाससौ, सुमनसौ, सुतापसौ,
सुवर्चसौ,
निरंतर विधिहुत जातवेदसौ
निजतनु प्रभातिरस्कृत तमसौ,
अविरत नवनव दृश्यमान वयसौ,
हेलाविलसित वचसौ, मालालंकृत शिरसौ,
वेला विरहित यशसौ,
भूयास्तामिति भवन्तो महान्तो अनुगृह्णंतु

इमौ दंपती रोहिणी चंद्रमसौ,
रती कुसुमशरासौ
लक्ष्मीपुरुषोत्तमौ, जानकी रघुनायकाविव,
परस्परानुरागयुक्तौ,
भूयास्तामिति भवन्तो महान्तो अनुगृह्णंतु

अनयोर्दंपत्योः अनवरत क्षेमस्थैर्य वीर्य
विजयायुरारोग्य
सौभाग्यप्रदो भूयादिति भवंतो महांतो
अनुगृण्हंतु

इमौ दंपती श्रीवर्चमायुष्यमारोग्य
माविधाच्चोभमानं महीयते,
धान्यं, धनं, बहुपुत्रलाभं,
शतसंवत्सरं दीर्घमायुरिति
भवन्तो महान्तो अनुगृह्णंतु

imau dampatī suvāsasau,
sumanasau, sutāpasau, suvarcasau,
nirantara vidhihuta jātavēdasau
nijatanu prabhātiraskṛta tamasau,
avirata navanava dṛśyamāna
vayasau,
hēlāvilasita vacasau, mālālamkṛta
śirasau, vēlā virahita yaśasau,
bhūyāstāmiti bhavantō mahāntō
anugṛhṇantu *

May you grant that this couple be always well clothed, of a similar mind, versed in practicing austerities, vigorous, always engaged in offering prescribed oblations to fire, radiant as light overcoming darkness, enjoying always new pleasures, eloquent in speech with ease, and successful without limit.

imau dampatē rōhiṇī candramasau,
ratī kusumaśarāsau, lakṣmī
puruṣōttamau, jānakī
raghunāyakāviva,
parasparānurāgayuktau,
bhūyāstāmiti bhavantō mahāntō
anugṛhṇantu *

May you grant this couple to be mutually as passionate as Rohini and Chandra (Moon), Rati and Kama (whose arrows are flowers), Lakshmi and Vishnu, and Rama and Sita.

anayōrdampatyō: anavarata
kṣēmasthairya vīrya vijayāyurārōgya
saubhāgyapradō bhūyāditi bhavantō
mahāntō anugṛṇhantu *

May you grant this couple everlasting wellbeing, courage, energy, success, health, longevity and prosperity.

imau dampatī śrīvarcamāyuṣya
mārōgya
māvidhācchōbhamānam mahīyatē,
dhānyam, dhanam,
bahuputralābham,
śatasamvatsaram dīrghamāyuriti
bhavantō mahāntō anugṛhṇantu *

May you grant this couple abundance in luster, vigor, longevity and health and wealth of grains, money and progeny and a hundred-year life span.

Two more chants of blessing by the priest as follows conclude the ceremony, at the end of which the priest may announce the names of the couple as husband and wife. The couple may at that point prostrate in front of their parents and other elders in both families and the priest.

नवॊ नवॊ भवति जायमानॊन्हान् कॆतुर् उषसां ऐत्य् अग्रं
भागं दॆवॆभ्यॊ विदध्यात् आयन् प्रचंद्रमास्थिरति दीर्घमायुः

navō navō bhavati jāyamānōnhān kētur uṣasāmētyu agram
bhāgam dēvēbhyō vidadhyāt āyan pra chandramāsthirati dīrghamāyu:

He, born afresh, is new and new for ever; ensign of days he goes before the Mornings

Coming, he orders for the Gods their portion. The moon prolongs the days of our existence. (Griffith, *RV*)

This mantra is used very often in blessings. A liberal interpretation may convey blessing for an ever fresh, vigorous and long life. It is included here for its popularity among priests.

And finally another very popular blessing:

शतमानं भवतु शतायुः पुरुषः
शतॆंद्रियः आयुष्यॆवॆंद्रियॆ प्रतितिष्ठति

śatamānam bhavatu śatāyu: puruṣa:
śatēndriya: āyuṣyēvēndriyē pratitiṣṭhati

May you be (bestowed) with a life of a hundred years, with senses a hundredfold virile and may your longevity equal that of Indra (himself).

With this the entire wedding ceremonial/ritualistic parts are complete.

After this the couple may walk down the aisle to the previously designated location outside the wedding hall. The ushers may now point to the rows of audience for an orderly and safe exit.

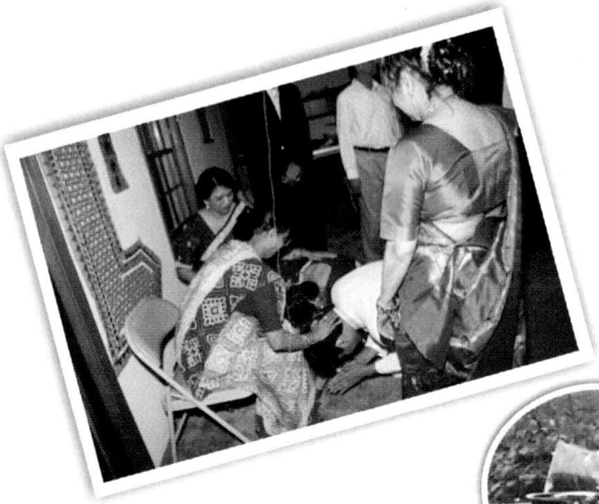

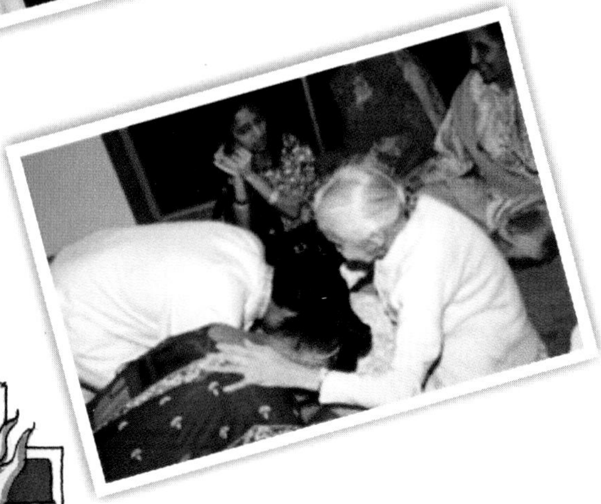

Bapu

Appendix I

Family Data Form

Today's date: ______________________ Place ____________________________________
Month/Day/Year

Wedding	Date/Time	Venue
Names	Bride	Groom
Father		
Mother		
Paternal grandfather		
Paternal great grandfather		
Gotras*		
Officiant(s)		
Phone/ email		
Address Dress**		
Transportation/Directions	Website/links	Address
Single Point of Contact	Phone#	email
Rehearsal	Date/Time	Address
Music/ DJ name	Live/CD/Other	DJ and/or Coordinator
Hotel name	Address	Phone/email
Ganapati Puja Gauri Puja Other	Date	Place
Expected # of guests		
Type of mantap	Indoor	Outdoor

* Gotra defines one's lineage. If a family does not know/remember their gotra, the priest will simply use the word "shubha" meaning auspicious.

** If there is a concern that akshata used during blessings may cause turmeric stains, alternatives such as using flower petals, plain rice or lightly colored akshata need to be discussed.

Planning ahead:

It is common for couples, especially in North America, to locate and book a place of their choice for the wedding ceremony a year or so before the date. It is also a good idea to arrange for an early meeting with the priest, including at least the couple and their parents or stand-ins. At such a meeting a systematic collection of the basic data as shown above is recommended. This is also the time to discuss family practices and develop a broad outline of the ceremony. It is best to agree that after a couple of iterations the program needs to be frozen and to avoid last minute changes. If it is an interfaith wedding, at least one meeting between the officiators is recommended in order to examine and agree to the logistics and sequence aimed at making the process a seamless one.

Fire Ceremony materials:

Havan or equivalent metal or metal-lined grille, about 18" x 18";
Small steady table, metal or tile-topped;
Bricks or tiles, aluminum foil;
Bunch of dry sticks; paper, 2 fire-starter cakes;
Matchsticks, small candle, fire lighter;
Havan samagree in small cup;
Puffed/parched rice in 4 small cups;
Small jar ghee, with spoon
A bucket of sand.

Wedding Materials:

The following list covers the quantity of materials needed, most of them contained in the boxed list of items given below.

General minimum quantities of material needed for wedding and pre-wedding ceremonies: water in 1 pitcher or kalasha; kumkum (2 tablespoons); haldi (4 tablespoons); 1 lb. akshata (yellow rice); 1 coconut, lightly coated with turmeric;

3 to 5 types of fruits and flowers; sweet or madhuparkam; perfume sprinkler (optional).

Recommended: paper towels or napkins; glass cover protection for deepas in outdoor ceremonies.

Prepare the akshata at least a day ahead of use, to allow it to dry, by mixing a flat tablespoon of turmeric and a very small amount of water as needed to coat the rice

WEDDING BASIC MATERIALS LIST

#	*ITEM*	*FUNCTION*
4	Small tables	2 (approx. 26" x 24" diameter) to hold, store, & assemble materials during the ceremony; 1 (approx. 26" x 18" diameter); 1 (approx. 18" to 26" high) to support the havan, with fire proof or tiled top.
7	Plates (thalis)	2 plates of five fruits & flowers, 1 each for Groom's & Bride's side; 1 plate with garland for Bride's side to give to Groom who will later give it to the Bride; 1 plate with Bride's garland for the Groom; 1 arati plate (with kumkum, haldi, water, deepa, akshata, flower or spoon, madhuparkam or sweet); 1 plate of fruits & flowers to be taken with the Bride's entourage; 1 small plate with silk piece for the mangalasutra; (2-3 extra thalis should always be available. Fruits and flowers can be carried separately.)
2-3	Kalashas	1 decorated for procession to meet Groom; 1 or 2 for consecrating water for the ceremony.
2	Bowls	1 medium, to hold akshata; 1 large, to receive water at Kanyaadaanam.
9	Cups	1 ritual water cup with spoon; 5 small, 4 with puffed or parched rice; 3 small, on arati plate, for haldi, kumkum, akshata; 1 small, for akshata.
6	Cloths	3, to cover materials tables; 1 large, for Antarpat; 1 small, silk, for mangalasutra
3+	Lamps (deepas), with wicks, oil	1 small, on arati plate; 1 or more for the Bride's entourage; (These may need glass mantle protection for outdoor ceremonies or use of battery-assisted substitutes)
2	Flower garlands	1 each for Bride and Groom (minimum; more may be needed for Swagatam or Milni)
1	Stone slab	For Ashmarohana.

Sample Cover Page for the Program

ॐ

The Auspicious Vedic Wedding Ceremony

of

Chiranjeevi Saubhagyavati (Bride's full name)...................

daughter of.............................

and

Chiranjeevi (Groom's full name).............................

son of.......................................

Parthiva Shraavana Shukla Prathama September......., 200X

Officiant: Dr. Amrutur V. Srinivasan

ऐकं सत् विप्राः बहुदा वदंति

Īkam sat vipra: bahudā vadanti

Truth is One, but the wise utter it many ways

The text of this Vedic wedding ceremony is arranged by
Dr. Srinivasan of Glastonbury, Connecticut

Sample Program

Swagatam/Milni

While the guests are seated, the bride's family* greets the groom* and his family and friends, in a ceremony known formally as Milni. The priest blesses the groom, the bride's mother performs an arati, the bride's father garlands the groom, and the group returns to the mantap escorting the groom and his family.

Overview

The officiant* begins by giving an overview of Vedic wedding rituals. The assembly is reminded of its obligation/role as witness.

Veda Mantras

The ceremony begins with a recitation of Vedic chants. Purification mantras invoking the Sacred Rivers mark the mantap as a sacred space.

Vara Puja

The bride's father* declares his intention to welcome and honor the groom* and his family.

Jayamala

The bride* walks down the aisle to musical accompaniment. She indicates her choice by garlanding the groom. He garlands her to show his consent.

Pravara/Hasta Milap

The ancestral lineages of the two families are announced. The bride's father* unites the couple by joining their right hands.

Kanyadanam

The bride's mother* pours water over a coconut held by the bride, groom and bride's father which consecrates their union and symbolically passes their daughter to the love and care of her new family.

Mangalasutra

The groom* ties the auspicious necklace blessed by both families around the bride's neck.

Exchange of rings/Sindhoor

The couple exchange rings. The groom* applies sindhoor at the parting of the hair on the bride's head.

Agni Homa

A sacred fire (Agni) is lit to receive offerings and to stand witness to the couple's vows.

Mangal Phera/Laaja Homa

The couple offer puffed rice to the fire as a symbol of the first hearth of their new home together. With garments knotted, the couple circle the fire four times, pledging to lead lives guided by Dharma (moral law), Artha (wealth), Kama (love) leading to Moksha (liberation).

Saptapadi

The bride and groom take seven steps around the fire, while they recite the vows.

Ashirvadam

Final blessings by the assembled conclude the ceremony. The couple seeks the blessings of all elders, family and friends as they embark on their new life together.

* Use actual names here

✣✣✣✣✣✣

Music

Music is an integral part of Hindu weddings and can be a great aid in structuring the flow of events into a delightful sequence when the renderings are chosen carefully. The choice of musical embellishments can be varied to suit the stage of the ceremony in progress: before the ceremony begins, before and during the bridegroom's arrival, the bride's arrival, garlanding, Kanyadanam, Mangalyadharanam, the homas and recessional. It is customary, especially in South Indian tradition, to use nadaswaram before the event starts and during certain processional parts of the ceremony, and play loud drums during the tying of the mangalasutra.

One can select from among a wide choice available these days on CD. Vibrant music with drums (tabla, or mrdangam) accompanying an instrument such as violin, mandolin, sitar or veena is appropriate while guests are being seated. The choice of festive nadaswaram or shehnai music as the bridegroom's party is greeted and brought to the mantap is appropriate. There are also some wonderful Tyagaraja compositions in praise of Mahaganapati that are relevant as the party comes in. Similarly, a very soothing composition on the flute may be chosen for the bridal procession. Some families with a South Indian background play or sing the famous devotional composition of Purandaradasa "bhagyaada lakshmi baaramma" (O prosperous Lakshmi, please do come) as the bride enters the wedding hall.

Some couples choose very traditional nadaswaram and/or shehnai music played by professionals or on CD/tape. More typical is an experienced DJ who has worked many weddings. A valuable recommended practice is to keep some appropriate music playing but to lower the volume considerably when the priest or other principals are speaking or chanting. This works well in allowing no silent gaps in sound and is very much appreciated by all.

Many couples prefer a DJ to be completely in charge of music arrangements. It is recommended that the DJ attend the rehearsal, especially if not familiar with Vedic wedding practices. This will assure that things go smoothly from one step to the next in the ceremony, even when there are unexpected delays. The right choice and sequence of music can keep an otherwise restive audience pleased and satisfied.

The basic recommendations may be summarized:

1) No silent gaps throughout the event, i.e. there shall be music when there is no chanting and/or any other verbal action taking place at the mantap,

2) selections are carefully made in consultation with the couple about the type/style of music to be played during the processionals and the recessional and other ceremonies,

3) the sound system should be thoroughly checked to be certain that sound levels and clarity are optimal, and

4) a clip-on microphone is provided to the officiator with proper checks made before the beginning of the ceremonies. Similar requirements should be observed if live musicians are participating. The basic and obvious expectation is pleasant, festive and appropriate music.

✣✣✣✣✣✣

Appendix II: Planning & Coordination

REHEARSAL/PREPARATORY STEPS

Stage Direction

At first glance one wonders about the need for stage direction in a religious ceremony. After all it is not drama. Upon some reflection, however, it should be clear that in a sense it IS drama, a real life one in fact, where the principals have specified roles that they need to "play" without missing a beat so that the series of steps do indeed blend together to reflect the meaning and symbolism of the culture and tradition of the families. Much time and money have been invested for many months by the couple and their families. Friends and relatives arrive at the ceremony with great expectation and excitement to watch the couple on their very special day. For these reasons it is important to designate one individual as the coordinator whose primary responsibility is to make sure that everyone and everything are in place as discussed during the weeks of planning and finalized at the rehearsal.

While the role of a wedding planner covers the preparations in terms of locating and booking the venue, photographer, videographer, selection of clothes, gifts, invitations, music and extraneous related activities up to and surrounding the ceremony itself, the role of the wedding coordinator covers the central event. The coordinator may be one of the principals: a parent, a friend or relative. He or she should be knowledgeable with the entire ceremony. It is a given that the coordinator should attend the rehearsal and be familiar with the geographical setting of the wedding site in order to visualize positioning of all the steps both in space and time. The goal is a smooth flow of steps at the ceremony. This is possible with a knowledgeable or experienced coordinator.

The principals required at the rehearsal

- Overall coordinator, director
- Bride, groom, and their parents and/or stand-ins
- Bride's entourage (at least five young women from among the bride's family and friends)
- Bridegroom's "best men" (at least five young men who will assist as discussed and identified during the rehearsal)
- Bride's brother(s)
- Five married ladies from the bride's family who will be in the processional to greet the bridegroom
- Fire managers (two selected from the "best men")
- Garland bearers (one from each side)
- A young boy or girl to collect water poured down during kanyadaanam
- Antarpat bearers (two selected from the "best men")
- Manager of mangalasutra blessing and akshata distribution (two selected from the five ladies above)
- Manager of sound/music/microphones
- Manager of pictures/videos
- Ushers (selected from the "best men" and/or bride's family)
- Manager of the mantap: arrangements, arrivals/departures
- Hall manager

Rehearsal Plan

1. Set a time when ALL of the above can be present, preferably the evening before the wedding

2. Introductions of principals (the barat, bride's entourage, bridal family meeting the barat) by either the bride or the groom or the parents
3. Determine locations and times (place where the bridegroom is to be met, place where the bride will start her processional, length of time needed to reach the mantap)
4. Set the time when the ceremony begins *
5. A description of what will take place step-by-step to be described by the officiant
6. Roles and responsibilities outlined
7. Meet at the site and walk through the main steps, discuss "difficult" steps, practice lighting fire
8. Assemble materials
9. Discuss role of Primary Coordinator (cues, communication, placement and movement of principals)
10. Understand when the ceremony begins and ends **

** The ceremony officially begins when the bride's party (priest, bride's parents, five ladies and any other group of elders and friends from the bride's side) assembles at and leaves the mantap and proceeds to receive the bridegroom and his party at the decorated gate or other designated location. This processional must arrive a few seconds earlier and wait for the arrival of the bridegroom's party.*

*** The ceremony ends when the officiator announces the couple as Mr. & Mrs.......... and the couple descend from the mantap to seek the blessings of elders from both families, prior to walking down the aisle.*

Fire Management

No Vedic ceremony is complete without an offer of oblation to Agni. This pleasant ceremony can take place without any mishap if planned carefully. The task is simple but requires care. Upon receiving the cue from the coordinator, the fire is lit and brought up to the mantap. It is best to assemble the kunda and the pedestal on which it sits ahead of time. The kunda may be covered in foil and placed on a table about 24" to 30" high topped with firebricks or tiles. A few pieces of dry wood sticks and a pinch of camphor may be placed inside the kunda. The whole assembly needs to be kept ready near the mantap. The day before at the rehearsal, the men in charge should practice lighting it up to test how to keep the flames neither too high nor too low. If the fire does go down too soon and begins to smoke, an additional pinch or two of camphor will restore the flame.

After the fire ceremonies are complete, and following the concluding Saptapadi step, it is best for the persons in charge to remove the fire vessel from the mantap and take it outside the wedding hall to be extinguished with a few handfuls of sand. Historically when a wedding was conducted at the bride's home, the kunda and small amount of flame would be preserved for the new home's hearth fire. This may not be practical in terms of weddings held away from the hometown.

Opening Ceremonies

As stated earlier the actual ceremony begins the moment the priest, the bride's parents, and selected relatives pick up the plates as described before and process towards the predesignated location for Milni. The ceremony continues after the parties arrive at the mantap with an overview by the officiant followed by chanting of Veda Mantras and Vara Puja as shown in the text. At this point and until after the Vara Puja is over the bride is not present. However a few families prefer to have the bride enter almost after the groom's processional has reached the mantap. This can be accommodated but it is necessary to bear in mind that the bride and her entourage have no role at this stage except to observe the proceedings and they may simply stand aside near the mantap, until the first few steps are taken, with no participation by her. Generally we have found that it adds to the drama to have the bride arrive, escorted traditionally by her maternal uncle or another male relative and her bridesmaids, as shown in the sample program above.

Closing Ceremonies

The closing ceremony also lends itself to a variety of approaches. Some possible variations include any or all of the following: ladies from both sides, especially close relatives, may come up and bless the couple, feed them sweets, give gifts, and whisper a wish or blessing or a prayer into the ear of the bride, and put bangles on the bride's hands. These gestures are described by the term "Saubhagyavati Bhava" (May you be fortune-favored). Occasionally, in another step, cooked rice balls are used by a few ladies from either or both sides, to ward off the "evil eye" as described later in Drshti. An arati is offered to the couple in a last step. In Andhra practice, the couple shower raw rice over each other in a playful mode. These steps are described in Appendix IV.

Any and all of these variations are appropriate in raising the level of comfort and satisfaction that familiar customs bring to the couple and the families. It is best to take care of these before the final blessings. Following the Ashirvadam (blessings) the couple may be declared husband and wife by the officiant upon which they can, if they wish, prostrate before the priest, parents and other elders briefly. Then beginning the recessional, they walk down the aisle followed by the parents, bridesmaids and finally by the officiant(s). It is not uncommon for the immediate families to gather and have the couple perform a major puja to their *ishtadevata* either the same night or a day or so later. Some families visit a local temple and have a special puja performed.

Appendix III : Vedic Calendar

Hindu Concept of Time

Hindu belief in regard to time is that it has no beginning and it has no end. It is an infinitely long continuous flow cycle that is periodic with creation, movement, rest, end of epoch, dissolution, rest and then a re-creation with a continuous repetition of the whole cycle. In human terms it can be compared to the soul leaving a body upon death of the physical being and entering a new body after a period of rest to begin a new earthly existence, living an active life and and then ending it to continue the cycle. We do not include here those perfected souls who attain moksha (salvation) and simply pass beyond the end of the cycle as they merge with the supreme Soul.

Reverence for nature has always been reflected in Hindu ritual. Invocation of sacred rivers and fire, references to the year, month, day, season, position and phase of the moon are all integrated into the specification of time and space necessary for a religious ceremony. The reckoning of time was based on the movements of the principal planets that could be observed. Further, ancient Hindus believed that the life of human beings is, to some extent, influenced by the position and movement of planets.

Sankalpam/Specification of Time for a Rite

At the beginning of a sacred ceremony, the officiant/priest and/or the person sometimes addressed as yajamaana (leader) who is conducting or sponsoring the rite must declare its position in time and space in order for the invoked godhead or deities to appear and be present in the objects of veneration (puja), and/or to sanctify the rite and to grant the blessings sought. A sacred space is delineated. In the case of a wedding, this space is the mantap. The declaration is called the sankalpam.

In a wedding ceremony, this important step known as sankalpam (declaration of intention), the location in time and space is to be specified by the giver of the bride. The basis of this specification is the Hindu reckoning of time and is referenced to the creator Brahma's day as will be defined below. The parameters used to precisely state the time are kalpa, manvantara, yuga, pada, samvatsara, aayana, rutu, maasa, paksha, tithi and vaasara.

While the ideal life span for humans is generally desired to be a hundred years, the time span for the creation cycle is on a different and vast scale. For example, Hindus reckon that a 100,000 years is a mere second in Brahma's time frame. With this scale in mind, we may define the length of time for the terms used in identification of time and space in the sankalpa specification as follows:

Brahma's day and life span:

1 daytime of Brahma = 14 Manus = 1,000 chatur yugas = 4,320,000,000 solar years.

1 night time of Brahma = 4,320,000,000 solar years, during which Brahma rests.

1 year of Brahma = 365 days x 8,640,000,000 solar years.

1 life span of Brahma = 100 x 365 days x 8,640,000,000 solar years.

When Brahma rests at night, during each kalpa, the three worlds (Bhuloka, Bhuvarloka & Suvarloka) are dissolved in a deluge (pralaya); when his life span ends, all seven worlds will perish. When a life span of Brahma ends, the cosmos ends but Brahman remains; another Brahma will begin the task of creation and the cycles will repeat.

Para = half of Brahma's term

Kalpa = day of Brahma = 4,320,000,000 years (four billion and three hundred twenty million years). We are now in what is known as Shweta Varaaha Kalpa, an epoch which belongs in the second half of the life of Brahma. According to the purana after which the kalpa is named, Lord Varaha (an incarnation of Vishnu) is said to have emerged from Brahma that day in the form of a white boar in order to rescue Bhu Devi (Mother Earth) from the deluge of that age and kalpa.

Manvantara = the period in the active daytime of Brahma ruled by a Manu. The current manvantara is ruled by a Manu known as Vaivasvata. The fourteen Manus who follow each other during a daytime of Brahma are: Swayambhuva, Sawosisha, Audhama, Thamasa, Raivatha, Sakshusha, Vaivasvata, Savarni, Daksha Savarni, Brahma Savarni, Dharma Savarni, Rudra Savarni, Rauchya and Bhautya. The present Kali Yuga is said to be the 28th in the present seventh, Vaivasvata Manvantara.

Yuga = one of four ages, often referred to in the epics and puranas or story cycles of the gods. Kali Yuga, a span of 432,000 years, is the current yuga. One day in the life-span of the divine creator Brahma is considered to be equivalent to 1,000 cycles of the four yugas or chaturyugas. The yugas consist of Krta or Satya Yuga, lasting 1,728,000 solar years, Treta Yuga, a duration of 1,296,000 years, Dwapara Yuga 834,000 years, and Kali, the present yuga, of 432,000 solar years. One cycle of the above four yugas is one mahayuga or divya yuga of 4.32 million solar years. Hindu astronomy identifies the current Kali Yuga (Iron Age) as beginning at midnight between February 17 & 18, 3102 B.C.

Pada = part of Brahma's day. Prathama pada is the first division of Dvitiya Parardha (second half) of the life of Brahma.

Aayana = the time period dominated by the direction of the sun. Uttarayana begins when the sun changes direction and begins his "journey" northwards on

Makara Sankranti day. When the direction of the sun's travel appears to be southern, away from the northern hemisphere, it is Dakshinaayana.

Paksha = fortnightly phase of moon. Upon passing the new moon day, the paksha becomes Shukla (bright) as the moon waxes, and upon passing the full moon day, the paksha becomes Krishna (dark), as the moon wanes.

Ritu (Rutu) = season (the 6 seasons of the 12 months in the lunar year as shown in the list below):

Shishira (Late winter: January and February)
Vasanta (Spring: March and April)
Greeshma (Summer: May and June)
Varsha (Rainy: July and August)
Sharad (Fall: September and October)
Hemanta (Early winter: November and December)

Samvatsara = year. The Hindu years or samvatsaras repeat in a cycle of 60 as shown in the table below:

Prabhava	1987--1988	Hevilambi	2017--2018
Vibhava	1988 1989	Vilambi	2018--2019
Shukla	1989--1990	Vikari	2019--2020
Pramoduta	1990--1991	Sharvari	2020--2021
Prajotpatti	1991--1992	Plava	2021--2022
Angirasa	1992--1993	Shubakritu	2022--2023
Srimukha	1993--1994	Shobakritu	2023--2024
Bhava	1994--1995	Krodhi	2024--2025

Yuva	1995--1996	Vishvavasu	2025--2026
Dhatu	1996--1997	Parabhava	2026--2027
Isvara	1997--1998	Plavanga	2027--2028
Bahudhanya	1998--1999	Kilaka	2028--2029
Pramathi	1999--2000	Saumya	2029--2030
Vikrama	2000--2001	Sadharana	2030--2031
Vishu	2001--2002	Virodhikritu	2031--2032
Chitrabanu	2002--2003	Paridhavi	2032--2033
Svabhanu	2003--2004	Pramadhicha	2033--2034
Tarana	2004--2005	Ananda	2034--2035
Parthiva	2005--2006	Rakshasa	2035--2036
Vyaya	2006--2007	Nala	2036--2037
Sarvajit	2007--2008	Pingala	2037--2038
Sarvadhari	2008--2009	Kalayukti	2038--2039
Virodhi	2009--2010	Siddharthi	2039--2040
Vikruti	2010--2011	Raudri	2040--2041
Khara	2011--2012	Durmati	2041--2042
Nandana	2012--2013	Dundubhi	2042--2043
Vijaya	2013--2014	Rudhirodgari	2043--2044
Jaya	2014--2015	Raktakshi	2044--2045
Manmatha	2015--2016	Krodhana	2045--2046
Durnmukhi	2016--2017	Akshaya	2046--2047

Maasa = Month. (See also the Glossary). There are 12 maasas in a year, lunar or solar. Since the lunar year is shorter than the solar year by about 11 days, once every 3 lunar years, an additional lunar month is added to realign with the solar year. It is called 'Adhika Maasa'. In other words, one of the lunar months will repeat.

Tithi = lunar day; this is the time it takes for the longitudinal angle between the moon and the sun to increase by 12 degrees. When the Sun and Moon are at the same longitude, it is Amavasya or new moon and when they are 180 degrees apart it is Poornima or full moon. In each paksha there are 15 tithis for a total of 30 tithis in a lunar month. The 15th tithi of Shukla Paksha is Poornima and the 15th of Krishna Paksha is Amavasya. Apart from the new moon and full moon, the other 14 tithis in each Paksha have the same names, which are literally numbers expressed in Sanskrit, from one through fourteen, i.e. Prathama, Dwiteeya, (First, Second, etc.), Triteeya, Chaturthi, Panchami, Shashti, Saptami, Ashtami, Navami, Dashami, Ekaadashi, Dwaadashi, Trayodashi, and Chaturdashi.

Vaasara = the day of the week; the names are adopted after the pattern of Western time keeping: See Glossary.

Rahukalam

An added feature in the selection of time of the ceremony is to avoid what is known as the time of Rahu which varies from day to day. While this particular time is readily available in Hindu almanacs, a general appreciation of how it is calculated is stated briefly here. The daily difference between the sunrise and sunset hours is determined for the region. This is divided into 8 segments and the first segment is discarded. Based on a 12-hour daylight schedule, the second interval is the Rahukaalam for Monday (generally around 7:30 a.m. to 9:00 a.m.), the third and successive segments are assigned to

Saturday (9 a.m. to 10:30 a.m.), Friday (10:30 a.m. to 12 noon), Wednesday (12 noon to 1:30 p.m.), Thursday (1:30 p.m. to 3:00 p.m.), Tuesday (3:00 p.m. to 4:30 p.m.) and Sunday (4:30 p.m. to 6:00 p.m.).

Sample Sankalpam

On this most auspicious time in the earliest part of the second half of Brahma's term of Vaivasvata in the White Boar's millennium, in the first segment of Kaliyuga, in North America, in the general region of America, in the island of Krauncha (Heron), specifying, under normal practice, among the sixty Chaandramana years beginning with Prabhava,.......... year,..........course of the sun,.............. season,........... month,.......... position of the moon,.......... lunar day,.............. constellation,.......... day, with such extraordinary time and day, I,............., along with............ my wife in dharma, declare my intention to welcome this bridegroom,............ , born in............gotra and his family in order to offer Vara Puja in connection with the auspicious wedding of my daughter, Chiranjeevi Saubhaagyavati............ Devi.

Additional Sankalpam: When families request the traditional approach in which the sankalpa is done before Vara Puja and later repeated at the time of Kanyadaanam, only the wording pertaining to the specific step needs to be changed or included.

Sankalpam/Specification of Place for a Rite

Generally only the greater region is specified as, for example, "bharata varshe bharata khande" in India. In North America similar reference is made by specifying "amerika varshe uttara amerika khande." If one wishes to include the local region (state/province, city etc.) that is acceptable. Krauncha is one of the seven island-continents or dvipas that constitute the land-mass of the earth in Hindu mythology. It is situated west of Mount

Meru. Meru, or Sumeru, the pivotal mountain at the center of the earth is located north of India (Bharatavarsha), possibly at the north pole. Because the sun was said to circle this mountain every day it has also been claimed by Hindu and Buddhist legend to be the center of the universe. Traditionally is is the home of the gods, Brahma in particular. The western location of Krauncha in respect to this mountain has made it a popular reference for sankalpams declared in North America.

Horoscopes

While it is true that ancient Hindus focused inwards while trying to unravel the mysteries of the self in their quest of the greater Self, they also turned their attention to the study of the outer universe. Thus the interest in constellations and the heavens, their relationships, and their influence on individual lives. Such influence was calculated on the basis of the position of planets at the precise time of birth of individuals. In a sense, one could look upon a life as being launched into a dynamic system, and the subsequent "movement" of that living system depended upon the initial conditions of the total system. This is what led to the writing of horoscopes, which sought to establish the general characteristics of the individual's life. It was an ingenious method of acknowledging our connection and linking our fate and fortune with the larger universe.

The positions of Surya (Sun), Chandra (Moon), Angaraka (Mars), Budha (Mercury), Guru (Jupiter), Shukra (Venus), Shani (Saturn) along with those of the "sub-planets" or malign influences, Rahu and Ketu, at the time of birth of an individual define the horoscope. Millions of Hindu families still consult a priest to have the horoscopes of the bride and groom studied in order to determine the probable influence of one course of life on another as predicted by the planetary positions and thus to project the compatibility of the union. It is part of the screening process in an arranged marriage, but is generally ignored in the case of marriages made by choice or interfaith marriages.

Appendix IV : Additional Ceremonies

- Ankurarpanam
- Anujna
- Rakshabandhan/Visarjan
- Sitting/Standing
- Engagement Ceremony
- Yagnopavitam
- Kashiyatra
- Groom's Arrival
- Padaprakshalana/Ritual cleansing
- Madhuparkam
- Antarpat
- Jeeriga/Bellam
- Mangalashtak
- Sitting on Father's Lap
- Hasta Milap
- Bride Moving From Right to Left
- Tying the Knot
- Ashmarohana
- Vows
- Talambralu
- Ceremonial Presentation of Clothing
- Dhruva/Arundhati Darshan
- Sindhur Application
- Drshti
- Unjal
- Games
- Presentation of Gifts
- Sashtanga/Blessings from Elders
- Vidai
- Grhapravesham

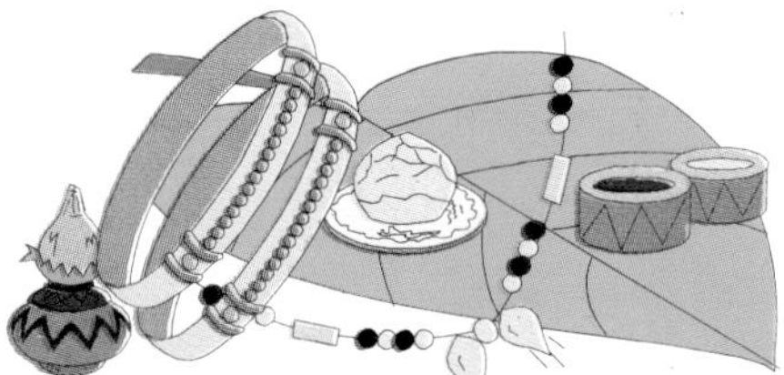

Ankurarpanam/Palikai

A day before a Vedic Wedding ceremony, some families, especially Tamilians, observe a tradition in which a few Sumangalis (married ladies) go through a ritual sowing of pre-soaked seeds in specially decorated small earthen pots containing fertile earth. It is common to use nine grains available in the region. This is sometimes called Palika Puja. The significance and interpretations vary. Some believe that eight of the grains are preferred grains of those gods that protect the eight directions of the future home of the couple. The ninth may represent the godhead that protects the center. Or the grains may represent the ones used in traditional Navagrahapuja. Another interpretation may be the expectation of potential new lives growing out of the union about to take place through the wedding ceremony. This is also an occasion in which, some believe, mother earth is worshipped. After the seeds sprout, the vessels are emptied into a body of water.

✣✣✣✣✣✣

Anujna/ Role of the Assembly

This is where the officiator seeks permission of the assembled to proceed. This requirement serves, not only as a mark of respect and acknowledgement of the authority of the assembled, but also implies their obligation to be witnesses to the wedding. Instead of down-playing this feature or taking it for granted, we have indeed integrated this feature into the ceremony and have benefited from it by using it at various times to keep the audience engaged because the assembly is required to respond and therefore is focusing on the proceedings at the mantap. During the overview, as seen earlier, the audience is alerted to this role and is asked to grant permissions when sought by responding with a Sanskrit word "tathaastu" meaning "it shall be so." This has worked out very well indeed as many feel connected and thus participate in the proceedings in an active way deriving some satisfaction from being a part of the event instead of mere spectators. Although this feature is not clearly spelled out as a Vedic requirement, in today's context it cleverly combines religious mandates and rituals taking place at the sacred space with social approval of friends and family.

✣✣✣✣✣✣✣

Rakshabandhan/Tying the Ritual Thread

It is a common Vedic practice to tie a turmeric-tinted yellow thread on the wrists of the right hand of those who are performing a ritual. In that context the bride and the groom may wish to take this step at the time the pujas are performed the night before or on the morning of the wedding day. The thread stays on until completion of the entire ceremonies.

Two versions are offered. The following mantras may be chanted by the bride and the groom.

Version 1:

गंगेच यमुनेच इत्यादि
अपवित्रः पवित्रोवा इत्यादि

सुरक्षा देवताभ्यो नमः
ध्यायामि, आवाहयामि, आसनं समर्पयामि
कुंकुम, हरिद्रा चूर्ण, अक्षतां समर्पयामि,
नानाविध परिमळ पत्र पुष्पाणि समर्पयामि

रक्षा बंधन मुहूर्तस्सुमुहूर्तोस्त्विति भवन्तो
महांतो अनुगृह्णन्तु

ॐ त्रयंबकं यजामहे
सुगंधिं पुष्ठि वर्धनं
ऊर्वा रुकमिव बंधनात्
मृत्योर् मुक्षीय मामृतात्

gangēca yamunēcaiva … ityādi
apavitra: pavitrōvā … ityādi

surakṣā dēvatābhyō nama:
dhyāyāmi, āvāhayāmi, āsanam samarpayāmi
kumkuma, haridrā cūrṇa, akṣatām samarpayāmi,
nānāvidha parimaḷa patra puṣpāṇi samarpayāmi

rakṣā bandhana muhūrtassumuhūrtōstviti bhavāntō
mahāntō anugṛṇhantu

ōm trayambakam yajāmahē
sugandhim puṣṭhi vardhanam
ūrvā rukamiva bandhanāt
mṛtyōr mukṣīya māmṛtāt

Tying of Raksha (protective thread)

Start with the invocation of the rivers and do the shuchi (cleansing) mantra as before:

Salutations to Ganga, Yamuna … etc.
May the impure be pure … etc.

Salutations to the godhead of protection
I meditate upon you, invoke you, offer you a seat here

I offer you kumkum, turmeric, akshata
And a variety of fragrances, leaves, flowers and fruits for your pleasure.

May the assembled grant this moment of tying of the protective thread
to be most auspicious.

Om. We worship the Three-Eyed Lord Shiva who is fragrant,
who enhances wellbeing. May he release us from death
as smoothly as severing a cucumber from the vine.

Version 2:

अवयो: रक्षणार्थं रक्षाधारणं करिष्ये
नमो अस्तु सर्पेभ्योयेकेच पृथिवीमनु
ये अंतरिक्षेये दिवि तेभ्य: सर्पेभ्यो नम:

अनयो: सूत्रयो: वासुकिं ध्यायामि
षोडशोपचार पुजा: समर्पयामि

avayō: rakṣaṇārtham rakṣādhāraṇam kariṣyē
namō astu sarpēbhyō yēkēca pṛthivīmanu
yē antarikṣēyē divi tēbhya: sarpēbhyō nama:

anayō: sūtrayō: vāsukim dhyāyāmi
ṣōḍaṣōpacāra pujā: samarpayāmi

We hereby wear the raksha thread to seek protection.
We salute all the reptiles residing on the earth, sky and the heavens.
We meditate on Vasuki, the serpent who can ward off all fears
and offer the traditional sixteen step puja to him.

✣✣✣✣✣✣

Raksha Visarjana/ Removing the Rakshsa

The practice is to undo the thread tied around the wrist of the right hand at the very end of the ceremonies. The following shloka may be recited while doing the visarjan.

सुरक्षा देवताभ्यो नमोनमः
कंकणमिदं विसृजामि विसृजामि विसृजामि

surakṣā dēvatābhyō namōnama:
kankaṇamidam visṛjāmi visṛjāmi visṛjāmi

Many salutations to the deity of protection
Let me the raksha thread undo, undo, undo.

✤✤✤✤✤✤

The Question of Sitting or Standing

Should the ceremonies be performed with the principals sitting at the sacred space, as is the usual custom in India, or standing, which is the Western mode? Wedding rental companies generally supply throne-like chairs for the principals and other decorative seats for relatives and officiants along with the mantap.

The author's experience is that the structured ceremonies which he has conducted over the years are dynamic and that the movement of the principals and handling of ceremonial items during the ceremony are greatly facilitated by having everyone on their feet. Some steps such as the homas and Saptapadi require the couple to stand anyway. Furthermore the guests assembled have a better and clearer view of what happens on the raised platform or mantap. Due to their familiarity with wedding rites as conducted in other faiths, young people growing up outside India appear to prefer it. However, if traditon and nostalgia prevail, and the families prefer to sit down for most of the rituals, and stand where needed, that can be accommodated.

✣✣✣✣✣✣

Engagement Ceremony

Introduction:

In the West, the time-honored practice is for the man, the groom-to-be, to ask his beloved, the bride-to-be, to marry him. This is often done in private, with or without the knowledge and approval of the families and is sealed with the gift of a ring to the lady. An engagement party may then follow. Such an engagement is considered a public announcement of the intention to marry.

The Hindu tradition also includes an engagement ceremony known as Vaagdaanam or Vaakdaana which means giving one's word (of honor). In fact it is an exchange of pledges by both families. The normal practice requires the families to assemble, approve and formalize the understanding between themselves or between the two young people. The words of honor or pledges are not exchanged between the principals but between the fathers. The bride-to-be and groom-to-be do indeed attend and participate, especially the prospective bride as she is welcomed and honored with gifts by the family of the groom-to-be. In this ceremony, in India, a ring may be presented to the groom-to-be by the family of the bride-to-be while the bride-to-be receives a set of jewelry and/or a saree and blouse.

Another version of the ceremony is common, especially in South India, and is known as Nischitaartham, the literal meaning being "firming up." The latter takes place usually the night before the wedding before an assembly of friends and relatives from both sides.

The focus is very clear and the rituals become a part of the imminent wedding ceremony.

In any case, the magic of love or its prospect brings two young people together and that circle of magic expands, bringing together the immediate families and friends, in a joyous ceremonial event. The ceremony is based on Vedic practices going back over 5,000 years. During the ceremony the basic "transaction" leading to the pledges is between the two fathers. This is done by proclaiming the lineages of the families and making a formal request for the alliance. Although there could be variations depending upon family traditions, one practice requires the father of the groom-to-be to make the first request. It is the affirmative response from the father of the bride-to-be that sets the stage for the remaining steps of the ceremony.

Materials needed:

Plates of fruits (five kinds), flowers, agarbatti, deepa with wick and oil, akshata, haldi, kumkum, engagement ring and/or saree and blouse piece, betel leaves, areca nuts, kalashas, raw rice, coconut, garlands, arati plate; paper towel roll, matches.

The Steps:

The following steps may be used with minor modifications depending on one's own family traditions. In this ceremony the groom-to-be and prospective bride to be will be designated the letters GTB and BTB for convenience.

1. A brief worship service to either Mahaganapati or an ishtadevata (family's chosen godhead) performed by or in behalf of the GTB is followed by the father of the GTB greeting and honoring the family of the BTB. The GTB's father (or his representative) identifies the families to be united by reciting the lineage of both and expresses his keen interest in this alliance. The BTB's father responds affirmatively "after consulting

his wife and elders in his family" ("*bhāryā jnātibandhvanumatim krutvā*" "भार्या ज्ञातिबंध्वनुमतिं कृत्वा").

2. The GTB's family now greets and welcomes the BTB and offers a variety of fruits, flowers and garments (a new saree, and blouse). Additional gifts such as the engagement ring, bangles, necklaces may also be given to the BTB at this time. She may then be requested to go and change into the presented garments.

3. Upon her return, the BTB's father does a sankalpam and specifies this moment in space and time (see Appendix III) and declares his pledge and invites the GTB's father to sit or stand by the side of the BTB.

4. With the GTB's father standing or sitting by her side, the BTB's family honors the GTB's father while repeating the lineages and declaring that they give their word to this alliance in the presence of this "godhead, fire god and the families" (devāgni dvija sannidhau; देवाग्नि द्विज सन्निधौ). Note: Even though an actual agnikunda may not be present, the power of the mantras is considered adequate.

5. The groom's family accepts this word of honor and in a 21st century improvisation, shaking of hands and/or hugging by family members may seal the deal.

6. Each father now expresses the wish that through this exchange of pledges each family will be happy.

7. The BTB and GTB are now each honored by members of the other family through an offer of garlands, and an arati is performed.

8. The ceremony concludes with blessings by the priest and the assembled.

The Ceremony:

The bride-to-be (BTB) is seated facing east; her father is to her left, her mother and other relatives to her right or behind her.

The officiant recites:

अविघ्नमस्तु
avighnamastu
May there be no obstacles.

शुक्लांबरधरं विष्णुं शशिवर्णं चतुर्भुजं
प्रसन्न वदनं ध्यायेत् रार्व विघ्नोपशांतये

śuklāmbaradharam viṣṇum
śaśivarṇam caturbhujam
prasanna vadanam dhyāyēt
sarva vighnōpaśāntayē

I meditate on Vishnu who wears white clothing,
the color of the moon, four-armed, of pleasant aspect,
so that all obstacles are minimized.

A prayer to Shiva whose very invocation is believed to clear out any troublesome vibrations follows:

ॐ नमः प्रणवार्थाय शुध्ध ज्ञानैक मूर्तये
निर्मलाय प्रशांताय दक्षिणामूर्तये नमः

ōm nama: praṇavārthaya śudhdha jnānaika mūrtayē
nirmalāya praśāntāya dakśiṇā mūrtayē namaha

I salute the Lord of the Southern direction who is the very embodiment of the sacred symbol Om and of pure knowledge and eternal peace.

Invocation of Mahāganapati, family Godhead and Guru

With folded hands the officiant and the assembled chant the following:

करिश्यमाणस्य कर्मणः निर्विघ्नेन परिसमाप्त्यर्थम्
आदौ महागणपति स्मरणं करिश्ये

kariśyamāṇasya karmaṇa: nirvighnēna parisamāptyartham
ādau mahāgaṇapati smaraṇam kariśyē

So that the ceremonies we are about to undertake proceed to completion without any obstacles we meditate on Mahaganapati.

गृहदेवतां ध्यायामि
ध्यानं समर्पयामि

gṛhadēvatām dhyāyāmi
dhyānam samarpayāmi

I respectfully contemplate our family Godhead.

गुरुर्ब्रह्मा गुरुर्विष्णुः गुरुर्देवो महेश्वरः
गुरुस्साक्षात् परब्रह्म तस्मै श्री गुरवे नमः

gururbrahmā gururviṣu gururdēvō mahēśwara:
gurussākṣāt parabrahma tasmai śrī guravē nama:

Salutations to the preceptor who is truly Brahma, Vishnu
and Maheshwara and who personifies the Supreme Being.

Shuddhi (Cleansing)

The sacred rivers are then invoked to fill the metallic vessel. This water is used to cleanse and offer throughout the worship. Water is poured from one vessel into the smaller one while chanting:

गंगेच यमुनेचैव गोदावरी सरस्वती
नर्मदा सिंधु कावेरी जलेस्मिन् सन्निधिं कुरु

gangēca yamunēchaiva godāvarī saraswatī
narmadā sindhu kāvērī jalēsmin sannidhim kuru

O Ganga, Yamuna, Godavari, Saraswati, Narmada,
Sindhu and Kaveri waters, please be present in this place

कोलंबिया कोलराडो चैव मिस्सौरि मिसिसिप्पी
रियोग्रान्डे च हड्संच कनेटिकट् नदीनां
जले: अस्मिन् सन्निधिं कुरु

kolambiyā kolarāḍō caiva missouri misisippī
riyōgrānḍē ca haḍsanca kaneṭikaṭ nadīnām
jalē: asmin sannidhim kuru

May the sacred waters of Columbia, Colorado, Missouri, Mississippi,
Rio Grande, Hudson and Connecticut rivers manifest themselves here.

A spoonful (uddharane) of water is now poured into the hands of the principals who, while wiping their hands, chant:

अपवित्रः पवित्रोवा सर्वावस्थाम् गतोपिवा
यःस्मरेत् पुंडरीकाक्षं स बाह्याभ्यंतरः शुचिः

apavitra: pavitrōvā sarvāvasthām gatōpivā
ya:smarēt puṇḍarīkākśam sa bāhyābhyamtara: śuci:

May anything unholy become holy, may all base tendencies depart,
cleansing both inside and out, as we recall the lotus-eyed Pundarikaksha.

GTB's father recites:

ॐ श्रीमन्महागणाधिपतये नमः
ॐ श्री सत्यनारायण स्वामिने नमः
ॐ श्री गृहदेवताभ्यो नमः

ōm śrīmanmahāgaṇḍhipatayē nama:
ōm śrī satyanārāyaṇa swāminē nama:
ōm śrī gṛhadēvatābhyō nama

Salutations to Mahaganapati.
Salutations to Satyanarayana.
Salutations to our family deity.

Pravara recital (reciting the lineage of both families):

प्रवर

त्रया ऋषयः प्रवरान्विताय .... गोत्रोत्पन्नयां ....प्रपौत्रं, ...पौत्रं,
श्रीमान् .... तथा श्रीमती सौभाग्यवती .... देवी पुत्रः, चिरंजीवी .... नाम्ने वराय,

त्रया ऋषयः प्रवरोपेतां .... गोत्रोत्पन्नां ....प्रपौत्रीं, ...पौत्रीं,
श्रीमान् .... तथा श्रीमति सौभाग्यवती .... देवी पुत्रीं, चिरंजीवी सौभाग्यवती
.... नाम्नी कन्यां, भार्यत्वाय वृणीमहे

trayā ṛṣaya: pravarānvitāya .... gōtrōtpannayām ....prapautāryām,
..............pautrāyām, śrīmān .... tathā śrīmatī saubhāgyavatī .... dēvī
putrāyā:, ciranjīvī .... nāmnē varāya,

trayā ṛśaya: pravarōpētām .... gotrōtpannām ....prapautrīm, ...
........pautrīm, śrīmān .... tathā śrīmati saubhāgyavati .... dēvī putrīm,
ciranjīvī saubhāgyavatī .... nāmnī kanyām, bhāryatvāya vṛṇīmahē

Descendent of three sages, born in the gotra ...., in behalf of the great grandson of ...., grandson of ...., son of .... and Saubhagyavati....................., Chiranjivi..........................,

I ask for the hand in marriage of Chiranjivi Saubhagyavati ....descendent of three sages, born in the ....gotra, great granddaughter of ....

granddaughter of ....and daughter of ....and Saubhagyavati ....

BTB's father:

वृणीध्वं, वृणीध्वं, वृणीध्वं

vṛṇīdhvam vṛṇīdhvam vṛṇīdhvam

It is my pleasure; It is my pleasure; It is my pleasure.

प्रदास्यामि, प्रदास्यामि, प्रदास्यामि

pradāsyāmi pradāsyāmi pradāsyāmi

I bestow her, I bestow her, I bestow her.

Vadhu Puja:

In this segment, the ladies of the GTB's family approach the BTB. Typically the GTB's mother picks up a plate of flowers, fruits, etc. and applies kumkum and haldi to the forehead of the BTB. This may be followed by a presentation of plates of gifts and garments. The BTB may be asked to change into the new clothing.

The families may now engage in additional pujas, chantings and songs until the BTB returns to the assembly.

Sankalpa/Declaration of Intention/Vaagdaana:

आचमनं

BTB's father sips water from the uddharana each time after chanting:

अच्युताय नमः
अनंताय नमः
गोविन्दाय नमः

अच्युतानंतगोविन्देभ्यो नमोनमः

ācamanam
acyutāya nama:
anantāya nama:

gōvindāya nama:

acyutānantagōvindēbhyō namōnama:

Salutations to Achyuta
Salutations to Ananta
Salutations to Govinda

Salutations to Achyuta, Ananta and Govinda

शुभे शोभन मुहूर्ते, आद्य ब्रह्मणः, द्वितीय परार्धे, श्री श्वेत वराह कल्पे, वैवस्वत मन्वन्तरे, कलियुगे, प्रथम पादे, क्रौन्च द्वीपे, अमेरिका वर्षे, उत्तर अमेरिका खंडे, व्यवहारिके, चांद्रमानेनस्य षष्ठि संवत्सराणां मध्ये, ... नाम संवत्सरे, ...आयने, ...ऋतौ,............ मासे, ...पक्षे, ...तिथौ, ...वासर युक्तायाम्, ऐवं गुण विशेषण विशिष्टायाम् अस्याम् शुभ तिथौ, ...नामधेयः अहं मम धर्म पत्नी ....देवी सहित मम पुत्री चिरंजीवी सौभाग्यवती ....देवी नाम्नि करिष्यमाण शुभ विवाहांगभूतं वाग्दानमहं करिष्ये.

śubhē śōbhana muhūrtē, adya brahmaṇa:, dvitīya parārdhē, śrī śvēta varāha kalpē, vaivasvata manvantarē, kaliyugē, prathama pādē, kraunca dvīpē, amerikā varṣē, uttara amerikā khaṇḍē, vyavahārikē, cāndramānēnasya ṣaṣṭhi saṁvatsarāṇām madhyē,.................. nāma saṁvatsarē, ... āyane, ...ṛtau................... māsē,............... pakṣē, ...tithau,............vāsara, yuktāyām, ēvam guṇa viśēṣaṇa viśiṣṭāyām asyām śubha tithau, ...nāmadhēya: aham mama dharmapatnī .... dēvi sahita mama putrī ciranjīvī saubhgyavatī........... dēvi nāmni kariśyamāṇa śubha vivāngabhūtam vāgdānamaham kariśye.

On this most auspicious time, in the earliest part of the second half of Brahma's term, of Vaivasvata manvantara, in the White Boar's millennium, in the first segment of

Kaliyuga, in North America, in the general region of America, in the island of Krauncha (Heron), specifying, under normal practice,
among the sixty Chaandramana years beginning with Prabhava .... year,
.... solstice, ...season, ...month,
.........................position of the moon, ...the lunar day,
..................day, with such extraordinary time and day, I
..............................along with ....my wife in dharma, give this pledge as a part of the upcoming auspicious wedding rites.

Puja to the GTB's father: sitting/standing next to where the BTB's father is seated, the BTB's father offers him a plate of flowers and fruits.

BTB's father declares:

पूर्वोक्त ऐवं गुण विशेषण विशिष्ठायं अस्यां शुभ तिथौ मम पुत्री अस्य सौभाग्यवती .... नाम्नीं
इमां कन्यां ज्योतिर्विदारिष्टे सुमुहूर्ते दास्ये इति वाचा संप्रददे
अव्यंगे अपतिते अक्लीबेदश दोष विवर्जिते इमां कन्यां प्रदास्यामि देवाग्नि द्विज सन्निधौ
.... गोत्र ....नामधेयः वर विषये भवंतो निश्चिता भवंतु.

pūrvōkta ēvam guṇa viśēṣaṇa viśiṣṭāyām asyām śubha tithau mama putrī asya
saubhāgyavatī .... nāmnīm imām kanyām
jyōtirvidāriṣṭē sumuhūrtē dāsyē iti vāchā sampradadē
avyangē apatitē aklībēdaśa dōṣa vivarjitē
imām kanyām pradāsyāmi dēvāgni dvija sannidhau
................gōtra .... nāmadhēya: vara viṣayē bhavantō niścitā bhavantu

As described previously, at this most auspicious time, I, in the presence of this godhead, the assembled elders and the fire altar, shall give this word of honor and bestow this young woman, my daughter Saubhagyavati ...., who is free of defects (perfect), single, healthy, free from any of the ten blemishes to proper alliance.

Acceptance by the father of GTB:

............गोत्रोद्भवस्य ....नामधेयः वर विशये भवंतो निश्चिता भवंतु.

.... gōtrōdbhavasya ....nāmadhēya: vara viśayē bhavantō niścitā bhavantu

In the matter pertaining to my son ....as the bridegroom born in the ....gotra, it is now firm and settled.

Both fathers shake hands.

BTB's father:

वाचादत्ता मया कन्या पुत्रार्थं स्वीकृता त्वया
कन्यावलोकन विधौ निश्चितस्त्वं सुखी भव

vācādattā mayā kanyā putrārtham svīkṛtā tvayā
kanyāvalōkana vidhau niścitastvam sukhī bhava

Having given the word of honor in regard to my daughter in this prescribed manner, please accept her for your son and be happy.

GTB's father:

वाचादत्ता त्वया कन्या पुत्रार्थं स्वीकृता मया
कन्यावलोकन विधौ निश्चितस्त्वं सुखी भव

vācādattā tvayā kanyā putrārtham svīkṛtā mayā
kanyāvalōkana vidhau niścitastvam sukhī bhava

Having heard your word of honor in regard to your daughter, I shall accept in this prescribed manner and wish you to be happy.

The bride-to-be is sprinkled with water and akshata by the priest and blessed with the following chants:

शिवा आपः संतु, सौमनस्यमस्तु अक्षतं चारिष्टं चास्तु दीर्घमायुः श्रेयः शांतिः
पुष्टिःतुष्टिः चास्तु ऐतद्वः सत्यमस्तु

ṣivā āpa: santu, saumanasyamastu akṣatam cāriṣṭam cāstu
dīrghamāyu: śrēya: śānti: puśṭi:tuśṭi: cāstu ētadva: satyamastu

May Parvati manifest here, may there be enjoyment, may she be secure,
may she live long, prosper, be at peace, well nourished and content.

The bride-to-be may chant the following or repeat after the priest:

देवेंद्राणि नमस्तुभ्यं देवेंद्र प्रियभामिनि
विवाहं भाग्यमारोग्यं पुत्रलाभं च देहिमे

dēvēndrāṇi namastubhyam dēvēndra priyabhāmini
vivāham bhāgyamārōgyam putralābham ca dēhimē

O Indrani, dear wife of Indra, please grant me
a prosperous married life, and health, with progeny.

The ceremony is complete with the following blessings by the priest.

नवो नवो भवति जायमानोन्हान् केतुर् उषसां ऐत्युग्रं
भागं देवेभ्यो विदधात्य् आयन् प्रचंद्रमास्थिरति दीर्घं आयुः

navō navō bhavati jyamānōnhān kētur uṣasām ētyugraM
bhāgam dēvēbhyō vidadhyāty āyan pracandramāsthirati dīrghamāyu:

He, born afresh, is new and new for ever; ensign of days he goes before the Mornings Coming, he orders for the Gods their portion. The moon prolongs the days of our existence. *(Griffith, RV, ibid)*

शतमानं भवतु शतायुः पुरुषः
शतेंद्रियः आयुष्येवेंद्रिये प्रतितिष्ठति

śatamānam bhavatu śatāyu: puruṣa:
śatēndriya: āyuṣyēvēndriyē pratitiṣṭati

May you live a hundred years, with senses a hundredfold strong,
may your length of life equal that of Indra himself.

✤✤✤✤✤✤✤

Yagnopavitam

Male children born and raised in traditional Hindu and orthodox families are initiated into the Vedantic fold through a ceremony known as Upanayanam. From a purely religious point of view this ceremony is perhaps the most significant step in the life of a man for a variety of reasons. First of all it is the step that ushers the boy out of childhood and in ancient times it meant that he was ready to begin the study of the Vedas under a guru in the latter's abode. Secondly upon taking this step the young person becomes eligible to receive the most sacred and "secret" mantra of Gayatri as it is whispered into his right ear by his father in a climactic step. This eligibility is declared publicly when the boy is allowed to wear the sacred thread of three strings made of cotton with a tight knot known as brahmamudi (knot of Brahma). This is deemed to be a life-changing event because the individual is initiated into a life of celibacy with total focus on learning the wisdom of the Vedas. This lifestyle may continue through the rest of his life until and unless interrupted by consideration of the next stage of life defined as Grihastha (householder) as discussed in the section known as Kashiyatra preceding the wedding ceremony. The child initiated thus is considered a dwija (twice-born).Thus the significance of the sacred thread known as yagnopavitam.

In the context of this book, if the groom has been thus initiated and if the family desires, then we need to consider the step in which he is required to wear the second set of the sacred thread that declares his new status in life, that of a householder. However if the groom has not already been through the Upanayanam ceremony and family tradition requires it, then it can be done the day before the wedding ceremony.

There is the question of when to add the second thread ceremony. One possibility is to take this step almost after the Vara Puja. But a question may then arise about its rationality. Since the groom has not gone through the marriage ceremony the second yagnopavitam may be worn immediately after. Immediately after what? Should it be after the tying of the mangalasutra or should it be when he has taken the seventh step of the Saptapadi which, according to Indian laws, confers married status. There is a choice which the families involved may have to discuss and settle.

This step may begin with a sankalpam as follows:

सन्कल्पं

शुभे शोभन मुहूर्ते आद्य ब्रह्मणः द्वितीय परार्धे श्री श्वेत वराह कल्पे वैवस्वत मन्वन्तरे कलियुगे प्रथम पादे क्रौन्च द्वीपे अमेरिका वर्षे उत्तर अमेरिका खंडे व्यवहारिके चांद्रमानेनस्य षष्ठि संवत्सराणां मध्ये
----------संवत्सरे, ------------ आयने, -----------, ऋतौ,------
मासे, ------पक्षे, ------ तिथौ, ------ नक्षत्रे ----------वासर युक्तायाम्,
ऐवं गुण विशेषण विशिष्टायाम् अस्याम् शुभ तिथौ, ________________
नामधेयः अहं मम गृहस्थाश्रम कर्मानुष्ठान योग्यता सिध्यर्थं श्वशुर दत्त
द्वितीय यज्ञोपवीत धारणं करिष्ये. तदंग यज्ञोपवीत परब्रह्म पूजां करिष्ये.

Sankalpam

śubhē śōbhana muhūrtē, ādya brahmaṇa:, dvitīya parārdhē, śrī śvēta varāha kalpē, vaivasvata manvantarē, kaliyugē, prathama pādē, kraunca dvīpē, amerikāvarṣē, uttara amerikā khanḍē, vyavahārikē, cāndramānēnasya ṣaṣṭi samvatsarāṇām madhyē, -------- samvatsarē, ------------āyanē, -----------, ṛtau,------------ māsē, ------- pakṣē, ----------- tithau, -------------nakṣatrē, ---------------vāsara yuktāyām, ēvam guṇa viśēṣaṇa viśiṣṭāyām asyām śubha tithau, ----------------- nāmadhēya: aham gṛhasthāshrama karmānuṣṭhāna yōgyatā siddhyartham śvaśura datta dvitīya yajnōpavīta dhāraṇam kariśyē.

tadanga yajnōpavīta parabrahma pūjām kariśyē

On this most auspicious time in the earliest part of the second half of Brahma's term of Vaivasvata in the White Boar's millennium, in the first segment of Kaliyuga, in North America, in the general region of America, in the island of Krauncha (Heron), specifying, under normal practice, among the sixty Chandramana years beginning with Prabhava ------------- year, -----------------solstice, ------------- season, --------------month, -------------- position of the moon, ------------------ the lunar day, -------------constellation, -------------- day, on such superior time and particular day, I ----------------------, in order to attain the eligibility to perform duties relevant to the status of a householder, I shall wear the second sacred thread offered by my father-in-law. As a part of that I shall perform puja to the Supreme Being present in this sacred thread.

अस्मिन् सूत्रे यज्ञोपवीत परब्रह्मणं आवाहयामि.
स्थापयामि पूजयामि. यज्ञोपवीत परब्रह्मणे नमः
षोडषोपचार पूजां करिष्ये.

asmin sūtrē yajnōpavīta parabrahmaṇām āvāhayāmi. sthāpayāmi pūjayāmi.
yajnōpavīta parabrahmaṇē nama: ṣōḍashōpachāra pujām kariśyē.

I invoke the Supreme Being in the sacred thread. I install him and offer prayer.
I perform the *shodashopachaara* (sixteen part) prayer.

The following mantra is chanted while holding the string with both hands. The string is stretched tight with the brahmamudi at the top, right palm up, and the lower part held with the left palm facing down. After chanting, the string is first worn around the neck like a garland and then the right arm is inserted through the loop such that the yagnopavitam rests on the left shoulder draping across the upper body from left to right.

(Here follow the same procedure as in the Ganapati Puja replacing that prayer by yajnōpavīta parabrahmanē nama:)

यज्ञोपवीतं परमं पवित्रं
प्रजापतेर्यत्सहजं पुरस्तात्
आयुष्यमग्रियं प्रतिमुंच शुभ्रं
यज्नोपवीतं बलमस्तु तेज:

yajnōpavītam paramam pavitram
prajāpatēryatsahajam purastāt
āyuṣyamagriyam pratimunca śubhram
yajnōpavītam balamastu tēja:

This, the most sacred thread, is sanctioned by Prajapati himself and is considered sacrosanct. This, the symbol of purity, shall enhance my longevity and bring strength and vigor.

द्वितीय यज्ञोपवीत धारण मुहूर्तः
सुमुहूर्तोस्त्वित्यनुगृह्णंतु

dvitīya yajnōpavīta dhāraṇa muhūrta
ssumuhūrtōstvityanugṛṇhaṇtu

May you please grant this moment when I wear my
second sacred thread to be auspicious.
The assembled respond with तथास्तु (*tathāstu;* It shall be so).

✤✤✤✤✤✤

Kashiyatra/ Ritual Journey to Kashi

"This young man is well-versed in all the four Vedas and is now on his way to Kashi (Benares) for advanced studies in Brahmacharya" said the priest in the course of a wedding ceremony when the entourage led by the priest, the groom and his relatives were stopped by a group of people from the bride's side led by her father. The groom was clad in a dhoti which had been drenched in turmeric water and dried (sign of a holy person or mendicant) with a similar upper cloth worn on a bare back adorned with the sacred thread. A bundle, presumably packed with scriptures on the shoulder, a staff, sandals, an umbrella, a small water vessel added to convey the impression of a long journey.

It is an amusing event and is indeed a part of most, if not all, Brahmin weddings to this day. There appears to be no reference to this step in the Vedas. However a simple dialog such as the one shown below may suffice if one incorporates this step into the wedding plans.

चरित ब्रह्मचर्योहं कृत व्रत चतुष्टयः
काशीयात्रां गमिश्यामि अनुज्ञां देहिमे शुभां

carita brahmacaryōham kṛta vrata catuśṭaya:
kāśīyātrām gamiśyāmi anujnām dēhimē śubham

Please wish me well and permit me to proceed on my pilgrimage to Kashi
in order to undertake the four-fold penance of celibacy.

According to custom, this permission is sought from a stranger, here the priest, who interrupts the journey.

Then the bride's father makes his age-old appeal:

सालंकारां ममसुतां कन्यां दास्यामि ते द्विज
पाणिं गृहीत्वा साग्निस्त्वं गच्छस्वागच्छमद्गृहं

sālankārām mamasutām kanyām dāsyāmi tē dvija
pāṇim gṛhītvā sāgnistvam gacchasvāgacchamadgṛuham

I offer you my daughter, fully adorned, in marriage. Please come to my home, hold her hand, partake in the fire rituals, and both of you may then proceed on your journey.

The sequence ends with an apparent acceptance of this offer as everyone turns around and proceeds towards the wedding hall.

V.S. Naipaul makes an interesting observation about a similar event, involving a thread ceremony, in his book, *An Area of Darkness:*

"I had no belief; I disliked religious ritual; and I had a sense of the ridiculous. I refused to go through the *janaywa,* or thread ceremony of the newborn, with some of my cousins. The ceremony ends with the initiate, his head shaved, his thread new and obvious, taking up his staff and bundle--as he might have done in an Indian village two thousand years ago--and announcing his intention of going to Kasi-Banaras to study. His mother weeps and begs him not to go; the initiate insists that he must; a senior member of the family is summoned to plead with the initiate, who at length yields and lays down his staff and bundle. It was a pleasing piece of theatre. But I knew that we were in Trinidad, an island separated by only ten miles from the South American coast, and that the appearance in a Port of Spain street of my cousin, perhaps of no great academic attainment, in the garb of a Hindu mendicant-scholar bound for Banaras, would have attracted unwelcome attention. So I refused; though now this ancient drama, absurdly surviving in a Trinidad yard, seems to me touching and attractive."

✣✣✣✣✣✣

Baraat/Groom's Arrival

It has been customary, especially among North Indian families, to bring the bridegroom to the wedding site on horseback. As discussed earlier in the chapter on Origins, this is the kshatriya practice which requires that the bride be "captured" as opposed to accepting her as a gift implied in the Kanyadana concept.

Variations on this theme involve a horse-drawn cart, or, nowadays, a highly decorated (usually with flowers) automobile. Some families even consider an elephant. In any case, this is clearly an opportunity for the groom's party to assemble outside the hall, celebrate with music and drums and dance to their heart's content as they approach the bride's family awaiting this arrival at a predetermined location. This ice-breaker and lighter moment has become a popular entry mode that is desired even by couples who have no North Indian connection and is enjoyed by all, and generally approved by family members.

✣✣✣✣✣✣

Pada Prakshalana /Washing of the Feet

Some families wish to observe this ritual in which a member of the bride's family (bride's father or brother) washes the feet of the groom upon his arrival at the entrance.

Viewed in the context of the belief that the groom is the embodiment of Vishnu for the duration, one can justify the observance as a part of a Shodashopachara Puja (16-part offering) practiced when worshipping deities. If this is a final choice, then the groom can be asked to step into a brass or stainless steel plate large enough to accommodate the feet comfortably. Into this plate just enough water is poured to symbolize washing. If the family wish to go through the actual motion of washing the feet, then the groom can step off onto a towel.

One variation is to simply dispense a few drops of water from the uddharana towards the feet and chanting "padyam samarpayami" (I offer water for your feet).

With the shuddhi mantra (cleansing prayer) that will be chanted soon after the parties arrive at the mantap, there is enough justification to skip this step if desired as the spirit of cleanliness in every sense is met by the shuddhi mantra step.

✣✣✣✣✣✣

Madhuparkam

Offering a sweet drink to the groom in a formal manner as he arrives at the bride's home appears to have been the practice in Vedic times. Colebrooke refers to this in his commentary included in the chapter on Origins in this book. The particular drink referred to in the treatises on weddings is known as madhuparkam, basically a mixture of honey and yogurt.

Apart from the normal practice of offering a drink to a guest, any guest, the reason attributed to this particular concoction is its apparent nourishing quality expected to enhance one's strength and virility.

There is an elaborate ritualistic viewing of the elements (honey and yogurt) and chanting as they are stirred to mix. Dipping three fingers once into the vessel and using what adheres to sprinkle in the four principal directions and the center prior to drinking from the same appears to have been the practice. In some traditions it is the bride that offers the drink later, but here, as in most cases, it is her father.

In this day and age it is enough to symbolically offer any sweet or sweet drink as a gesture upon first meeting with the groom at the Milni. As there is usually a crowd accompanying the groom this appears to be an adequate gesture. It is best to include a plate of sweets in the paraphernalia carried by the bride's family welcoming the groom. This shows a clear intent. However, if one wishes, the groom may be offered madhuparkam itself.

✣✣✣✣✣✣

Arrival of the Bride; The Antarpat

Some families practice a tradition in which the view of the arriving bride is shielded from the awaiting groom. Upon cue, two men (best men) pick up a large piece of cloth (a saree for example), unfold it and hold it in front of the groom to obstruct the view of the bride from him. If this step is to be included, the chosen assistants are requested to hold up the cloth until the priest instructs them to remove it. With the previously selected music playing as the bride enters the hall, the bridal procession approaches the mantap where the bride is received by the priest and the entourage take places previously agreed to. The bride should stand facing the groom such that they are both visible to the assembly but not to each other.

The ceremony begins with the following mantra uttered by the groom and/or officiator:

आनः प्रजां जनयंतु प्रजापतिः
आजरसाय समनक्त्वर्यमा
अभ्रातृघ्नीं वरुणा

अपतिघ्नीं बृहस्पते
इन्द्रा पुत्रघ्नीं
लक्ष्म्यंतामस्यै सवितस्सुव

अघोर चक्षुर् अपतिघ्न्येधि
शिवा पतिभ्यस्सुमना स्सुवर्चाः
वीरसूर् देवकामा स्योना शंनो भव
द्विपदे शंचतुष्पदे

āna: prajām janayantu prajāpati: ājarasāya samanaktvaryamā
abhrātṛghnīm varuṇā apatighnīm bṛhaspatē
indrā putraghnīm lakṣmyatāmasyai savitassuva

aghōra cakṣur apatighnyēdhi shivā patibhyassumanā ssuvarcā:
vīrasūr dēvakāmā syōnā śamnō bhava dvipadē śamcatuṣpadē

May Prajaapati bless her with children, May Aaryama bless her jewelry, May Varuna and Brhaspati protect her husband and his brothers, May Indra protect her children, May Savitr grant her wealth.

O Bride, may your peaceful demeanor and compassion provide peace in my family. May you bear brave children and bring happiness to both humans and animals. *(Griffith)*

The priest concludes this step by chanting the qualities of the bride as follows.

संज्ञानं विज्ञानं प्रज्ञानं जानदभि जानत्
संकल्पमानं प्रकल्पमानं उपकल्पमानं
उपक्लुप्तं क्लुप्तं
श्रेयोवसीय आयुस्संभूतं भूतं

चित्रकेतुः प्रभानाथ्संभानां
ज्योतिष्मागं्स्तेजस्वानातपग्
स्तपन्नभितपन्
रोचनो रोचमानश्शोभन
श्शोभमानः कल्याणः

सुमंगलीरियं वधूरिमां समेत पश्यत

samjnānam vijnānam prajnānam jānadabhi jānat, sankalpamānam prakalpamānam upakalpamānam upakluptam kluptam śrēyōvasīya āyussambhūtam bhūtam citrakētu: prabāhnāthsambhānām jyōtiṣmāgmstējasvānātapag stapannabhitapan rōcanō rōcamāna śśōbhana śśōbhamāna kalyāṇa: sumangalīriyam vadhūrimam samēta paśyata

This bride possesses superior intelligence to bring harmony between the two families; decisive, honorable, desirous of and ready to make a home. She arrives truly beautiful, distinguished as a bright shining light, resplendent, charming, pleasing and lovely; Hail this bride. Let all look at this bride who is auspicious.

Immediately after this chant the curtain is removed and the couple face each other. A bridesmaid offers a garland to the bride while at the same time the best man assists the groom to take off the garland that is now on his neck. The bride is now instructed to offer the garland to the groom who in turn takes the garland in the hand of the best man and garlands the bride. With both garlanded now they face the audience with the bride standing to the right of the groom.

✣✣✣✣✣✣✣

Jeelakarra-Bellum / Cumin-Brown Sugar

This is a tradition observed in some families and is considered a climactic event scheduled to take place at a time corresponding to the muhūrtam (auspicious moment). Some families prefer this to be the first act upon arrival of the bride.

If the couple include this in the ceremonies, it is best to have them take this step when the antarpat is up. As the bride arrives and stands in front of the curtain, the priest instructs the couple to apply the paste of cumin seeds (jeera or jeelakarra) and brown sugar (bellam) to each other's heads reaching over the curtain. This symbolizes that the couple will become inseparable much as the mixture of cumin and sugar, and also be ready to experience both the bitter and sweetness of life. The curtain is removed and they exchange garlands. The bride's parents now unite the couple by joining their hands.

✤✤✤✤✤✤

Mangalashtak

Mangalshtak consists of songs in praise of the gods, praying for the well-being of the bride. They are traditionally sung upon arrival of the bride at the mantap. These eight verses vary from region to region in India.

✤✤✤✤✤✤

The Bride Sitting on her Father's Lap

"Why did you not ask the bride to sit on her father's lap during the tying of the mangalasutra?" This question was posed a couple of decades ago by an elderly relative of the bride. This practice clearly originated during those periods when marriages took place between couples at a very young age and the step is still in vogue in some families. This practice is outdated these days when the principals are in their twenties and older.

Furthermore, if the entire ceremony takes place with everyone standing, then this becomes even less relevant. Again, there is an element of nostalgia, of custom, and a father-child bond that may require the addition of what is now an option rather than a necessity.

✣✣✣✣✣✣

Hasta Milap/ Joining Hands

Subsequent to Jai Mala or Jayamala (garlanding) and as the bride and groom turn to face the audience, the bride's father steps up and places the right hand of his daughter in the right hand of the groom.

The groom is instructed to chant the following:

गृभ्णामि ते सौभगत्वाय हस्तंमया पत्या जरदश्टिर्यथाअसः
भगोअर्यमा सविता पुरंधिर्मह्यंत्वादुर्गार्ह पत्याय देवाः

gṛbhṇāmi tē saubhagatvāya hastammayā patyā jaradaśṭiryathāasa:
bhagōaryamā savitā purandhirmahyam tvādurgārha patyāya dēvā

(RV X.85.36)

O bride, I shall hold your hand in order to live long with you and our progeny through the grace of Aŗyama, Savitr and Indra who have granted us the status of householders.

(VP)

✣✣✣✣✣✣

The Bride Moves from Right to Left

"I will come to your left if..." says the bride, extracting certain promises, during the wedding ceremony in some traditions. The basis for this procedure may be explained as follows: after the tying of the mangalasutra or a similar climactic step, it is the generally accepted practice for the priest to ask the bride, who up to this point stands or sits to the groom's right, to change sides. This possibly has its origin in the belief that Mahalakshmi, the consort of Mahavishnu resides in his vakshasthala, i.e. close to his heart, a stance which may be viewed in many pictorial and sculptural representations of Vishnu. In any case, this later step is also the basis for managing the early positioning of the groom and bride upon arrival at the mantap. It is best to guide the groom and his party to stand (or sit) on the left of the mantap facing the audience. When the bride and her party arrive, they are then stationed to the right of the groom's family. Thus when the indicated change does occur and she moves to his left, she has now moved from her family of birth to join her new family.

✣✣✣✣✣✣

Gatha Bandhana/ Tying the Knot

It is common to tie the edge of the bride's saree or scarf or shawl to an upper garment of the groom to signify their bond before they circle the fire. It is best to have the couple repeat the following mantra during the tying:

बध्नामि सत्यग्रंथिना मनश्च हृदयं च तॆ
यदॆतद् हृदयं तव तदस्तु हृदयं मम
यदॆतद् हृदयम् मम तदस्तु हृदयं तव

badhnāmi satyagranthinā manaśca hṛdayam ca tē
yadētad hṛdayam tava tadastu hṛdayam mama
yadētad hṛudayam mama tadastu hṛdayam tava

(Sama Brahmana 1.3.89)

I shall tie this knot of truth to tie our minds and hearts together.
May your heart be mine and may my heart be yours.

✤✤✤✤✤✤

Ashmarohana/ Stepping on Stone

Many families observe the tradition in which the bride is requested to touch a stone or step on to a stone slab with her right foot to emphasize the need for her to be a stable component of the new family. A small slab of stone may be placed for the bride to step on as she completes leading the groom on the last round of Laaja Homa. As this is a blessing the priest may chant the shloka as the bride touches the stone.

आरोहेममश्मानं
अश्मेव त्वं स्थिराभव
अभितिष्ठ पृतन्यतो
अवबाधस्व पृतनायत:

ārōhēmamaśmānam
aśmēva tvam sthirābhava
abhitiṣṭha pṛtanyantō
avabādhasva pṛtanāyata:

Mount this rock here
Be as firm as this rock
In the midst of any conflict
Remain as stable as this rock

(ParasGS 1:7:1)

✤✤✤✤✤✤

Vows

Any or all of the following mantras may be chosen by the couple. There are several suitable moments to insert these into the program: directly following the Mangalyadharanam or ring exchange or before or after Saptapadi. The couple may exchange the vows directly or they may both repeat after the priest who can have them repeat the mantras in Sanskrit and/or the translations in English.

ॐ मम व्रते हृदयं ते ददामि
मम चित्तमनुचित्तं ते अस्तु
मम वाचं ऐक मना जुषस्व
प्रजापति स्त्वानि युनक्तु मह्यं
पारस्कर गृह्यसूत्र

ōm mama vratē hṛudayam tē dadāmi
mama cittamanucittam tē astu
mama vācam ēka manā juṣasva
prajāpati stvāni yunaktu mahyam

(ParasGS 1.8.81)

Our hearts and minds, may they be one, may our words delight each other. May divinity unite us both.

✤✤✤✤

पश्येम शरदःशतं
जीवेम शरदः शतं
शृणुयाम शरदः शतं

paśyēma śarada: śatam
jīvēma śarada: śatam
śṛṇuyāma śarada: śatam

(VS 36-24)

Let us live together in each other's sight,
in each other's company,
listening to each other,
for a hundred years.

✤✤✤✤

अहमस्मि सहमानातो त्वमसि सासहिः
मामनुप्रते मनो पथा वारिव धावतु
सम्नौ भगासो अग्मत संचित्तानि समव्रता
यथा सम्मनसौ भूत्वा सखायाविव सचावहै

ahamasmi sahamānātō tvamasi sāsahi:
māmanupratē manō pathā vāriva dhāvatu
samnau bhagāsō agmata sancittāni samavratā
yathā sammanasau bhūtvā sakhāyāviva sacāvahai

May my mind move with your mind in love,
Let us move like flowing water on the path of life:
My life is linked to your life, my mind with your mind, my vows with your vows
Let us work together like two friends, like two seekers of the same goal.

(Lal, P. The Vedic Hindu Marriage Ceremony, 1996)

✤✤✤✤

ॐ क इदं कस्मा अदात्
कामः कामायादात्
कामो दाता कामःप्रतिगृहीता
कामः समुद्रमाविशात्
कामेन त्वा प्रतिगृह्णानि
कामैतत् ते
ॐ स्वस्ति

(SSSRatnamala)

ōm ka idam kasmā adāt
kāma: kāmāyādāt
kāmō dātā kāma: pratigṛhītā
kāma: samudramāviśāt
kāmēna tvā pratigṛhṇāni
kāmētat te
om svasti

Om Who is giving to whom?
Love is giving to Love
Love is the giver and Love is the receiver
Love is the inexhaustible ocean
You come to me with love O Love, this is all your doing
Om All is holy

(Lal, ibid)

✣✣✣✣✣✣

Talambraalu

This practice is common in Andhra weddings and appears to be related to the abundance of rice grown on the fertile fields of Andhra Pradesh, courtesy of the two great rivers Krishna and Godavari. In this ceremony raw rice is poured in large handfuls by the groom and the bride over each other's head in a joyful manner conveying prosperity and abundance now and for ever. It is best to play a musical selection which is joyous and vibrant while this takes place.

✣✣✣✣✣✣

Ceremonial Presentation of Clothing to the Bride by the Bridegroom's Family

Some families have a tradition in which the bridegroom's mother presents clothing to the bride (a saree and blouse) after the Kanyadanam ceremony. The bride then retires for a few minutes to change into those clothes and return for the climactic step of Mangalyadharanam. Clearly this provides a break in the sequence and is an opportunity for a musical interlude or offering of song.

✣✣✣✣✣✣

Dhruva Darshanam/ Sighting the Pole Star and Arundhati

Towards the end of the main ceremony, it is customary to include the step known as Dhruva darshanam, the sighting by the bride of the pole star. Dhruva (Polaris) is seen near the constellation group known as the Saptarishi Mandala (Seven Sages; L. Ursa Major, the Great Bear) in Sanskrit. Because this star appears stationary at the same location irrespective of the earth's movement, Hindus have incorporated this feature into a ceremony where Dhruva is acknowledged with a prayer seeking such stability be granted to the bride in her new world.

The Sapta Rishis are the following: Kasyapa, Atri, Bharadwaja, Viswamitra, Gauthama, Jamadagni and Vasishta. (This list may vary. See Glossary) The wives of these sages consider Vasishta's wife, Arundhati (also a star), to be a model of chastity, a pativrata. Therefore in addition to viewing the pole star, the bride is asked by the priest to imagine sighting yet another star in the sky, i.e. Arundhati, and pray for a chaste life.

ध्रुवं ते राजा वरुणो
ध्रुवं देवो बृहस्पति:
ध्रुवंत इंद्रश्चाग्निश्च
राष्ट्रं धारयतां ध्रुवं

dhruvan tē rājā varuṇō
dhruvam dēvō bṛhaspati:
dhruvanta indraṣāgniṣca
rāṣtram dhārayatām dhruvam

(RV X. 173. 5)

Steadfast, may Varuna the king,
Steadfast, the god Brhaspati,

Steadfast, may Indra, steadfast too,
May Agni keep thy reign steadfast.

(Griffith)

Bride's prayer addressing Dhruva:

ध्रुवमसि ध्रुवाहं पतिकुले भूयासं

dhruvamasi dhruvāham patikulē bhūyāsam

You are forever stable. May I be as stable in my husband's home.

✤✤✤✤✤✤

Sindhura Danam/ Sindhur Application

A practice prevalent in many North Indian families is the application of sindhur (vermillion powder similar to kumkum) by the groom to the hair parting on the bride's head. Some use a coin, slightly wetted, so that the powder adheres to its rim which is drawn over the parting for easy transfer. This is done close to the end of the ceremony. An appropriate mantra is the following:

सुमंगलीरियं वधूरिमां
समेत पश्यत
सौभाग्यमस्यै दत्वायाथास्तं विपरेतन

sumangalīriyam vadhūrimām
samēta paśyata
saubhāgyamasyai datvāyāthāstām viparētana

May good fortune attend this bride. Gather here one and all
and bless her before you depart.

✤✤✤✤✤✤

Drshti/Warding off the Evil Eye

Those who grew up in villages in India will undoubtedly recall the fear of some mothers that children might be subjected to the peril known as the "evil eye" and consequently suffer illnesses, injuries or even death. This was considered especially likely if the child/youth was a boy or an only child or considered good-looking. This is an inherited belief and weakness prevalent in many ancient cultures and in India was given prompt attention after a young person returned from outside the home.

One of the several methods practiced in South India was to take a handful of red chilies held tightly in the right hand and move the hand in front of the "victim" three times in a large circle clockwise as if performing an arati. After the last round the entire contents in the hand are thrown on to the fire in the kitchen on which some cooking might be in progress. Lo and behold, the individual was now freed from any possible harm! The procedure was declared to be especially successful if the resulting smoke, which under ordinary circumstances would result in fumes and coughs, produced no such effects on the onlookers. Everyone was satisfied and life returned to normal.

Another example is to use a coconut, instead of red chilis, shattering the same after the third round. This is commonly practiced when a deity is taken out in procession around the village or when a groom/bride/couple return from a similar procession. The offering and shattering of watermelons in front of new cars or farm vehicles (during the Dasara festival) is part of this custom. Similarly one sees very often, especially in villages, a small black dot on the cheek of a child dressed up for the day. The theory is that bad disturbances are distracted by the sight of this "blemish" and minimized.

These ideas have naturally crept into wedding ceremonies although the practice is gradually disappearing. Because the bride and the groom are always especially attractive in their wedding attire (as is evident from the appended photographs!), it is not uncommon to see a variety of practices even now. Sometimes, a group of ladies will approach the couple near the end of the ceremony with a vessel containing colorful rice balls and go through the same motion described above. The rice balls are supposed to draw in the evil designs and are later discarded. And in his village, the author remembers seeing a bride dressed in a man's suit and taken out in procession on the presumption that she could not possibly look beautiful in men's clothing and therefore would attract no evil eye consequence!

If the families wish this step to be included in the ceremonies, it is best to allow them the practice before the final blessings. It is recommended that some music be chosen to play while this goes on for a few minutes at the mantap.

✣✣✣✣✣✣

Unjal/ Oonjal

Unjal is a ceremony popular among South Indians and sometimes discussed in the course of planning a wedding. This is a practice in which women take a special interest and sing a variety of songs appropriate to the occasion while the couple swing gently back and forth, seated on a swing. Flower petals may be sprinkled on the couple while they swing. It is not uncommon for relatives and friends to persuade other young couples to take turns on the swing in a joyous celebration by the whole group of families. This practice may have its origin in certain sevas (service) offered to deities at major temples. Special halls are built in the open for this very purpose where a divine couple, Rama and Sita, Krishna and Rukmini, Srinivasa and Padmavati, for example, are taken in procession, seated on a swing, and swung gently to music rendered by the devotees and/or the nadaswaram ensemble at the temple.

✣✣✣✣✣✣

Games

In arranged marriages, not so long ago, when the young people to be wedded were virtual strangers to each other and when wedding ceremonies and entertainment were conducted over a week, it was customary to include certain games. These games might include throwing flower balls at or to each other. They involved mock fights or tests over snatching a ring out of a tray/vessel filled with water or rice or milk. They could include mutual feeding of sweets or pouring rice over each other. Pouring bowls of rice on each other's heads is discussed in Talambraalu.

We have avoided adding these games to the main ceremony except as optional for several reasons: (1) the objective of such games was, as stated above, to "break the ice" when the couples barely knew each other, (2) the framework proposed in this book has a Vedic basis with very meaningful and joyous mantras that create an obvious and appropriate sense of solemnity, and (3) the time constraints of the modern wedding ceremony.

Understanding that there may be a nostalgic need to see the couple play these games, we recommend that they take place before or after the formal ceremony. There is often ample opportunity for more fun, music and dance in the days and hours leading up to the wedding.

✣✣✣✣✣✣

Presentation of Gifts

Some families have the custom of presenting gifts to the couple at the mantap as a part of the ceremony. It is recommended that this practice be restricted to immediate family members as it is likely to disengage and distract the wedding assembly, and detract from what may so far have been an enjoyable and disciplined event. If certain relatives need to offer gifts at the mantap, the person in charge of music is well advised to play some appropriate music. Some relevant songs or performances could be added here.

✣✣✣✣✣✣

Sashtanga / Blessings from Elders

Sashtanga or prostration before the elders in the family and the priest seeking their blessings is a traditional Hindu way of receiving blessings after any major ritual. If the couple chooses to observe this, then right after the announcement of their names as husband and wife, they may be directed to prostrate before the priest and previously designated elders from both families, beginning with the eldest. The elders in turn may throw a few grains of akshata on the heads of both, and touch the couple's heads with both hands.

✣✣✣✣✣✣

Vidai/ Farewell to the Bride

A practice commonly observed in Gujarati weddings is bidding goodbye to the bride at the end of the ceremony. Even though she may not actually be leaving for her new home at that moment, her departure is observed symbolically. Members of the bride's family conduct her to the entrance door of the wedding hall and perform the send-off formalities (hugs and kisses, etc.) and let her leave with a plate of flowers, fruits and sweets in the company of the groom. Normally the couple enter a decorated car and go around the building and return to the same entrance which now serves as the entrance to her new home. The priest may then have them do the puja to the threshold and follow the procedures outlined in the Grhapravesham ceremony described below.

✣✣✣✣✣✣

Grhapravesham/ Ceremony at the New Home

Some families wish to conduct this step upon returning to their own home when the bridegroom's family formally receives the bride into their home or they may choose to complete the formality right after the wedding in a pre-designated section of the wedding hall.

Grhapravesham is performed when the new bride enters her new home for the first time. The format suggested below assures that she is now placed in charge of her own home (unless she lives with her husband's family) and ceremoniously makes her grand entrance blessed by the assembled.

The bride and groom along with her family (parents and other selected family members) approach the new home with Vedic chants and carrying plates of fruits, flowers, kalasha, uddharane, and deepa (lamp). The bridegroom's family stands ready to greet the bride and the groom into the new household.

The priest chants:

ॐ नमस्सदसे, नमस्सदसस्पतये
नमस्सखीनां पुरोगाणां चक्षुषे
नमो दिवे नमः पृथिव्यै
सप्रथसभांमे गोपाय येचसभ्यास्सभासदः
तानि इंद्रियावतः कुरु सर्वमायुरुपासतां
सर्वेभ्यः श्री महान्तेभ्यो नमः

ōm namassadasē, namassadasaspatayē
namassakhīnām purōgāṇām cakśuṣē

namō divē nama: pṛthivyai
saprathasabhāmē gōpāya yēcasabhyāssabhāsada:
tāni indriyāvata: kuru sarvamāyurupām satām
sarvēbhya: mahāntēbhyō nama:

Salutations to the assembly and its leader (presider), friends, family
and other notables present here. Salutations to heaven and earth.
May all the honorable and powerful belonging to the family, present or absent,
in this assembly be blessed with long life and be protected .

Just before entering, the bride and the groom should worship the threshold as follows by offering the upacharas (refer to Pujas, Appendix VI) by using akshata, water, incense, deepa, fruits, flowers). Begin with either or both mothers applying kumkum and haldi to the threshold as the groom begins to chant:

द्वारश्रियै नमः

dvāraśriyai nama:

Salutations to the goddess presiding over this entrance.

ॐ इंद्राय नमः
ॐ अग्नये नमः
ॐ यमाय नमः
ॐ नैरुतये नमः
ॐ वरुणाय नमः
ॐ वायुवे नमः
ॐ कुबेराय नमः

ॐ ईशानाय नम:

इति दिक्पालक पुजां समर्पयामि

ōm indrāya nama:
ōm agnayē nama:
ōm yamāya nama:
ōm nairutayē nama:
ōm varuṇāya nama:
ōm vāyuvē nama:
ōm kubērāya nama:
ōm īśānāya nama:

iti dikpālaka pujām samarpayāmi

Salutations to Indra, Agni, Yama, Nairuta, Varuna, Vayu, Kubera and Ishana, the lords of the East, Southeast, South, Southwest, West, Northwest, North and Northeast. Thus I offer puja to the lords of these directions.

The groom may now do the sankalpam as follows:

पूर्वोक्त ऐवंगुण विशेषण विशिष्ठायां अस्यां शुभ तिथौ
श्री भगवदाग्नया श्रीमन्नारायण प्रीत्यर्थं
नूतनागार प्रवेशं करिष्ये

pūrvōkta ēvamguṇa viśēṣaṇa viśiṣṭhāyām asyām śubha tiṭhau
śrī bhagavadāgnayā śrīmannārāyaṇa prītyartham
nūtanāgāra pravēsham kariṣyē

With the sacred features of the day mentioned as before, I shall now,
on this auspicious day, under the orders of the gods and to please the
supreme god Narayana, enter the new home.

The party may now enter as music is rendered with the bride leading, with her right foot inside first, followed by the groom and rest of the party.

The bridegroom recites the following Veda mantra (or repeat after the priest):

इह प्रियं प्रजयौ ते॒ समृध्यतामस्मिन् गृहे॒ गार्हपत्याय जागृहि
ऐ॒नापत्या तन्वं सं स्पृशस्वाथ जिर्विर्विदथमा वदासि

iha priyam prajayau tē samṛdhyatāmasmin gṛhē gārhapatyāya jāgṛhi
ēnāpatyā tanvam sam spṛśasvātha jirvirvidathamā vadāsi

Happy be thou and prosper with thy children here: be vigilant to rule
thy household in this home. Closely unite thy body with this thy husband.
And may you both rule this house (give orders to your household).

(Griffith, Apte, RV X. 85. 27)

Version 2.

Enter this your household to rule with vigilance. May you be happy
and prosper with offspring. Unite with your husband
and may you both be lords of this dwelling.

Previously sanctified water (See Pujas, Appendix VI) is sprinkled towards the four directions (east, south, west and north) and finally at the center with appropriate mantras shown below chanted by either the priest or the groom repeating after the priest.

ब्रह्मचतेक्षत्रंच पूर्वेस्थूणे अभिरक्षतु
यज्ञश्च दक्षिणाश्च दक्षिणे
इषश्चोर्जश्पापरे मित्रश्चवरुणश्चोत्तरे
धर्मस्ते स्थूणाराज श्रीस्ते स्तूपः

brahmacatēkṣatranca pūrvēsthūṇē abhirakṣatu
yajnaśca dakśiṇāṣca dakṣiṇē
iṣaścōrjaśpāparē mitraścavaruṇaścōttarē
dharmastē sthūṇārāja śrīstē stūpa:

(PP, 245)

Let this sprinkling [with sanctified water] be on Brahma and his dominion on the Eastern post, this on the Southern post south of the sacrificial fire, this on the

Western post wishing wealth and vigor, this on the Northern post representing the Sun and Varuna, and this at the center pillar representing the queenly dharma.

The ceremony may conclude with the following mantra chanted by the couple

ॐ सहना ववतु
सहनौ भुनक्तु
सहवीर्यं करवावहै
तेजस्विनावधीतमस्तु
मा विद्विशावहै
ॐ शांतिः शांतिः शांतिः

ōm sahanā vavatu
sahanau bhunaktu

sahavīryam karavāvahai
tējaswināvadhītamastu
mā vidviśāvahai
ōm śānti: śānti: śāntihi

May Brahman protect us both
May he bestow on us both the fruit of knowledge
May we both obtain the energy to acquire the knowledge
May what we both study reveal the truth!
May we cherish no ill feeling toward each other
Om Peace, Peace, Peace!

The bride is blessed finally by the priest with the following mantra

साम्राज्ञी श्वशुरो भव
साम्राज्ञी श्वश्रुशां भव
ननंदारी साम्राज्ञी भव
साम्राज्ञी अधिदेव्रषु

sāmrājnī śvaśurō bhava
sāmrājnī śvaśruśām bhava
nanandārī sāmrājnī bhava
sāmrājnī adhidēvraśu

Be queenly with your father-in-law
Be queenly with your mother-in-law
Be queenly with his sisters
Be queenly with his brothers

Appendix V: Indian Bridal Attire.

1. Indian Bridal Jewelry.

As befits a civilization that traded textiles, gold and gemstones to the Roman Empire, India still places an emphasis on these accessories to a wedding. Bridal attire is resplendent with color, richness of fabric, and adornments in jewels from head to toe.

The ancient tradition of *Sola shringaar* or the sixteen traditional adornments for all parts of the body may still be a step in the preparations for a Rajasthani wedding, but it can be expected to make an appearance at any wedding:

"I offer you my daughter, standing by my side, foremost among young women, covered in jewels,..." says the would-be father-in-law in that well known line from the wedding ceremony.

This jewelry was, historically, a large part of the Indian bride's dower, her "stridhan," and on her wedding day she might wear essentially all of it. In fact the variety of bangles, earrings, necklaces, armlets, nose-pins, rings (for fingers and toes) in sets and unique pieces is so vast and generally available that only jewelry that might be worn by a North or South Indian bride on her special day will be reviewed here:

- *maangatika/ tika/ tikli,* a pearled or gold chain hooked to the center hair parting with a small or elaborate jewelled pendant that hangs on the brow; this is specifically bridal or classical dancer's jewelry.
- *matha patti/ nethi chutti,* hairline ornament similar to the tika, but with 3 gold chains that support it at the hairline and parting.
- *jhoomka/ jimmikki,* the dangling jewelled earrings, also supported on chains that

attach to the hair. Again, this is formal bridal jewelry, often in meenakari (enamelled gold) and bead work. Smaller earrings of this type are not uncommon for regular wear.

- *nath/ mookuthi,* large jewelled gold or silver nose-ring, with dependent chain that attaches to the hair on one side for support. This, along with the wedding sari and tika pendant, were and still are in the Punjab, the traditional gift of the bride's maternal uncle.

- *mangalasutra, or maangalyam,* generally a gold chain necklace, often with additional gold or black beads and/or pendant(s) with caste/subcaste/ community significance, tied around the neck of a bride by the groom during a significant moment in the wedding ceremony. Also called a *tali* or *thali,* it can be a simple gold pendant on several, usually three, tumeric-tinted threads, knotted by auspicious, i.e. married women with living husbands, sumangalis, and then tied with three knots around the neck of the bride by the groom. It fulfils the purpose of a Western wedding ring, and will be put aside and not worn again by a widowed woman.

- *haar,* decorative gold, jewelled necklace in many lengths and designs.

- *baajubandh,* gold or silver jewelled armlet; this item formerly held an amulet.

- *mekhala, kardhani,* waist chain, often silver, with silver key-chain holder.

- *kamarband/ oddiyanam,* gold wedding belt, worn with a sari, lehengha or lengha; more often seen worn with classical dance attire.

- *arsi,* thumb-ring with inset mirror. This carries a heavy weight of romance as it was once the means of the first view a veiled bride had of her new husband, seated beside her at her wedding ceremony.

- *anguti,* a gold ring, worn on the index finger, with or without gemstone.
- *hath panja,* wristlet with five rings attached, decorated with gems and tiny bells.
- *choodamani,* large round gold bejewelled hair ornament fixed at the crown and circled with a wreath of jasmine buds.
- *sooryan chandran,* gold ornamental hair brooches, in the shape of sun and moon, fixed on either side of the hair parting.
- *kankan/ bala/ kada,* decorative thick bangles and cuff bangles in gold or elaborate kundan work (gems and precious beads set in gold) and/or ornamented in meenakari.
- *churi,* slender gold or colored glass bangle, worn in sets of 12.
- *mama chura,* the red and white ivory bangles worn by a Punjabi bride, presented by her maternal uncle; they are placed on her arms, up to four dozen, in a special ceremony, with silver and beaten gold ornaments (*kaleeras*) attached at the wrist.
- *nupur/ payal,* anklet, usually a silver chain or cuff and chains with tiny bells; sometimes with one to five toe rings attached. Gold anklets are not common as silver has been preferred for a lowly body part such as the foot.
- *bichwa/ amvat/ nupur,* also, silver toe-rings, traditionally two simple silver bands.
- *jhoomar,* silver or gold hair ornament with spreading chains.
- *parandi/ kunjalam/ pinnal,* beaded, silk ornament for the end of a braid.

Some family traditions do include the ceremony in which the bridegroom fixes silver rings on the toes (usually the second toe of both feet) of the bride as an essential step in the later part of the main ceremony. It was a widely recognized sign of her new wifely status. Modern young women have hesitated in recent decades to include this tradition and have tended not to wear toe rings. But, like multiple ear piercings and nose-studs, they are now part of a fashion trend that comes and goes, and even vary in design.

Folklore attributes the use of toe rings or anklets to none other than Sita in the Ramayana. Rama's brother is asked if he recognizes the jewelry which Sita had dropped unnoticed by Ravana as she was being abducted at great speed. In a hyperbole of modesty, Lakshmana simply replies that the only jewelry he does recognize are her anklets which he sees as he prostrates in front of his elder brother's wife seeking her blessings!

This episode is included in P. Lal's prose transcreation of the Ramayana (Lal, P. *The Ramayana of Valmiki* , p. 89, 1989) citing Kishkindha, 6-22:

ऐवं उक्तः तु रामेण लक्ष्मणो वाक्यमिदमब्रवीत्
नाहम् जानामि केयूरे नाहम् जानामि
कुन्डले नूपुरेतु अभिजानामि नित्यम् पाद अभिवन्दनात्

ēvam ukta: tu rāmēṇa lakshḥmaṇō vākyamidamabravīt
nāham jānāmi kēyūrē nāham jānāmi kuṇḍalē
nūpuretu abhijānāmi nityam pāda abhivandanāt

Upon hearing Rama, Lakshmana responded thus: I cannot
recognize her bracelets, nor her earrings but I do
recognize her anklets on her feet as I see them while
prostrating in front of her (to seek her blessings)

Addenda:

There are distinct regional ornaments worn nowadays mainly by brides. Besides the Punjabi mama chura, these include the Kashmiri cord earring extensions, iron bangles (loha) and silver filigree in eastern India, and red lac bangles, and pearl strings in Maharashtra. Designs range from geometric to natural motifs of flowers, leaves, seeds, bird, serpentine, butterfly and animal shapes. While gold has always been the preferred metal and diamond the preferred gemstone, jewelry in India has generally been made of many substances: silver and other metals and auspicious metallic combinations such as panchalohana; wood and bamboo; lac; glass and ceramic.

Historically Indian men have not been backward in adorning themselves in ropes of pearls, gold chains, armlets and cuffs, and jewelled rings. The modern groom is more likely to sport a good watch and possibly a gold ring with a lucky gemstone. If he has chosen to wear a turban, he might also add such turban ornaments as such as the *sarpech* or jewelled aigret brooch fastened to the front, or a gold chain set (*kalagi*) for draping over the turban.

2. Indian Bridal Clothing.

Western guests at a Hindu wedding are likely to marvel at the rainbow river of silks visible in the ranks of the guests alone. What could a bride wear to stand out in this riot of color? Generally not white, although a richly gold-embroidered red or green bordered white or ivory-colored saree is often worn in the south of India. Traditionally, the color for Indian brides has always been a shade of red or gold. Nowadays fashion dictates what shade and what decoration. The current trend is for heavily beaded, gold and/or silver embroidered attire which can range from saree and blouse to skirt, blouse and veil or tunic, pant and veil combinations from one part or day of the celebration to the finale.

Clothing for the bride includes:

- *ghomta/ odhani,* veil or shawl in varying lengths and drapes; there are many more regional names for this item; in the Rig Veda, Suryaa's shawl is the only bridal garment that is defined with any clarity as she is otherwise clothed in metaphors (See Origins chapter) and it remains, in North India, the quintessential garment that is or used to be draped over whatever else the bride was wearing, be it saree or skirt or salwar kameez. In Vedic times it was gifted after the wedding to the officiating priest. In historic times it was one of the gifts of the maternal uncle to the bride. It was generally red, trimmed with gold lace or tinsel ribbon. More often now it is integrated into the total outfit.

- *anchal,* skirt, with an attached or extended wraparound veil or shawl, worn with a choli; the loose end of the saree or veil.

- *choli,* short, close-fitting blouse, traditionally with short sleeves, otherwise elbow-length or sleeveless; worn under sarees and with skirt outfits.

- *sari/ saree,* draped garment of usually 6 (sometimes 9) yards of silk or silk interwoven with gold thread, usually in shades of red or gold for weddings, with a gold thread border or embroidery.

- *salwar kameez,* in red velvet or silk; this is the two piece outfit of the Punjabi bride: tunic, matching pants gathered at the ankle, with added veil or shawl (*dupatta*), all gold and bead embroidery, and edged with gold lace.

- *lehnga/ lehenga* outfit, ankle-length paneled skirt, with matching choli and veil; a heavily embroidered, bejwelled version is now a wedding favorite. It can also be worn with a kameez or sleeved tunic. The traditional Rajasthani *ghagara* is a many pleated or gathered, almost circular, skirt, worn with choli and veil.

- *garara/ gagra* outfit, as above except with a divided skirt or pant effect from waist to knee, flouncing out from knee to ankle, worn with tunic top and veil.

Clothing for the Groom:

The modern mid twentieth century urban Indian groom was inclined to turn up in a Western-style suit, topped with a turban or decorated white pith and tinsel coronet, further decorated with a small veil of jasmine bud strings. But just as weddings in India have become more elaborate in the past few decades and a complete bridal industry has sprung forth to meet the need, so has the idea of attire for the groom evolved. Unlike in the West, the role of groom is not eclipsed by the role of the bride. He shares an equal footing, a procession of his own, and a larger speaking role. His clothes are still less elaborate in color and style but can be equally elegant. While a suit may still be preferred for a wedding reception, some of the following garments for the main event:

- *dhoti/ antariya/ lungi,* a 6-yard length of fine cotton or silk, white or natural, unstitched, draped from the waist to the ankle and tied in front; often passed through the legs for a pant effect, with one end hanging in folds at the front. This garment can have a simple gold or elaborate colored silk and gold woven border. Worn with an upper cloth, this is still the wedding garment of choice for South Indian brahmins.

- *uttariya,* upper cloth, usually worn with a dhoti, across the bare upper body, or as a waist band, or over the shoulder with a kurta or jacket.

- *kayabandhan,* waist cloth, for tying or wrapping.

- *sherwani* outfit, a tunic-style coat or long shirt, differing in length, worn over a dhoti, drawstring straight pants or churidhar pants. Worn long in embroidered heavy silk with matching pants or churidhars, with or without a matching vest or kamarband, this is the favorite current wedding attire for the average groom.

- *churidhar,* origin of the pants style known as jodhpurs in the West; silk or cotton pants tight from the knee down.

- *achkan,* a fitted jacket, better known as a Nehru jacket in the West, with high collar, long sleeve, in light wool, heavy silk or cotton; for a wedding this jacket can be in white, ivory, natural, brown, or light pastels; with gold brocade or embroidered detail.

- *kamarband/ patka,* the groom's waist band is usually brocaded silk.

- *sadri/* vest, vest or waistcoat in embroidered light wool or silk brocade.

- *pagari/ safa/ turban,* fitted headgear or a long unstitched length of cloth, usually fine cotton, wound around a cap or coiled hair. This is a historical hallmark of Indian men's attire, and at one time each Indian state had its distinct style in terms of color, fabric, pattern and method of tying. For weddings, it is worn in bright cotton or rich silk brocade. Some grooms do not cover their heads at all, and some traditions call for small coronets or caps in varying styles.

- *jootis/ mojaris,* leather shoes with pointed toes made of leather in camel, goat or sheepskin; first described for the West by Alexander's historians, these are a traditional favorite for wedding wear, especially at their finest, worked with gold embroidery and beads.

3. Floral adornments:

Flowers probably preceded jewelry as ornaments for the bride in ancient India. They are still an important part of the ceremony. Aside from the flowers used to bedeck the mantap, and petals used to sprinkle on the bride, flower accessories include:

- *malas,* wedding garlands for bride and groom to exchange with each other at a signal part of the ceremony, Jai Mala; and for other members of the wedding party to exchange, if desired, at the time of Milni or Swagat(am).

- *malli poo,* jasmine buds roped around the full chignon (*juda*) or small side chignon in the case of some South Indian brides.

- *kondai,* jasmine, and other flowers mounted onto stiff paper, cane or cloth to construct floral coronets or the long *moggina jade* that covers the braid of a Mysore bride.

- headpiece or coronet, of the Bengali bride and groom, crafted of white pith.

- jasmine bud "veil" screen for a North Indian bridegroom: short vertical strings attached to the front of the turban or coronet.

4. Indian Bridal Cosmetics.

- *sindhur or sindhoor,* the red vermillion powder or paste that is another hall mark of the traditional bride when applied to the simanta, the parting of her hair, during the wedding ceremony. It is also used for the bindu.

- *bindu, tilaka,* the round mark or streak on the forehead of the bride which used to denote a married woman. The bindu is now a fashion trend, varied by color, shape and substance. Jewels, beads and sequins have been popular more recently for brides and for general wear. It has also been a fashion not to wear it at all, except for weddings, pujas and special events. A black dot, made with kohl or a modern eyebrow pencil is sometimes applied somewhere on the bride's face to ward off the evil eye.

- *alaktak,* bright red foot paint, seen mainly now on the soles and edges of feet of classical Indian dancers, has largely been supplanted by the use of mehndi or henna.

- *mehndi,* a paste made from the dried leaves of the henna plant is used for elaborate tattoo-like decorations on hands and feet in a delicate shade of reddish brown. The patterns last for around three weeks, and the application process for the bride and her wedding party is now a popular pre-wedding event.

- *haldi,* turmeric; the yellow powder made from the root of this plant was an important part of beauty preparations for the bride-to-be. After the pre-wedding ritual bathing, turmeric was rubbed into her skin to give her a much admired golden glow. Turmeric still has a ritual use during weddings as well as other Hindu rites. It is applied to color the coconut for Kanyadanam and to tint the rice (*akshata*) used for blessings.

- *kohl/ kajal/ anjana,* sulfide of antimony used for lining the eyes; usually in powder form or made from carbon and herbs mixed into a paste. Nowadays it is usually replaced by modern makeup.

- *sandal* paste, from the naturally aromatic roots and heartwood of the sandalwood tree (Latin s*antalum album*), used to create the line of white dots that follow the twin arches of the eyebrows and accentuate this recognized item of beauty as well as the bindu for Bengali and other North Indian brides. Nowadays this is also sometimes replaced by a line of colored designs, either painted, natural leaf or petal, or sequins or jewels.

It is important to keep in mind that terminology for clothing and jewelry differs from one end of India to the other, expressed in many languages and traditions. Only the most common terms are included here.

Appendix VI : Pujas

Note that the materials and other ritual arrangements used at the pujas may be brought to the mantap later for use during the processionals and the main ceremony. Abbreviated pujas to Mahaganapati and Gauri are included below:

Preparation of the altar:

First and foremost begin with cleansing, i.e. clean the area where the altar is to be set up. This should face the eastern direction if possible. A small bench or a wooden table or a cardboard box covering an area no larger than 36" x 24" and about 15" to 24" tall is adequate. Cover it with a clean cloth and arrange a picture of the god/goddess to be worshipped. Similarly pictures or images of the family godhead and guru may also be arranged on the altar.

Materials and arrangement:

- Prepare one or two deepas (lamps) with cotton wicks soaking in oil. Place the lamp/s about 6" in front of the picture if it is one lamp, or about 10" apart if two lamps. Do not light these until you are ready to begin the puja.
- Prepare a worship plate (stainless steel, silver or other metal, 12" to 24" diameter) by placing on it small vessels (cup-like, preferably metallic) of kumkum, turmeric, one square of camphor, sandal powder or paste, a dozen agarbatti sticks (incense sticks), a bell, and a matchbox.
- Prepare another plate, 12" or 24" diameter, metallic or wicker and put a variety or five kinds of fruits (bananas, apples, oranges, etc.) and a variety of leaves and flowers.
- You will need an arati plate. This can be a small metal plate with one or five wicks soaking in oil or ghee.

- You will also need a small cup of akshata (raw rice dampened slightly with water and colored with turmeric.) This mixture should be prepared a day earlier so that it is completely dry.
- Covered dishes of your favorite prasaadam or sweets may be placed in front of the altar.
- A metallic urn large enough to contain a couple of mugs of water should be filled with water and placed in front of the altar. You will need a smaller vessel, preferably a metallic straight-walled tumbler into which water will be poured during the service.
- A dispenser, called uddharana, or a simple metallic spoon to dispense water from the tumbler will be needed.
- You will need a piece of cloth, white for a male deity and colorful cloth for a goddess for an offering during the puja.

Now you are ready to begin. Light the lamps and a couple of agarbattis. In a few moments you will be invoking and receiving a godhead and therefore the principal mood should be one of joy and bhakti, but the mind should be relaxed.

PUJA TO MAHAGANAPATI

It is customary for the bridegroom to perform, with his family and friends attending, a puja to Mahaganapati and to pray for a successful wedding ceremony without any vighna or obstacle.

After ringing the bell to ward off any bad vibrations and tendencies in the area and before starting the puja proper, it is essential to contemplate Mahaganapati to assure ourselves that no obstacles interfere with a smooth performance of the puja rituals. Thus, with folded hands chant the following:

करिष्यमाणस्य कर्मणः निर्विघ्नेन परिसमाप्त्यर्थं

आदौ महागणपति स्मरणं करिश्ये

kariśyamāṇasya karmaṇa: nirvignēna parisamāptyartham
ādau mahāgaṇapati smaraṇam karishyē

So that the ceremonies we are about to undertake proceed to completion
without any obstacles we meditate on Mahaganapati

Similarly the grhadevata, i.e. the family godhead, who is ever present bestowing protection to the family at all times is now invoked. Chant as follows:

गृह देवतां ध्यायामि
ध्यानं समर्पयामि

gṛha dēvatām dhyāyāmi
dhyānam samarpayāmi

I respectfully contemplate our family Godhead.

Finally, it is necessary to pay respect to the family guru (guru here refers to aachaaryaas such as Adi Shankarachaarya, Ramanujaachaarya, Madhvaachaarya or others) and offer prayer before beginning the ceremony by chanting:

गुरुर्ब्रह्मा गुरुर्विष्णुः गुरुर्देवो महेश्वरः
गुरुस्साक्षात् परब्रह्म तस्मै श्रीगुरवे नमः

gururbrahmā gururviṣṇu: gururdēvō mahēśwara:
gurussākśhāt parabrahma tasmai śrīguravē nama:

Salutations to the preceptor who is verily Brahma, Vishnu
and Maheshwara and who personifies the Supreme Being

Shuddhi (Cleansing)

In order to assure ourselves that any and all evil tendencies are removed from the worship room, we start with a prayer to Shiva whose very invocation is believed to clear out any troubling vibrations:

ॐ नमः प्रणवार्थाय शुद्ध ज्ञानैकमूर्तये
निर्मलाय प्रशांताय दक्षिणामूर्तये नमः

ōm nama: praṇavārthāya śuddha jnānaika mūrtayē
nirmalāya prashāntāya dakśhiṇā mūrtayē nama:

I salute the Lord of the Southern direction who is the very embodiment of the sacred symbol Om and of pure knowledge and eternal peace.

Next we need to invoke and invite the sacred rivers to fill the metallic vessel.

This water is used to cleanse and offer throughout the worship. Start pouring water from one vessel into the smaller one as you chant:

गंगेच यमुनेचैव गोदावरी सरस्वती
नर्मदा सिंधु कावेरी जलेस्मिन् सन्निधिं कुरु

gamgēcha yamunēchaiva gōdāvarī saraswati
narmadā simdhu kāvērī jalēsmin sannidhim kuru

O Ganga, Yamuna, Godaavari, Saraswati, Narmada, Sindhu and Kaveri waters, please present yourselves in this place.

Now that we have received the sacred waters, it is time to symbolically cleanse our hands by offering a spoonful (uddharane) of water into the hands of the principals (bridegroom, his parents) by wiping the hands with reverence as we chant:

अपवित्रः पवित्रोवा सर्वावस्थां गतोपिवा
यःस्मरेत् पुंडरीकाक्षं स बाह्याभ्यंतरः शुचिः

apavitra: pavitrōvā sarvāvasthām gatōpivā
ya:smarēt pumḍareekākśham sa bāhyābhyamtara: śuchi:

May anything unholy become holy, may all lower tendencies depart, cleansing both inside and out as we remember Pundareekaaksha.

Prayer

वक्रतुंड महाकाय सूर्यकोटि समप्रभ
निर्विघ्नं कुरु मे देव सर्व कार्येषु सर्वदा

vakratumḍa mahākāya sūryakōṭi samaprabhā
nirvighnam kuru mē dēva sarva kāryēshu sarvadā

My Lord, who has a curved tusk, immense body and whose brilliance matches that of a million Suns, please remove all obstacles in all my undertakings all the time.

Upachaaraas (Puja offerings)

Now we are ready to invoke Ganapati and offer Upachaaraas (reception with reverence). With folded hands focus on the picture of the deity as you chant the following:

ॐ श्रीमन्महागणाधिपतयेनमः

ōm śrīmanmahāgaṇādhipatayēnama:

I offer my salutations to Mahaganapati.

Now offer a few grains of akshata with your right hand such that the grains fall on the picture gently as you chant:

ॐ श्रीमन्महागणाधिपतयेनमः

ōm śrīmanmahāgaṇādhipatayenama:

आवाहनं समर्पयामि

āvāhanam samarpayāmi

I offer an invocation to you.

Offer akshata as before such that the grains fall on the altar as you chant:

ॐ श्रीमन्महागणाधिपतयेनमः

ōm śrīmanmahāgaṇādhipatayenama:

आसनं समर्पयामि

āsanam samarpayāmi

I offer a seat for you.

Offer an uddharana-full of water at the feet of the deity or picture as you chant:

ॐ श्रीमन्महागणाधिपतयेनमः

ōm śrīmanmahāgaṇādhipatayenama:

पाद्यं समर्पयामि

pādyam samarpayāmi

I offer water to your feet.

Offer an uddharana-full of water to the hands of the deity or picture as you chant:

ॐ श्रीमन्महागणाधिपतयेनमः

ōm śrīmanmahāgaṇādhipatayenama:

अर्घ्यं समर्पयामि

arghyam samarpayāmi

I offer water to your hands.

Offer again an uddharana-full of water to the hands of the deity or picture as you chant:

ॐ श्रीमन्महागणाधिपतयेनमः

ōm śṛīmanmahāgaṇādhipatayenama:

आचमनीयं समर्पयामि

āchamanīyam samarpayāmi

I offer water to quench thirst.

Offer some sweet drink (fruit juice or honey) as you chant:

ॐ श्रीमन्महागणाधिपतयेनमः

ōm śrīmanmahāgaṇādhipatayenama:

मधुपर्कं समर्पयामि

madhuparkam samarpayāmi

I offer some sweet drink.

Symbolically offer water to bathe or pour water over the deity to bathe as you chant:

ॐ श्रीमन्महागणाधिपतयेनमः

ōm śrīmanmahāgaṇādhipatayenama:

शुद्धोदकस्नानं समर्पयामि

śuddhōdakasnaanam samarpayāmi

I offer clean water to bathe.

Offer again an uddharana–full of water to the hands of the deity or picture as you chant:

ॐ श्रीमन्महागणाधिपतयेनमः

ōm śrīmanmahāgaṇādhipatayenama:

स्नानानंतरं आचमनीयं समर्पयामि

snānānamtaram āchamanīyam samarpayāmi

I offer water to drink after the bath.

Symbolically offer a clean piece of cloth to represent gifts of clothing:

ॐ श्रीमन्महागणाधिपतयेनमः

ōm śrīmanmahāgaṇādhipatayenama:

वस्त्रान् समर्पयामि

vastrān samarpayāmi

I offer clothing.

Symbolically offer a clean piece of string to represent a new yagnopaveet:

ॐ श्रीमन्महागणाधिपतयेनमः

ōm śrīmanmahāgaṇādhipatayenama:

उपवीतं समर्पयामि

upavītam samarpayāmi

I offer a new yagnopaveet.

Apply to the forehead some sandal paste:

ॐ श्रीमन्महागणाधिपतयेनमः

ōm śrīmanmahāgaṇādhipatayenama:

गंधान् धारयामि

gamdhān dhārayāmi

I offer sandal paste.

Offer some akshata:

ॐ श्रीमन्महागणाधिपतयेनमः

ōm śrīmanmahāgaṇādhipatayenama:

अक्षतान् समर्पयामि

akshatān samarpayāmi

I offer akshata.

Offer flowers or petals of flowers to the picture or the deity:

ॐ श्रीमन्महागणाधिपतयेनमः

ōm śrīmanmahāgaṇādhipatayenama:

पुष्पाणि समर्पयामि

puṣpāṇi samarpayāmi

I offer flowers in worship.

With folded hands chant the several names of Mahaganapati:

ॐ सुमुखाय नमः ऐकदंताय नमः कपिलाय नमः गजकर्णकाय नमः
लंबोदराय नमः विकटाय नमः विघ्नराजाय नमः विनायकाय नमः
धूम्रकेतवे नमः गणाधिपाय नमः फालचंद्राय नमः गजाननाय नमः
वक्रतुंडाय नमः शूर्पकर्णाय नमः हेरंबाय नमः स्कंद पूर्वजाय नमः

ōm sumukhāya nama:, ĕkadamtāya nama:, kapilāya nama:, gajakarṇakāya nama:, lambōdarāya nama:, vikaṭāya nama:, vighnarājāya nama:, vināyakāya nama:, dhūmrakētavē nama:, gaṇādhipāya nama:, phālacamdrāya nama:, gajānanāya nama:, vakratumḍāya nama:, shūrpakarṇāya

shūrpakarṇāya nama:, hērambāya nama:,
skamda pūrvajāya nama:

I salute that Lord who has a beautiful face, single tusk, red color, elephant ears, large belly and who is a source of happiness, ruler of obstacles, supreme, fire-like in stature, head of the army, with crescent moon for crest, face of an elephant, a curved tusk, sharp ears, powerful, and elder brother of Skanda.

ॐ श्रीमन्महागणाधिपतयेनमः

ōm śrīmanmahāgaṇādhipatayenama:

Offer incense by motioning incense smoke with your right hand towards the altar:

धूपं आघ्रापयामि

dhūpam āghrāpayāmi

I offer fragrance in worship.

Lift the lamp and show it to the picture or deity such that it illuminates the face:

ॐ श्रीमन्महागणाधिपतयेनमः

ōm śrīmanmahāgaṇādhipatayenama:

दीपं दर्शयामि

dīpam darshayāmi

I offer sacred light.

Lift the plate of fruits, leaves and flowers in reverence and offer them:

ॐ श्रीमन्महागणाधिपतयेनमः

ōm śrīmanmahāgaṇādhipatayenama:

नानाविध परिमळ पत्र फल पुष्पाणि समर्पयामि

nānāvidha parimala patra phala pushpāṇi samarpayāmi

I offer a variety of flowers, leaves and fruits.

Now lift the cover off the sweets/prasaadam and offer it as you chant:

ॐ श्रीमन्महागणाधिपतयेनमः

ōm śrīmanmahāgaṇādhipatayenama:

नैवेद्यं निवेदयामि

naivēdyam nivēdayāmi

I offer delicious food to you.

Sprinkle a few drops of water with the uddharana on the food as you chant:

प्राणाय स्वाहा, अपानाय स्वाहा, व्यानाय स्वाहा,
उदानाय स्वाहा, समानाय स्वाहा, ब्रह्मणे स्वाहा

prāṇāya swāhā, apānāya swāhā, vyānāya swāhā,
udānāya swāhā, samānāya swāhā, brahmaṇē swāhā

These are invocations and hails to the various wind elements in our body which promote digestion. The final hail is to the creator Brahma.

Continue to offer water as you chant:

ॐ श्रीमन्महागणाधिपतयेनमः

ōm śrīmanmahāgaṇādhipatayenama:

मध्ये मध्ये आचमनीयं समर्पयामि

madhyē madhyē āchamanīyam samarpayāmi

I offer more water as you partake the foods.

Offer a coin as you chant:

ॐ श्रीमन्महागणाधिपतयेनमः

ōm śrīmanmahāgaṇādhipatayenama:

सुवर्ण पुष्पं समर्पयामि

suvarṇa pushpam samarpayāmi

I offer gold to you.

This completes the Upachaaraas.

Pradakshina

Now stand up and do a *pradakshina* (circumambulation) turning three times to your right.

ॐ श्रीमन्महागणाधिपतयेनमः

ōm śrīmanmahāgaṇādhipatayenama:

यानिकानिच पापानि जन्मांतर कृतानि च
तानि तानि विनश्यंति प्रदक्षिणं पदे पदे

yānikānicha pāpāni janmāmtara kṛutāni cha
tāni tāni vinashyamti pradakśhiṇam padē padē

Whatever sins I have committed in all my lives,
May all of them be absolved as I circumambulate in worship of you

Conclusion

Now the Puja can be completed with an aarati. *Om jayajagadeeshahare* is recommended.

If the ashtoththara (108 names) is to be chanted then the aarati follows that. After the aarati is complete, take the aarati plate around so that the devotees can receive the blessing by reverentially cupping their hands downwards to receive the warmth of the flame and touching their eyes with the cupped hands.

We conclude the puja ceremony by chanting the following two shlokas.

त्वमेव माताच पिता त्वमेव
त्वमेव बंधुश्च सखा त्वमेव
त्वमेव विद्या द्रविणम् त्वमेव
त्वमेव सर्वं मम देव देव

tvamēva mātācha pitā tvamēva
tvamēva bamdhuścha sakhā tvamēva
tvamēva vidyā draviṇam tvamēva
tvamēva sarvam mama dēva dēva

You alone are our mother and father
You alone are our sibling and friend
You alone are our knowledge and prosperity
You alone are everything to us
My Lord, my Lord

कायेन वाचा मनसेंन्द्रियैर्वा
बुध्यात्मनावा प्रकृते स्वभावात्
करोमि यद्यत् सकलं परस्मै
नारायणायेति समर्पयामि

kāyēna vācā manasēmndriyairvā
budhyātmanāvā prakṛutē swabhāvāt

karōmi yadyat sakalam parasmai
nārāyaṇāyēti samarpayāmi

Whatever I have performed through my action,
speech, thought, knowledge, or my natural habit,
may all that be surrendered to Srimannarayana.

The prasaad (consecrated food) may now be distributed and enjoyed after the Shanti Mantra (Peace) chant:

ॐ सहना ववतु
सहनौ भुनक्तु
सहवीर्यं करवावहै
तेजस्विनावधीतमस्तु
मा विद् विशा वहै
ॐ शान्तिः, शान्तिः, शान्तिः

ōm sahanā vavatu
sahanau bhunaktu
sahavīryam karavāvahai
tejaswināvadhītamastu
mā vid vishā vahai
ōm shānti:, shānti:, shānti:

May Brahman protect us
may we dine together
let us work together with great energy
let us be illumined together
let us live in harmony
peace, peace, peace!

✣✣✣✣✣✣

PUJA TO GAURI BY THE BRIDE

Materials and arrangement: All the preliminaries required for Gauri Puja are identical to those shown above for the Puja to Mahaganapati. Changes begin from the section designated as Prayer and continue as shown below. Also note in the list of materials, a set of ornaments such as necklace, bangles etc., relevant as offering to a goddess replace the yagnopaveet listed in the Ganapati Puja.

Prayer

सर्व मंगळ मांगल्ये शिवे सर्वार्थसाधिके
शरण्ये त्र्यंबके देवी नारायणी नमोस्तुते

sarva mamgala māmgalyē śivē sarvārthasādhikē
śaraṇyē tryambakē dēvī nārāyaṇī namōstutē

O Naaraayani, embodiment of prosperity, personification of the Shiva aspect, accomplished, protector, Mother of the Three Worlds and known as Gauri.

Upachaaraas

Now we are ready to invoke Gauri and offer Upachaaraas (reception with reverence). With folded hands focus on the picture of the deity as you chant the following:

ॐ नमो भगवत्यै सकल देवता शक्तात्मिकायै श्री गौर्यै नमः

ōm namō bagavatyai sakala dēvatā śaktātmikāyai śrī gauryai nama:

Salutations to Sree Gauri that goddess who personifies
the strengths of all godheads in herself.

Now offer a few grains of akshata with your right hand such that the grains fall on the picture gently as you chant:

ॐ नमो भगवत्यै सकल देवता शक्तात्मिकायै श्री गौर्यै नमः

Salutations to Sree Gauri that goddess who personifies
the strengths of all godheads in herself.

आवाहनं समर्पयामि

āvāhanam samarpayāmi

I offer an invocation to you.

Offer akshata as before such that the grains fall on the altar as you chant:

ॐ नमो भगवत्यै सकल देवता शक्तात्मिकायै श्री गौर्यै नमः

Salutations to Sree Gauri that goddess who personifies
the strengths of all godheads in herself.

आसनं समर्पयामि

āsanam samarpayāmi

I offer a seat for you.

Offer an uddharana-full of water at the feet of the deity or picture as you chant:

ॐ नमो भगवत्यै सकल देवता शक्तात्मिकायै श्री गौर्यै नमः

Salutations to Sree Gauri that goddess who personifies
the strengths of all godheads in herself

पाद्यं समर्पयामि

pādyam samarpayāmi

I offer water to your feet.

Offer an uddharana-full of water to the hands of the deity or picture as you chant:

ॐ नमो भगवत्यै सकल देवता शक्तात्मिकायै श्री गौर्यै नमः

Salutations to Sree Gauri that goddess who personifies
the strengths of all godheads in herself.

अर्घ्यं समर्पयामि

arghyam samarpayāmi

I offer water to your hands.

Offer again an uddharana-full of water to the hands of the deity or picture as you chant:

ॐ नमो भगवत्यै सकल देवता शक्तात्मिकायै श्री गौर्यै नमः

Salutations to Sree Gauri that goddess who personifies
the strengths of all godheads in herself.

आचमनीयं समर्पयामि

ācamanīyam samarpayāmi

I offer water to quench thirst.

Offer some sweet drink (fruit juice or honey) as you chant:

ॐ नमो भगवत्यै सकल देवता शक्तात्मिकायै श्री गौर्यै नमः

Salutations to Sree Gauri that goddess who personifies
the strengths of all godheads in herself.

मधुपर्कं समर्पयामि

madhuparkam samarpayāmi

I offer a sweet drink.

Symbolically offer water to bathe or pour water over the deity to bathe as you chant:

ॐ नमो भगवत्यै सकल देवता शक्तात्मिकायै श्री गौर्यै नमः

Salutations to Sree Gauri that goddess who personifies
the strengths of all godheads in herself.

शुद्धोदकस्नानं समर्पयामि

śuḍhōdakasnānam samarpayāmi

I offer clean water to bathe.

Offer again an uddharanafull of water to the hands of the deity or picture as you chant:

ॐ नमो भगवत्यै सकल देवता शक्तात्मिकायै श्री गौर्यै नमः

Salutations to Sree Gauri that goddess who personifies
the strengths of all godheads in herself.

स्नानानन्तरं आचमनीयं समर्पयामि

snānānamtaram āchamanīyam samarpayāmi

I offer water to drink after the bath.

Symbolically offer a clean piece of cloth to represent gifts of clothing:

ॐ नमो भगवत्यै सकल देवता शक्तात्मिकायै श्री गौर्यै नमः

Salutations to Sree Gauri that goddess who personifies
the strengths of all godheads in herself.

वस्त्रान् समर्पयामि

vastrān samarpayāmi

I offer clothing.

Symbolically offer ornaments as you chant:

ॐ नमो भगवत्यै सकल देवता शक्तात्मिकायै श्री गौर्यै नमः

Salutations to Sree Gauri that goddess who personifies the strengths of all godheads in herself.

सकलाभरणानि समर्पयामि

sakalābharaṇāni samarpayāmi

I offer all ornaments.

Apply to the forehead some sandal paste:

ॐ नमो भगवत्यै सकल देवता शक्तात्मिकायै श्री गौर्यै नमः

Salutations to Sree Gauri that goddess who personifies the strengths of all godheads in herself.

गंधान् धारयामि

gamdhān dhārayāmi

I offer sandal paste.

Offer some akshata:

ॐ नमो भगवत्यै सकल देवता शक्तात्मिकायै श्री गौर्यै नमः

Salutations to Sree Gauri that goddess who personifies the strengths of all godheads in herself.

अक्षतान् समर्पयामि

akśatān samarpayāmi

I offer akshata.

Offer flowers or petals of flowers to the picture or the deity:

ॐ नमो भगवत्यै सकल देवता शक्तात्मिकायै श्री गौर्यै नमः

Salutations to Sree Gauri that goddess who personifies the strengths of all godheads in herself.

पुष्पाणि समर्पयामि

puṣhpāṇi samarpayāmi

I offer flowers in worship.

With folded hands chant the several names of Gauri:

ॐ श्री गणेशजनन्यै नमः ॐ स्वर्णगौर्यै नमः ॐ शंकर्यै नमः ॐ मांगल्यदायिन्यै नमः
ॐ सर्वकाल सुमंगल्यै नमः ॐ त्रिपुरसौंदर्यै नमः ॐ रूपसौभाग्यै नमः ॐ परमानंददायै नमः
ॐ आद्यंतरहितायै नमः महामात्रे नमः सर्वैश्वर्यै नमः ॐ महेश्वर्यै नमः ॐ दीनरक्षिण्यै नमः
ॐ पापनाशिन्यै नमः ॐ जगन्मात्रे नमः ॐ कृपापूर्णायै नमः ॐ श्री गौरीमातायै नमः

ōm śrī gaṇēshajananyai nama: ōm svarṇagauryai nama: ōm śamkaryai nama: ōm māmgalyadāyinyai nama: ōm sarvakāla sumamgalyai nama: ōm tripurasaumdaryai nama: ōm rūpasaubāgyai nama: ōm paramānamdadāyai nama: ōm ādyamtarahitāyai nama: mahāmātrē nama: sarvaishvaryai nama: ōm mahēśvaryai nama: ōm dīnarakśiṇyai nama: ōm pāpanāśinyai nama: ōm jaganmātrē nama: ōm kṛupāpūrṇāyai nama: ōm śrī gaurīmātāyai nama:

Salutations to the mother of Ganesha, the Golden Gauri, consort of Sankara, the bestower of the Mangalya, one who is good fortune forever, the beauty of the Three Worlds, prosperous in beauty, bestower of bliss, one who is free of beginning and end,

Great Mother, possessor of all wealth, consort of Maheswara, protector of the poor, destroyer of sins, mother of the universe, full of compassion,

Om Salutations to Mother Gauri!

ॐ नमो भगवत्यै सकल देवता शक्तात्मिकायै श्री गौर्यै नमः

Salutations to Sree Gauri that goddess who personifies
the strengths of all godheads in herself.

Offer incense by motioning incense smoke with your right hand towards the altar:

धूपं आघ्रापयामि

dhūpam āghrāpayāmi

I offer fragrance in worship.

Lift the lamp and show it to the picture or deity such that it illuminates the face:

ॐ नमो भगवत्यै सकल देवता शक्तात्मिकायै श्री गौर्यै नमः

Salutations to Sree Gauri that goddess who personifies
the strengths of all godheads in herself.

दीपं दर्शयामि

dīpam darshayāmi

I offer sacred light.

Lift the plate of fruits, leaves and flowers in reverence and offer them:

ॐ नमो भगवत्यै सकल देवता शक्तात्मिकायै श्री गौर्यै नमः

Salutations to Sree Gauri that goddess who personifies
the strengths of all godheads in herself.

नानाविध परिमळ पत्र फल पुश्पाणि समर्पयामि

nānāvidha parimala patra phala pushpāṇi samarpayāmi

I offer a variety of flowers, leaves and fruits.

Now lift the cover off the sweets/prasaadam and offer it as you chant:

ॐ नमो भगवत्यै सकल देवता शक्तात्मिकायै श्री गौर्यै नमः

Salutations to Sree Gauri that goddess who personifies
the strengths of all godheads in herself.

नैवेद्यं निवेदयामि

naivēdyam nivēdayāmi

I offer delicious food to you.

Sprinkle a few drops of water with the uddharana on the food as you chant:

प्राणाय स्वाहा, अपानाय स्वाहा, व्यानाय स्वाहा,
उदानाय स्वाहा, समानाय स्वाहा, ब्रह्मणे स्वाहा

prāṇāya swāhā, apānāya swāhā, vyānāya swāhā,
udānāya swāhā, samānāya swāhā, brahmaṇē swāhā

These are invocations and hails to the various wind elements in our body which promote digestion. The final hail is to the creator Brahma.

Continue to offer water as you chant:

ॐ नमो भगवत्यै सकल देवता शक्तात्मिकायै श्री गौर्यै नमः

Salutations to Sree Gauri that goddess who personifies
the strengths of all godheads in herself

मध्ये मध्ये आचमनीयं समर्पयामि

madhyē madhyē āchamanīyam samarpayāmi

I offer more water as you partake the foods.

Offer a coin as you chant:

ॐ नमो भगवत्यै सकल देवता शक्तात्मिकायै श्री गौर्यै नमः

Salutations to Ṣree Gauri that goddess who personifies
the strengths of all godheads in herself.

सुवर्ण पुष्पं समर्पयामि

suvarṇa puṣpam samarpayāmi

I offer gold to you.

This completes the Upachaaraas.

Pradakshina

Now stand up and do a pradakshina (circumambulation) three times, turning to your right:

ॐ नमो भगवत्यै सकल देवता शक्तात्मिकायै श्री गौर्यै नमः

Salutations to Sree Gauri that goddess who personifies
the strengths of all godheads in herself.

यानिकानिच पापानि जन्मांतर कृतानि च
तानि तानि विनश्यंति प्रदक्षिणं पदे पदे

yānikānicha pāpāni janmāmtara kṛutāni cha
tāni tāni vinaśyamti pradakśiṇam padē padē

Whatever sins I have committed in all my lives,
May all of them be absolved as I circumambulate in worship of you.

Conclusion

Now the Puja can be completed with an aarati.

If ashtoththara (108 names) is to be chanted then the aarati follows that. After the aarati is complete, take the aarati plate around so that the devotees can receive the blessing by reverentially cupping their hands downwards and receiving the warmth of the flame and touching their eyes with the cupped hands inwards.

The conclusion part of the ceremony is identical to that shown above for Mahaganapati Puja, ending with distribution of prasaad (consecrated food) and the Shanti Mantra (Peace) chant:

ॐ सहना ववतु
सहनौ भुनक्तु
सहवीर्यं करवावहै
तेजस्विनावधीतमस्तु
मा विद् विशा वहै
ॐ शान्तिः, शान्तिः, शान्तिः

ōm sahanā vavatu
sahanau bhunaktu
sahavīryam karavāvahai
tejaswināvadhītamastu
mā vid vishā vahai
ōm shānti:, shānti:, shānti:

May Brahman protect us
may we dine together
let us work together with great energy
let us be illumined together
let us live in harmony
peace, peace, peace!

GLOSSARY of NAMES & TERMS

PLEASE NOTE: the term within parentheses below is transliterated for correct pronunciation, where needed, using the conventional diacritical marks for Indic languages. The lead word reflects common usage. (For further terms related to jewelry and clothing, see Appendix V)

aarati/arati(ārati), ritual in which a plate or thali with a deepa (oil lamp) and other items of ritual purification such as flowers, incense, kumkum and turmeric, are waved at least three times clockwise around a venerated person or object. Sometimes the plate may contain just water with kumkum dissolved in it and a few grains of akshata.

aayana/ayana (āyana), course or journey; refers to the apparent direction of the sun's course through the sky, uttarayana (north) or dakshinayana (south); cited in a sankalpam.

adhika masa (adhika māsa), an extra month added (a consecutive repetition) once every 3 lunar years, to realign with the solar year; Shunya.

Adityas (ātlityās), the devas or Vedic gods.

agarbatti, incense stick.

Agni, Vedic god of fire; invoked for all domestic rituals, especially a wedding in which he is considered to be the bride's first guardian and chief performer of the rite itself as well as the recipient of offerings.

Agni Pratishtapana (Agni Pratiṣṭhāpana), the setting up of a fire vessel/altar ready for a fire ritual.

akshata (akṣata), rice tinted with turmeric.

amavāsya, new moon.

Anasūya, a pativrata, wife of the sage Atri.

Angāraka, Mars; one of the Navagrahas, the Nine Planets of Vedic astrology.

Arjuna, chief warrior among the Pandava princes (sons of Pandu) and skillful archer, spiritual son of Indra; hero of the epic Mahabharata.

Arundhati darshanam (ārundhati darśanam), a ceremony in which the bride views Arundhati, a star named after the wife of a sage, noted for her fidelity.

Aryaman/Aaryaman (āryaman), rules of conduct, social code, personified in the Rig Veda, as Aaryama.

Ashirvadam (āśirvādam), traditional set of blessings on the couple, accompanied by sprinkling of akshata by the priest and family elders.

Ashmarohana (aśmārohana), ceremonial stepping onto a stone by the bride to symbolize stability in marriage.

Ashwins (Aśvins), the Heavenly Twins, connected with the care of animals, agriculture and medicine; Suryā's escort at her bridal.

Atri, a rishi, one of the Seven Sages of the Saptarishi constellation (L. Ursa Major). His wife, Anasuya, is one of the pativratas evoked along with him in the final ashirvadam or blessing of the couple.

baraat (barāt), groom's arrival at the wedding venue on foot, horseback or by automobile, accompanied by his relatives, and usually by musicians.

Bhāga, ancestral share, personified, according to Griffith *(RV. 10.85.23.);* also good fortune..

Bhagavad Gīta, literally Song of God, the discourse given by Krishna to Arjuna on the battlefield of Kurukshetra in the Sanskrit epic Mahabharata; a crystallization of the meaning of dharma, and now accepted as central to Hindu dogma.

Bhishma (Bhīsma), hero of the Mahabharata, patriarch of the Kuru clan.

Brahma (pronounced *Bramha),* the divine creator, whose age is used to mark the time and moment in Vedic rituals. His day covers 1,000 mahāyugas or 4.32 billion solar years. It is divided into Adi Sandhi (1,728,00 solar years), 14 manvantaraṣ, and 14 Sandhi Kālas; during the latter the earth is covered with water. At the end of each life-span of 100 Brahma years, the cosmos dies. Another Brahma comes into being to recreate life and the worlds again.

brahmin (brāhman), one of the four castes, the priestly or scholarly class, learned in the Vedas.

Brihaspati (Bṛhaspati), also called Guru (Jupiter), one of the Navagrahas; the preceptor of the gods.

chaturyuga (caturyuga), the Four Yugas (Kṛta, Treta, Dwāpara, Kali) or world-ages, as a unit, also known as a mahāyuga.

dakshinayana (dakśināyana), see *āyana.*

deepa (dīpa), lamp fuelled by ghee or oil; mainly for ritual use; a small brass, silver or clay deepa with cotton wick which can be placed on an ārati plate, or a larger size with a handle.

Deṣṭrī, a form of Saraswati as "Instructress" (according to Griffith's footnote to *RV.10.85.47)*

dharmapatni, wife-in-dharma, equivalent of the term 'lawfully wedded wife.'

drushti (dṛṣti), ceremony to ward off the "evil eye."

Dhruva darshanam, ceremony in which the bride views Dhruva (Polaris) the North Star, a symbol of stability.

Dwāpara Yuga, second in the yuga cycle, lasting 834,000 (432,000 x 2) solar years.

Ganapati, elephant-headed god, remover of obstacles; the groom and his family usually perform a puja to this deity, also known as Ganesha, before the wedding.

Gandharva, Vishvavasu guardian of the bride in her first home, before marriage *(RV)*; later a class of heavenly beings.

*Gāthā,*sacred song, personified in the Rig Veda (Griffith reference to X. 85. 6.) along with other types of meter and verse; source of Suryā's bridal garment.

Gauri Pūja, ceremony of worship offered to the Devi, mother of Ganesha by the bride and her family the day before the wedding, for a good outcome for the ceremony and her new life.

ghee (ghī), butter clarified to preserve it; used to fuel lamps (deepas) of all sizes.

gotra (gōtra), spiritual lineage; each Hindu is considered to be the descendant of a sage, three or five of whom are cited in pravara recitals or in formal identification of the individual.

Grihapravesham (Gṛhapraveśam), homecoming ceremony for the bride.

Gṛhasthāshrama, one of the four stages of life for a Hindu, that of the householder, which begins with the wedding rite. The others are Brahmacharya (student life); Vanaprastha (hermit stage or retirement); and Sanyasashrama (renunciation).

haldi, turmeric in powder form, used as a tinting medium for textiles, food and, formerly, complexion; an auspicious yellow gold color.

Harishchandra and Chandramati, an ideal couple of legend, including the Mahabharata, whose names are evoked in the Ashirvadam.

Hasta Milāp, ceremony in which the bride's father joins the right hands of bride and groom.

havan, fire altar.

Hindu, originally a geographical term given by the Persians to the people who lived around and beyond the River Indus; now used to denote an adherent of Hinduism or Sanātana Dharma.

Hinduism, major religion of India, Sanātana Dharma, a set of beliefs derived primarily from the Vedas and related scriptures.

homa, fire ceremony.

Indra, Vedic King of Heaven, wielder of the thunderbolt; regent of the east.

Jai Mala (Jayamāla), ceremony in which the bride first garlands the groom, signifying her choice, and the groom garlands the bride in consent.

Jeeriga/Jeelakarra-bellam (Jīriga/jīlakarra-bellam), regional custom, in which the couple offer each other a mixture of cumin seed and brown sugar, symbolizing willingness to share the bitter and the sweet in life together.

kalasha (kaḷaśa), rounded water vessel, serving as an essential part of the Vedic purification rites and providing sanctified water throughout the ceremony.

Kali Yuga, fourth in the 4-yuga cycle, lasting 432,000 solar years, ending in the destruction of the world, and re-cycling of the chaturyugas.

kalpa(m), generally, a day in the life of the creator Brahma. Brahma's life covers 7 kalpas: Matsya, Kūrma, Lakshmi, Shweta Varaha, Shiva, Brahma and Vishnu Kalpa. We are now (2006) halfway through the fourth kalpa in the lifetime of the current Brahma.

Kanyadanam (Kanyādānam), ceremony of the giving away of the bride by her parents.

Kashiyatra (Kāśīyātra), the ritual journey to Varanasi (Benares).

Kāshyapa, the son of the rishi Marichi, married the 13 daughters of Daksha; he is named in the Ashirvadam to evoke the birth of many children.

Ketū, one of the Navagrahas; lunar node; Cauda Draconis; a malign influence connected with comets.

Krishna (Kṛṣṇa), avatar of Vishnu; in the epic Mahabharata he is prince of Dwaraka, a cousin of the Pandavas; he is also the charioteer who addresses Arjuna on the battlefield of Kurukshetra, delivering the Bhagavad Gita.

krishṇa paksha, dark fortnight, immediately leading into the new moon.

Krita Yuga (Kṛta Yuga), also called Satya Yuga, first in the 4-yuga cycle, lasting 432,000 x 4 = 1,728,000 solar years; an Age of Gold.

Kshatriya (kṣatriya), one of the four castes, the warrior.

Kubera, Vedic lord of wealth, regent of the North; he is invoked in the Ashirvadam for the blessing of wealth and happiness.

kuladharma, family tradition.

kumkum, powder in vermillion and other shades of red used extensively in ritual ceremonies and for cosmetics.

Laaja Homa (Lāja Homa), fire ceremony in which parched rice is offered to Agni.

loka, world: seven worlds are inhabited by gods, humans and all other celestial and terrestrial beings (Bhuloka, Bhuvarloka, Suvarloka, Maharloka, Janaloka, Tapoloka and Satyaloka). The first three, the Triloka, are invoked in rituals; they are deluged and reborn in each kalpa.

Mātarisvan, conception, personified, according to Griffith *(RV.10.85.47).*

madhuparkam, sweet drink or mixture of honey and yoghurt, presented to the groom on his arrival.

Mahābhārata, second great epic of India, featuring the dynastic quarrel between the descendants of Bharata, the Kurus and the Pandavas, which becomes a war between good and evil.

Mahāganapati Pūja, a ceremony of worship offered to Ganapati by the groom and his family, the day before the wedding wishing for prevention of obstacles and a successful start to the new stage in life.

mahāyuga, a span of the 4-yuga cycle; also chaturyuga, 4.32 million solar years.

Mangala, Mars; one of the Navagrahas (Nine Planets).

mangaḷashtak, the prayers and songs recited at the time of the bride's arrival at the mantap.

Māngalyadhāranam, ceremony of the tying of the mangalasutra or tāli/thali around the bride's neck by the groom.

Mangal Phera, also Lāja Homa, in which the couple circle the fire altar four times, and the bride makes offerings of parched rice.

mantap (mandapam), sacred space prepared for the wedding, usually four pillars, often with young banana trees fastened to them, with a canopy, decorated with flower garlands and a string of mango or other leaves across the front.

Manu, mythical progenitor of the human race; 14 Manus rule over one day in the life span of Brahma; the first Manu is Svayambhuva; the current Manu is Vaivasvata.

manvantara, the reign of each Manu; – 71 mahayugas or 306,720,000 solar years.

masa/maasa (māsa), lunar month of approximately 29.5 days; there are 12 lunar or solar months in the year:

1. Chaitra (March-April);
2. Vaishakha (April-May);
3. Jyeshta (May-June);
4. āshādha (June-July);
5. Shrāvana (July-August);
6. Bhādrapada (August-September);
7. āshvayuja (September-October);
8. Kārthika (October-November);
9. Mārgasheera (November-December)
10. Pushya (December-January);
11. Māgha (January-February);
12. Phālguni (February-March).

The names here are given in Sanskrit. Certain months are considered less auspicious for wedding ceremonies: āshādh, Bhadrapad, and Shunya (the month added to the lunar year every 30 months to bring it in line with the solar year, the adhika māsa).

mehndi, henna; a powder made from the leaves of the henna plant are used to create elaborate decorative patterns on the hands and feet of the bride, and her friends, usually the day before the wedding (See Appendix 5, Makeup).

Milni, means meeting, often called Swagatam or greeting; refers to the ceremonial meeting between the groom and his family and the bride's family at a point outside the bride's home or wedding venue which begins the main ceremony.

Mitra, Vedic god; Friendship; social bond.

Mṛkanda, father of the rishi Markandaya, is recalled in the Ashirvadam as an example of longevity.

muhūrtam, an auspicious time range selected by a qualified priest or person versed in the sacred calendar to be the best interval for beginning or performing the highlights in a wedding or other sacred rite.

nakshatra, constellation; 27 Nakshatras are contained in the Zodiac, at 13.20 degrees each. Horoscopes are based on the position of the moon in a particular nakshatra at birth.

Nala and Damayanti, an ideal couple, named in the Ashiravadam; their story is told in the epic Mahabharata.

Nārāśamsī, hymn of praise, personified (Griffith footnote to *RV*, 10.85.6).

Navagrahas, the Nine Planets of Vedic astrology: Surya (Sun); Chandra (Moon); Angāraka or Mangala (Mars); Budha (Mercury); Brhaspati or Guru (Jupiter); Shukra (Venus); Shani (Saturn); Rahu (lunar node; eclipse); Ketu (lunar node; comet).

Oonjal (Ūnjal), a South Indian custom in which the bride and groom sit in a swing.

pāda, part of Brahma's day; Prathama pāda is the first part of Dvitīya parārdha (the second half) of Brahma's life.

Pādaprakshālana, ritual washing of the groom's feet.

paksha (pakṣa), fortnight, defined by the prevailing phase of the moon: either the bright fortnight or two-week period ending with the full moon (Shukla Paksha), or the dark fortnight (Krishna Paksha) leading to the new moon.

Pāndu, a king of the Kuru race; in the epic Mahabharata his five sons, the Pandavas, are embroiled in a feud with their cousins, the Kauravas.

para, half the life-span of Brahma.

parārdha, half a para.

pativrata, a devoted and virtuous wife, for example, the wives of the sages as evoked in the Ashirvadam. See *Saptarishi.*

pooja (pūja), ceremony of worship.

Poornima (Pūrṇima) , full moon.

Pradhāna Homa, principal fire ceremony, observed first at a fire ritual.

Prajāpati, lord of progeny.

pralaya, chaotic floods which engulf the Three Worlds (Triloka) at the end of each kalpa.

Pravara, recital of the spiritual lineage of the bride and groom, usually accompanied by recital of their ancestry going back three generations.

Pundareekaaksha (Pundarīkākṣa), epithet of Vishnu, i.e. the lotus-eyed.

purāṇa, a story poem or collection of stories which covers creation, destruction and recreation/salvation of the world, centered around the saga of a principal god or avatar and royal house, and the history, customs and beliefs of the age or manvantara.

Purandara, a name of Indra.

Purandhi, Abundance (Griffith, *RV*).

Pūshan, Protection and guidance.

Rahu (Rāhu), one of the Navagrahas; lunar node; Caput Draconis; a malign influence connected with eclipses.

Rāhukalam, a period of time each day which is considered inauspicious for beginning a rite. Rahu, in Hindu legend is a snake which swallows the sun; in astrology it marks a path of intersection of the sun and moon, the north lunar node, during which eclipses occur. (See Rahukalam, Appendix III)

Raibhī, ritual verse (Griffith footnote to *RV*, 10. 85. 6).

Rakshā Bandhana, ceremony in which turmeric-tinted threads are tied around the right wrists of bride and groom to signify that they are taking part in a rite, and for protection.

Rama/Raama(Rāma), hero of the Ramayana, prince of Ayodhya; avatar of Vishnu.

Rakshā Visarjana, ceremony of removing the raksha thread.

rāshis, signs of the Zodiac:

1. Maisha (Aries) Ram;
2. Vrushabha (Taurus) Bull;
3. Mithuna (Gemini) Couple;
4. Karka (Cancer) Crab;
5. Simha (Leo) Lion;
6. Kanya (Virgo) Maiden;
7. Tula (Libra) Scales;
8. Vrushchika (Scorpio) Scorpion;
9. Dhanu (Saggitarius) Bow;
10. Makar (Capricorn) Sea Monster;
11. Kumbha (Aquarius) Pot;
12. Meena (Pisces) Fish.

Rig (ṛg) Veda, the oldest of the four Vedas. Mandala X, Hymn LXXXV contains the reference to the bridal of Suryā, daughter of the sun, to Soma, the moon, in lines which are still used in modern Vedic wedding rituals.

ritu or rutu (ṛtu), season; the 6 seasons of the 12 lunar months in the year: Vasanta (Spring); Greeshma (Summer); Varsha (Monsoon); Sharad (Autumn); Hemanta (Winter); Shishira (Dewy).

samskāra, Hindu rite of passage; 16 in all, of which marriage is one.

samvatsara, the Vedic year; these repeat in a cycle of 60 (see Samvatsara Table, Appendix IV).

Sankalpa/sankalpam (samkalpam), ritual declaration of place and time for a religious rite, as in a wedding ceremony.

Sanskrit (Samskrit), oldest extant Indo-European language, related to the oldest classical languages of Europe, Latin and Greek; it is now mostly liturgical, especially the Vedic Sanskrit used in wedding rituals; the many modern languages of North India (Hindi, Marathi, Bengali, etc.) have developed mainly from Prakrits, less formal regional derivations from Sanskrit.

Sanyās, the life of the renunciate, the last of the four stages of life.

Saptapadi, (also Hindi. *Sapta Padi),* the seven steps taken together, by the couple with the groom leading the bride, either around the fire once, or, near it while she steps into seven circles or seven mounds of rice, according to family tradition. Each step is taken with a purpose. After the seventh step, the marriage is legally ratified, by law, according to the Manava Dharma Shastra and the Hindu Code Bill.

Sapta Rishi (Saptarṣi), the constellation (L. Ursa Major; Big Dipper); also the Seven Sages of legend. The sages' names may differ in the separate scriptures and other writings which refer to the constellation. The rishis (and their wives) mentioned in the Ashirvadam as examples of ideal couples are: Kashyapa (and his thirteen wives), Agastya (and Lopamudra), Atri (and Anasuya), Gautama (and Ahalya), Rishyashringa (and Shanta), Vasishta (and Arundhati). The father of rishi Markandaya is included as a type of longevity.

Sāshtānga, ceremony in which the couple bend down to touch the feet of elders in the family, to be blessed, at the end of the rite.

Saubhāgyavatībhava, ceremony in which married ladies bless the bride.

Saubhari, sage whose name is mentioned in the Ashirvadam, together with his wives, in a blessing for the birth of healthy children.

Savitar (*Savitr*), sun.

shodashopacharas (śodaśopacārās), the 16 traditional methods of worship.

Shringar (śṛingar), female adornments, usually in the many forms of jewelry, flowers, and traditional makeup which were used to beautify the bride (See Appendix V); this has often taken the part of a separate ceremony or party for ladies; the application of mehndi is included here.

shukla paksha (śukla pakṣa), the bright fortnight, ending with the full moon day.

Shukra, Venus; one of the Navagrahas; preceptor of the asuras (titans).

Shunya (śūnya), literally zero; adhika māsa; the extra month added to the lunar year every three years; not considered auspicious for weddings.

sindhoor (sindhūr), auspicious red powder used by married women to apply the bindu or tika (round forehead mark); also used by her groom to mark the hair parting of the bride.

Sita/Seeta(Sīta), heroine of the Ramayana, faithful wife of Rama.

Soma, Vedic god of the moon and of plants; his wedding to Suryā, daughter of the sun, in the Rig Veda, provides many of the earliest wedding-related verses still in use.

Sūrya, the sun.

Suryaa/Sooryaa (Sūryā), daughter of the sun.

Svāgatam, the ceremonial greeting of the groom and his entourage, including his family, in which he is garlanded, and honored by the bride's family.

Shweta Varaha Kalpa (śvētavarāha) the current, fourth kalpa in Brahma's life-span; the White Boar's time, in which, according to legend, Lord Varaha (an incarnation of Vishnu) emerged from Brahma in the form of a white boar in order to rescue the earth from the bottom of the cosmic ocean after a flood.

Talambraalu (Talambrālu), regional custom from Andhra Pradesh in which the bride and groom pour rice over each other in a playful mode.

tali (tāḷi), wedding pendant, equivalent to a mangalasutra.

thali (thāli), metallic plate or tray; also a wedding pendant.

tithi, lunar day, the time taken by the moon to move 12 degrees from the sun. When the sun and moon are at the same longitude, it is amavasya (new moon); when they are 180 degrees apart, it is full moon (Pūrnima). There are 30 tithis in each lunar month, 15 in each paksha.

Treta Yuga, second in the yuga cycle, lasting 432,000 x 3 = 1,296,000 years.

Triloka, also Trailokya, the three worlds: Bhuloka (Earth), Antariksha Loka (Cosmos), and Dyuloka/ Devaloka or Swarga (Heaven); these are the material worlds, accessible to humans, and all creatures as well as gods, which are destroyed and remade in each kalpa.

turmeric, see *haldi.*

uttarayana (uttarāyana), northward course of the sun; cited in a sankalpam.

vaasara (vāsara), day of the week; named after the first 7 navagrahas:

1. Indu vāsara (Sunday);
2. Soma vāsara (Monday);
3. Mangala vāsara (Tuesday);
4. Budha vāsara (Wednesday);
5. Guru vāsara (Thursday);
6. Shukra vāsara (Friday);
7. Shani vāsara (Saturday)

Vara Pūja, ceremony in which the groom is honored by the bride's father as a personification of Vishnu.

Varuṇa, Vedic lord of waters and of destiny; regent of the west.

Veda (Vēda), one of four books which form the bedrock of Hinduism or Sanatana Dharma: Rig Veda, Yajur Veda, Sama Veda, and Atharva Veda.

Vedic, pertaining to Hindu religious rites; to the historic period (dating still to be decided), the language (early Sanskrit) and literature, the culture, and beliefs derived from the Vedas.

Vidaī, ceremony of leave-taking when the bride is about to depart for her new home.

Viśvavāsu, the Gandharva named in the Rig Veda as guardian of the bride in her home before marriage.

Vivāha, wedding, as ceremony or a samskara (one of the 16 rites of passage for a Hindu).

Yagnopavītam (yajnopavītam), the "thread ceremony" by which a brahmin (by tradition) or other Hindu who has studied the Vedas attains the status of "twice-born." At the time of marriage, the thread needs to be renewed and doubled in a separate ceremony.

yaksha (yakśa), woodland spirit.

Yama, Lord of the dead, of ancestors; Justice; regent of the south.

Yudhishtira (Yudhiṣṭhira), hero of the epic Mahabharata, eldest of the five Pandava brothers, renowned for his adherence to dharma.

yuga: an age or era in the history of the world: Krita Yuga or Satya Yuga: 432,000 x 4 years; Treta Yuga: 432,000 x 3 years; Dvapara Yuga: 432,000 x 2 years; Kali Yuga: 432,000 years. The 4 ages collectively are called a chaturyuga, a period of 4,320,000 years. They have been popularly referred to as Ages of Gold, Silver, Bronze and Iron, with each age manifesting a deterioration in dharma or strength of moral values, intellect and physical wellbeing. As in many time periods tied to Vedic astrology, different traditions ascribe variations in these measurements.

NOTE: Most of the above terms are transcribed from languages with differing alphabets. Over the years the best known among them have been spelled (or misspelled) in varying ways. For the sake of accuracy the international system of diacritical marks has been used in the longer ritual Sanskrit sequences and the terms in parentheses in the Glossary. However, for the general reader's comfort, these are included only where obvious in the general text and appendices. We have reverted in many cases, especially for personal and place names, to familiar usage. The general attempt has been to balance accuracy with ease of use, even when there might be a small loss in consistency.

ABBREVIATIONS

AV	*Atharva Veda*
AGS	*Ashvalayana Grihya Sutra*
H.	*Hindi*
L.	*Latin*
MBh	*Mahabharata (epic)*
MDS	*Manava Dharma Shastra (Laws of Manu)*
ParasGS	*Paraskara Grihya Sutra*
RA	*Ramayana (epic)*
RV	*Rig Veda*
SV	*Sama Veda*
SSSR	*Sartha Shodasha Samskrta Ratnamala*
VS	*Vajaseya Samhita*
YV	*Yajur Veda*

Select Bibliography

Apte, Vinayak Mahadev. RgVeda Mantras in Their Ritual Setting in the Grhyasutras, reprint from *The Bulletin of the Deccan College Research Institute,* Poona, Vol. I 14-44, 127-152, [1940].

Bhatta, K. (tr.) *Saartha Shodasha Samskara Ratnamala*. Nagalinga Swami Samskritha Veda Pathashala, 1979.

Bose, A.C. *The Call of the Vedas.* Bharatiya Vidya Bhavan, 1970.

Buhler, G. *Laws of Manu.* (Volume XXV, Sacred Books of the East series, edited by Max Muller) Oxford, 1886).

Chand, Devi. *The Atharvaveda.* Munshiram Manoharlal Publishers, New Delhi, 2002.

Chand, Devi. *The Samaveda.* Munshiram Manoharlal Publishers, New Delhi, 2004.

Colebrooke, H.T. *Miscellaneous Essays,* Second Edition. Higginbothams & Co., Madras, 1872.

Tagore, R.; Choudhury, Rabindra Nath (transl.). *Love Poems of Tagore.* Vision Books, Delhi, 1975.

Daniclou, Alain. *The Complete Kama Sutra.* Park Street Press, 1994.

Danielou, Alain. *Hindu Polytheism.* Pantheon Books, Bollingen series, 1964.

Griffith, Ralph T.H. *The Rig Veda.* Benares, 1896, rev. 1899. 1992 reprint.

Griffith, Ralph T.H. *The Hymns of the Atharva-Veda, Volumes I & II.* Benares, 1894/1897; E.J. Lazarus, 1916 & 1917 reprint.

Jamison, Stephanie W. "Draupadi on the Walls of Troy: Iliad 3 from an Indic Perspective" *Classical Antiquity,* Volume 13, No. 1. August 1994.

Keshavadas, Sadguru Sant. *Gayatri:The Highest Meditation.* Motilal Banarasidass, Delhi, 1994.

Krishnamaachaarya, S.M. *Yaajusha Purva Prayoga.* Srivaishnava Sabha, Bangalore, 1988.

Kumar, Ritu. *Costume and Textiles of Royal India.* Antique Collectors' Club, Ltd., 2005.

Lal, P. *The Mahabharata of Vyasa, Volume 23: The Svayamvara & Vaivahika in the Adi Parva.* Writers Workshop, Calcutta, 1970.

Lal, P. *The Mahabharata of Vyasa.* Vikas Publishing House, 1980.

Lal, P. *The Vedic Hindu Marriage Ceremony.* Writers Workshop, Calcutta, 1996.

Lal, P. *The Ramayana of Valmiki.* Vikas Publishing House, 1989.

Monier-Williams, M. *A Sanskrit-English Dictionary.* Clarendon Press, Oxford, 1899. 1996 reprint.

Oldenberg, Hermann. *The Grihya-Sutras, Part I.* Oxford, 1886. (Volume 29, Sacred Books of the East series, edited by Max Muller) 1964/1997 reprint.

Prasad, R.C. *The Vivaha.* Motilal Banarasidass, Delhi, 1995.

Rao, D.H.; Murthy, KMK. *Valmiki Ramayana* on line translation, 2003.

Srinivas, M.N. *Marriage and Family in Mysore.* New Book Co., Bombay, 1942

Srinivasan, A.V. *A Hindu Primer:Yaksha Prashna,* 2nd Edition. E. Glastonbury, CT: Parijata Publication, 2002.

Ramakrishna Sastry, Banavati. *Vivaahaartha Pradipika.* Banavati Prakashana, Bangalore, 1988.

Vyasa Rao, R. *Vivaha-Mangala.* Sahitya Sindhu Prakashana, Bangalore, 1997.

Dear Dr & Mrs. Srinivasan,

Thank you so much for officiating and being a part of one of the most important days of our lives. The words spoken on our special day will always be with us. Thank you again.

With love
Seju & John Mulvaney

9/1/04

Dear Dr. Shrinivasan,

We cannot begin to express how wonderfully you officiated the wedding ceremony of Radhika & Praveen. Our family and friends have not stopped talking about how well organized the entire ceremony was. We can only imagine your difficulty in giving up your own family event to keep your commitment to us. We did miss your wife Kamala's presence due to this fact.

Do not be surprised if you get some requests from India as well for future events.

Again, thank you for officiating an organized, well articulated event. Also enclosed find a copy of the marriage certificate for your records.

Sincerely,
Hema & Harshwardhan Panke

Dear ~~Mrs.~~ Dr. and Mrs. Sreenivasan,

Thank you both very much for all your advice and patience in helping us plan the wedding ceremony. Your vast wealth of knowledge and experience really helped all of us sift through the traditions to understand the meanings behind them.

Thank you for the wonderful gifts of cooking and puja books as well.

Sincerely,
Ratna Purohit
Vandana Purohit

R&S

oct 2004

Dear Dr & Mrs Srinivasan,

We cannot express our gratitude for the part that you played in the start of our life together. The ceremony was both beautiful & meaningful, and yet still retained a sense of humor – we couldn't have asked for anything more. Thank you, and thank you also for the kind gift of the bookends; they went into immediate use! Please join us for a meal next time you're in NYC.

With all best wishes, Rachel & Sandip

8/26/04

Dear Srinivasan,

Thanks for performing an extraordinary Wedding Ceremony. Everybody loved it because they understood it, participated in it and found the miniature version very appealing.

Thanks & love

6.16.99

Dear Dr Srinivasan,

Thank you so much for all the time and effort you gave to Seju & John's wedding ceremony. The ceremony was beautiful and we all enjoyed it very much. Again thank you.

Sincerely,
Indu Jitendra Bhatt

Dear Dr & Mrs. Srinivasan,

Thank you so much for officiating and being a part of one of the most important days of our lives. The words spoken on our special day will always be with us. Thank you again.

With love
Seju & John Mulvaney

Thank You

Dear Dr. Srinivasan and Kamla,

We are truly blessed to know you, and we can't thank you enough for everything you've done for us. Your advice and guidance have helped set the foundation for the rest of our lives as a married couple.

Thank you for helping to bridge the two families together in a beautiful and memorable ceremony. And thanks for the gift of the brass bookends. They will look great on our shelf, and we'll think of you every time we see them.

Sending our Love and Warmest Regards,

Salim and [illegible]

Dr: Mrs. Srinivasan

Thank you for the beautiful gift. We both love the tray. Also, thank you for making our ceremony beautiful... and working with us. We appreciate everything you did.

Love-
Vasu : Ryan

October 2004

Dear Dr. Srinivasan,

We would like to sincerely thank you for presiding over our wedding ceremony and for marrying us. We heard so many comments that our ceremony was the most organized and interesting one our guests had ever attended, and all the thanks goes to you! You managed us all very well prior to the wedding - we were amazed and impressed how smoothly it all went! You really did a tremendous job and all of our expectations were surpassed.

Hope to meet you again sometime. Thank you so much!

Sincerely,
Radhika & Praveen

Dear Dr Shrinivasan & Kamala Aunti,

Thank you for all of your help & guidance through out the whole wedding process. The wedding was a success thanks to all of your efforts! We received many compliments on the ceremony and your performance! We really appreciate everything you have done for us! Thank you also for the wonderful books. George would love to spend some time talking to you about the Hindu religion!

Thanks again Daya & George

Dear Dr Srinivasan + Kamala -

We want to thank you for performing such a nice + organized wedding ceremony. Also thank you for the wedding gifts. I enjoy reading religious books and I am sure as soon as I get settled in I will start to explore one of them.

Sincerely
Bhavine
& Samir

Dr. & Mrs. Srinivasan,

Thanks so much for preforming our wedding ceremony. Kevin & I were very happy to have you celebrate "our day" with us!

Love Always,
Tina
&
Kevin

Dear Dr & Mrs Srinivasan,
Thank you for conducting our beautiful wedding ceremony and for the enlightening books.

Thank You for Sharing in Our Special Day

Sapna Gupta
& Sean Westley

Dear Dr. Srinivasan and Kamala Auntie,

Thanks so much for helping to make our wedding such a wonderful event. From the very beginning of the planning, you were so generous with your time, helpful with your advice and inspiring with your wisdom in putting together our ceremony. And, it all came together so well! Srinu, your delivery of the service was incredible, and Kamala Auntie, your stage direction and advice were invaluable.

You will always be a central part of our memory of that great day. Thanks again.

Love

Daniel

Dear Dr Srinivasan,

We wanted to thank you for all that you have done for us. You've been there from the beginning from helping us to make the programs to your kind, reassuring words when I was a nervous bride. Also thank you for taking time out of your night on Friday to preform the Ganeesh Puja. We were all very stressed by that point but the Puja had a calming affect on us.

Your planning and rehearsals helped us to execute a wonderful event, I think your wife really helped to coordinate and cue the family, especially when some of us forgot what was next. The ceremony was simply beautiful. I remember walking down the aisle to the gazebo feeling rather nervous, but once you began the ceremony I felt at ease and very happy. We both truly enjoyed the ceremony. I think it set a festive tone for the rest of the evening. This was a truly memorable day for us, thank you for helping to make our wedding an event that we will remember for the rest of our lives. We hope you had as wonderful a time as we did.

Sincerely,

Anjali & Peter

Dear Dr. Srinivasan,

Thank you for the beautiful ceremony + for your blessings! Thank you for the lovely book! It is quite inspirational.

Both of us appreciate
Much more
than we can say
The extra joy
you added to
Our happy wedding day!

We could not have imagined a more beautiful + meaningful ceremony. Thanks again.

Love,

Priti + Peter

Dear Srinu and Kamala auntie,

At the expense of being self-congratulatory, I'd like to say that our wedding ceremony was the most meaningful, most beautiful, and most interesting ceremony I have ever experienced. It was all of these things thanks to you, Srinu. Your interest and knowledge of Hinduism transcends ritual; your voice and delivery brings life to a language from which most people feel disconnected; your presence and manner embody spirituality and intellectuality. Thank you also for all of your time, your interest and willingness to understand exactly what we wanted and why, and your constant calm (despite my nervous ramblings).

Kamala auntie, thank you for your constant support and your expert orchestration of events on Sunday.

A bonus that I received from working with both of you is your example of a solid, good marriage. It is easy to see that you two are best of friends and companions; that you support each other's spiritual and intellectual growth and projects; that you look to each other for guidance; that you listen to each other.

Thank you both for helping to make our wedding the most special day of our lives (to date).

Love, Shilpa

Acknowledgments

It is with great pleasure and appreciation that I thank Professor Michael Witzel of Harvard University for writing the Foreword to the book; and Karen Anderson of Wesleyan University, and Dr. Subhash Kak of Louisiana State University for their encouragement and scholarly reviews.

My very special thanks go to my wife, Kamla, who first recommended this project and who took the meticulous task of helping edit this complex text and contributing several appendices, bibliography and the glossary. And many thanks to my daughter Asha and her husband Stephen for their active support during the development of several drafts, posting relevant parts of the treatise on the publisher website. Similarly many thanks to my daughter Sandhya for taking on the responsibility for marketing the book.

Our grateful thanks go to Chennai-based artist S. Lakshmi Narayana, better known as Bapu, for the fine kalamkari illustrations in his inimitable, graceful Andhra style.

It is a pleasure to acknowledge and thank those photographers who permitted the use of photos taken at weddings the author performed: Gary Allen Photography, Rocio Honigmann and Joe Madri, Agahuda Khanii, Cindy Patrick, Capture the Moment Photography by Grace Cribbins, Lynn Norgren Photography, A. Vincent Scarano, George Hartzell, Jay Sheth, and Shirley Speer. And thanks to the individuals who sent the pictures taken by them and/or family and friends: Roger Cole, the Raghuvirs, Parashar Patel, Margot Mindich, Daya Patel, Thakorbhai Patel, V.R. Garimella, Janine & Sunjay Patil, Sapna Gupta, Arun Basu, Praveen & Radhika Ramamurthy, Madhuri Gogineni, Aditi Saxena, and Kavita & Rahul Panke.

Also my sincere thanks go to Allynn Wilkinson of Wesleyan University for her enthusiastic support in preparing the illustrations and photographs for inclusion in the text. I appreciate Dr. Tiruvengadan Seshan's review of the slokas. Many thanks to priest Krishna Murthy of the Satyanarayana Temple in Middletown, Connecticut, for his comments on the ceremonial aspects covered in the book.

Special thanks to those friends for their keen interest in and encouragement of this project; they include the Gupta family (Sushma, Arvind and Sherene), Devika and Mohan Kasaraneni, Usha and Hem Kanithi; and last but not least, Sri. H.R. Ananth, CEO of The Bangalore Press, for his unflagging interest, patience and cooperation in the production of the book.

A. V. Srinivasan
Glastonbury, Connecticut
August 2006